D0984428

An Introduction to African Criminology

An Introduction to African Criminology

W. CLIFFORD

Nairobi
OXFORD UNIVERSITY PRESS
Dar es Salaam Lusaka Addis Ababa
1974

Oxford University Press, Ely House, London W.1

GLASGOW NEW YORK TORONTO MELBOURNE WELLINGTON
CAPE TOWN IBADAN NAIROBI DAR ES SALAAM LUSAKA ADDIS ABABA
DELHI BOMBAY CALCUTTA MADRAS KARACHI LAHORE DACCA
KUALA LUMPUR SINGAPORE HONG KONG TOKYO

Oxford University Press, P.O. Box 72532, Nairobi, Kenya

Cover design by Chris Higson

Made and printed in East Africa

CONTENTS

PERSPECTIVE

Crime in Africa is no unusual phenomenon. Like divorce, prostitution, drunkenness or adultery it is to be found wherever men are grouped in social organizations: and in Africa, as anywhere else, such problems mount, multiply and become less manageable as populations grow and as people concentrate into a few overcrowded, continually expanding, urban centres.

What is unusual in Africa, however, is the rate of development in this part of the world. Economically, but more especially politically and socially, the recent movement of the newly independent countries of Africa south of the Sahara has been at a quicksilver pace—a pace previously unknown in world history. All of this has deep significance for criminal conduct. If, as we believe, crime is associated with social mobility, population densities, family instability and urban growth, then we have a special case of such developments in Africa.

Many people, now settled in the modern towns of Africa, were reared in 'traditional', tribal, subsistence economies where status was determined by birth and where production was only for immediate family needs; where behaviour was group-oriented and where social controls were strict and effective. They have frequently leap-frogged whole stages of economic development (such as cash cropping and peasant production) to arrive abruptly at wage employment in modern industry. They have straddled centuries of social adaptation as the older extended family has been abruptly reduced to the nuclear proportions demanded by urban and industrial life.[1] Even in those areas where peasant production was reached years ago and has a longer history (for example in West Africa) the process of industrialization and urban growth has been swift and has given precious little time for any leisurely adaptation.

The material benefits of this development, however, have usually accrued to a minority of the people in each country. The continent has a collection of dual economies instigated by colonial development, or the industrial exploitation of limited areas—or both. Thus it is generally true, in sub-saharan Africa, that some seventy to eighty per cent of the people are still dependent on the simplest forms of agriculture and the *per capita* income for the countries as a whole remains low. In Mali the average urban income is three to five times as high as the rural income. In Zambia the industries employ only about ten per cent of the available labour in the country. Whilst Zaïre has an average income per inhabitant of seventy-seven dollars, the Congolese average has been only forty-one dollars and for most people in the rural areas it has been less than twenty-nine dollars.[2]

All this indicates that the centres of improvement and the areas of the most marked social changes have tended to follow the patterns of industrialization and urban growth. The rural areas have benefited, of course, from some injections of capital and there have been sporadic attempts at more deliberate and extensive rural development. It remains true, however, that the problem for most countries in this area today is to augment and generalize economic improvements—increase production and to give the majority of the people a greater share of a higher national income.

Significantly, the problems of crime are centred on those very areas where the most development has occurred. Crime is growing in the cities and larger towns and only to a lesser extent in those more accessible rural districts which have already felt the effects of industrialization and commerce. The implication is that where countries have invested the greatest amount in agriculture, commerce, industry, health and education they have sown unwittingly some prolific criminal seeds. In the areas where they have pushed for more improvements they have also generated crime. But the problem is not nearly so simple if only because crime, like any human or social phenomenon, has to be considered not only as it is now but as it might have been. It is not only a question of what crime has resulted from what investments but of what crime there would have been if there had been no investments.

There are other sides to the same question. The low level of living outside the towns, not to mention the high rate of unemployment in the towns themselves, means that few countries in Africa have, as yet, the means to provide those services for the prevention and treatment of crime which are common in the richer parts of the world. It might therefore be argued that the rates of crime could be decreased if more prevention could be afforded. If Africa could provide itself with the elaborate crime control and prevention services common to affluent nations then it could keep its crime rates at a lower level than they are and so reduce the undesirable by-products of its struggle to advance materially.[3]

In Africa it is obvious that where funds become available from inside or outside a country they are not likely to find their way into direct crime prevention. They need to be devoted in nearly every country to those services which will increase production and raise the means to provide better incomes. This investment in itself may create opportunities and favourable conditions for crime. Dense populations, increasing commerce and material possessions, all make crime easier to commit and more difficult to prevent or detect. On the other hand this concentration on the improvement of living standards can also be regarded as a vast programme to prevent that amount of crime which has its roots in ignorance and deprivation. Again it is necessary to look not only at the amount of crime that exists but at the amount there could well have been if standards had not been raised.

What is abundantly clear is that the countries of Africa are so vast and their populations still so very widespread that a rather different approach to crime and its prevention is called for. As things are, the expense of providing anything like that coverage of social services for crime prevention and treatment which is usual in developed countries would be grossly disproportionate. Nor may these services be necessary in their known form. The limited resources available for general development in Africa make it essential for these countries to husband their means and to court ingenuity. For this they need to understand more precisely how crime can be bred by the investments they are making in economic and social growth. If African countries, by making a virtue of their necessity, can learn from the mistakes of more developed countries—and if they succeed thereby in preventing crime more effectively—they will both improve social conditions and be serving their own economic interests. Moreover they could possibly give a lead to the more 'advanced' and crime-afflicted countries. This, incidentally, was a role which Africa was urged to assume by the Fourth United Nations Congress on the Prevention of Crime and the Treatment of Offenders held at Kyoto, Japan, in August 1970. There the possibilities of developing areas being in an advantageous position to plan for less crime was underlined and emphasized.[4]

It should also be noted that in sub-saharan Africa the struggle for economic growth is a struggle against time. Populations are increasing at a brisk rate; not less than 2.5 per cent per annum and probably much higher than this rather conservative estimate. Therefore the populations of most of the countries with which we are concerned can be expected to double in twenty-five to thirty years—if not sooner. The population surge also gives the age group pyramid an unusually wide base, i.e. most of the people are young. As yet demographic data is imprecise and we have only 'guestimates'; but there is adequate confirmation that some 40 per cent of the populations of the newly independent countries are under fifteen and some 60 per cent under twenty-one. Since crime is pre-eminently a problem of youth, and very large numbers of young people are idle and unemployed in the African towns, a steady rise in crime may be expected over the period in which the number of people will be doubling and this rise in crime may be expected to be more than proportionate to the rise in population, if our experience elsewhere in the world counts for anything.

It is for such reasons that the study of crime in Africa assumes importance for the countries of the continent south of the Sahara. It is, unfortunately, an importance which is not always appreciated. For despite its steady and troublesome growth in the urban areas of Africa, present day crime on this continent may quite reasonably be regarded as one of the lesser problems of these countries struggling manfully with, what seem to be, the more urgent problems of feeding the ever-growing numbers of people and raising their basic living standards.

However, it is not usually possible to ignore crime. As we have seen, it thrives on development expenditures and it could, if neglected, undo, in the future, all that is being done now to help and advance modern Africa. No one would suggest that priority should not be given to economic measures to raise levels of living, but experience now shows that care must be taken to avoid the growth of crime wasting a great deal of this effort and channelling the benefits into undeserving pockets. There is also the possibility that some of the disappointments in the results of the investments already made could be traceable to too little attention having been paid to the criminal potential. Corruption, profiteering and administrative malpractices can be forms of 'white collar' crime.

Fortunately, it is true that crime in Africa has not yet reached the proportions with which we are familiar in developed areas of the world. But if it is still not an impossible problem, it is important for Africa to see that it remains that way—if only to avoid it undermining the national efforts to improve. Where it is becoming serious in Africa its effect on the national struggle will already be apparent; and the loss in materials, in funds spent on its control and in man-hours of valuable labour, if not yet being calculated on the debit side of national recovery, will soon have to be counted.

In any case, crime is more than a national loss in materials or productive capacity. It is usually a real danger to peace-loving citizens, a dissipation of scarce human resources and, of course, above all, a personal tragedy both in victims and offenders. No state can ignore its obligation to protect its citizens and most are concerned to help offenders to find a better way of life. It is, indeed, a mark of civilization that nations everywhere seek to prevent crime and reform offenders. These, we may be sure, have been traditional preoccupations for Africans of every level of living and at each stage of history. It is a mistake to suppose that such concerns arise only at the more complicated levels of society or to believe that the simplest tribes do not have crime or an interest in reforming their offenders. The approaches may differ, but crime and its intelligent treatment attracts a fair amount of attention in the smallest and least complex situations in Africa. For the more advanced and complex tribes it is an important state concern. It would therefore be strange if such matters did not now assume more importance as the new countries of Africa make their way into the family of nations and begin to make their weight felt in world affairs.

It behoves us, therefore, to study the problems, to see how Africa differs, if at all, from other parts of the world in its crime and criminals. We need to devise now the measures which are necessary to prevent as many offences as possible, to reform offenders effectively and to ensure that measures are adequate to segregate and neutralize those criminals who are unlikely to respond to the best efforts made on their behalf. In all this, the complex of different cultures, the geography and the economic underdevelopment of the region make it necessary to find practical adaptations of old remedies if not in fact new solutions to the old problems—solutions as important for the world understanding of crime as they are for the building of the new Africa.

[1] This is a general statement which remains true despite the kinship links which have been shown by social anthropologists to survive in towns. cf. Clyde Mitchell on the Copperbelt and Leslie who found 'a network of kinship ties criss-crossing the town' in Dar es Salaam.

[2] Figures relate to pre-1970.

[3] This assumes, of course, that such services are really effective preventatives in the developed countries—an assumption that rising crime rates may not support.

[4] This same emphasis on the value of developing areas as 'pathfinders' in planning to prevent crime was made by the writer as a member of the Research Panel for the Third UN Congress held in Stockholm in 1965.

PART ONE

I
CRIMINOLOGY

Criminology is, quite simply, the science of crime. This is both the literal meaning of the word and what most people understand when they use it: even when we are trying to be more scientifically precise or more consciously academic, it is usually adequate to describe a criminologist as one who studies crime.

THE MEANING OF CRIME

This accuracy has a deceptive simplicity. It arises from our familiarity with the word 'crime' and from the general currency of the term in our everyday language. We may assume too readily that since everyone knows what 'crime' is then most people can understand very generally what is meant by criminology.

Crime, however, is a very common word with some uncommon connotations. It is a conventional label not always used in conventional ways. Crime is relative and can mean different, even opposed, things according to one's point of view. It is also an umbrella term covering a wide range of different circumstances and situations. It is only when one begins to examine the word, its ramifications and its possible meanings, that a first view is obtained of the depth, the extent and the complexity of criminology. When we think of crime, we have a general notion of theft, murder, assault, rape, fraud and other deleterious behaviour—the kind of conduct which cannot be allowed free rein without a disruption of order, a decline of public security and a steady descent into social chaos. Obviously, then, to protect lives and property and safeguard the social order such offences should be controlled.

Each one of these terms is difficult to define, however. There is an obvious difference between killing in self-defence, killing by accident and killing deliberately. Theft may seem simple enough until it has to be differentiated from various forms of temporary borrowing or the taking of things to which we believe we have a right. The intangible nature of consent sometimes makes rape no easy offence to prove whilst fraud and some of the more questionable practices in ordinary business are not always easy to separate.

For this reason—and for there to be any precision in what we mean by crime—we have to outline distinctly and specifically the actions which will not be tolerated. This defining of offences is the province of the law and it accounts to a great extent for its technicality. Sometimes, the line drawn between what the law allows and what it forbids is very fine. Not infrequently the difference lies only in the intention with which an action is performed. Again, the enacted laws may change over a perod of time forbidding some actions previously allowed and now permitting behaviour which might formerly have been prosecuted. This has happened fairly recently with respect to attempted suicide, homosexuality and the purchase of narcotics by addicts in England. During a war the killing of certain people may even be encouraged whilst free buying and selling, ordinarily allowed, may be prohibited. According to the economic situation the exportation of capital might sometimes be allowed whilst at other times the transfer of money is punishable. Or again, outmoded laws are repealed from time to time as they cease to have social meaning.

It can be argued, therefore, that the law itself creates crime. Actions once legal are now illegal whilst the law now smiles at behaviour once regarded as criminal. Laws can be made, unmade, changed or amended and, all the time, they are changing the meaning of crime. It is the law, we may say, which labels certain types of behaviour as criminal. If there were no laws there would be no crimes.

Alternatively, one may well maintain that it is crimes which create law. One may argue that crimes precede the law, that it is because crimes are commited that laws become necessary. It will be observed however, that in this case we have given the word 'crime' a different meaning. It is no longer dependent on a legal definition: it is not merely those actions forbidden by the law but those which are, by some other standard, so detrimental to society that laws have to be invoked against them. We are suggesting that behind all law-making there is a concept of what is socially permissible and should not be interfered with by legal rules—and what is socially dangerous or detrimental and requires legal control. We are implying that a 'reasonable man' can see when legal intervention is required—and when it is not—from the innocent or detrimental nature of the behaviour.

Now, quite obviously, individuals will not always agree on what is right or wrong, harmful or beneficial. How then do we conceive of an action which is detrimental to society? What is this new standard which we are using? Do we merely follow the majority or the weight of public opinion? Do we follow the dictates of a moral code? If so, there are of course many kinds of action of which public opinion or the moralities disapprove but which are still outside the law. People usually disapprove of profiteering, and the moral codes condemn promiscuity, but these are not usually illegal. In these cases it seems that the law has not followed the rules. Gambling, business monopolies, drunkenness, economic exploitation, are often denounced as anti-social but are frequently outside any legal regulation. These general ideas on crime then, are unsure guides. As we well know, public opinion is often fickle and the law tends to lag behind: ideas on the behaviour which is anti-social may change considerably over the years. Adultery, vagrancy and abortion, once criminal, are now permitted in some countries because of changes in the law promoted by organized public pressure. Moral precepts are not always suitable as legal rules if only because they include private behaviour beyond the normal reach of the law. It is therefore too simple to imagine that the law can be invoked according to recognized and precise underlying principles as to what should and what should not be allowed.[1]

This is not to say that some such general frame of reference does not exist at all. The clear, if still imprecise, answer to this complication in defining crime, is that law, public opinion and social habit or custom all reflect to some extent certain basic values or standards; a consensus of fundamental principles prevailing in a society at any given time.[2]

Obviously the laws which define crime are intended to preserve certain types of order and standards which are treasured, or at least favoured, by the social system and the laws seek to punish or otherwise discourage any non-conformity with these. Historically a country rarely lost this background consensus of values except by conversion to a new religion, by social transformation (both of which took many generations) or by revolution. Until modern times, therefore, the law was relatively unchanging, reflecting an underlying system of values which evolved only very slowly. Now the pace of change has greatly increased and difficulties arise when we have to define the deeper values in a changing modern state which may have no unifying ideology or generally accepted moral system.

This difference in values and law is also a function of size. In a small, integrated simple society such as the smaller tribes of Africa, social controls like laws, customs and morals are largely undifferentiated. Here the basic values are much the same whether reflected in laws, morals or immemorial custom. Thus right or wrong behaviour is clearly defined. It is difficult for crime to flourish in such small groupings because wrongful behaviour is immediately recognized and deplored by everyone. Detection is easy where people live closely together and non-conformity immediately arouses concern, opposition, outrage, antagonism and social action. In such conditions, deviant behaviour is the direct concern not simply of the authorities but of everyone in the group, and families have their own recognized ways of training the young for submission and expressing their disapproval of the non-conformist. One who follows the customs is respected, given prestige and encouragement. Another who tries to break out of the established pattern of conduct is shunned, disdained, perhaps even feared. He will find himself regarded with suspicion, animosity—perhaps disgust; he is likely to be excluded from group councils, denounced, scolded, derided, ridiculed—or in serious cases, expelled altogether. This social ostracism is usually much worse than any physical punishment or any obligation to compensate his victim. Moreover these social and physical sanctions may be reinforced by the supernatural. The outraged spirits may be invoked, striking terror into the heart of the offender whose family will blame him for any misfortune or sickness which ensues.

However, as a society 'evolves', becomes functionally diverse or grows in size; as its organization becomes more internally complex and its people's interests diverge, laws, customs and morals gradually separate. Education creates new preoccupations and status symbols. Contacts with other peoples of different habits and customs enjoin toleration of the extraordinary. Basic values are still maintained but these are not everywhere supported to the same extent. Moral behaviour no longer inevitably bolstered by law and custom may sometimes become irrelevant and dated. Society has to embrace many divergent patterns of life and provide for people of different views. Nor can the old sense of belonging to a family or community always be preserved. Social solidarity is diminished as one has to learn to support oneself amongst strangers and tolerate different ways of living in one's neighbourhood. Changes come more frequently, crime or deviant behaviour becomes more difficult to detect and even people in the same street are less united about what they will encourage or disapprove. The opportunities for the individual deviation of behaviour are vastly increased—often tolerated to an extent; and offensive behaviour is easily misrepresented to those who were not there or who do not know the whole story. With so much going on which can only be followed through newspapers or radio, the people now depend upon established institutions like the courts or the police to ensure conformity with the law. They themselves are no longer involved unless they happen to be directly affected. In the streets there is nothing to distinguish the offender from the non-offender. This anonymity both covers and justifies: where victims are not personally known to their assailants it is easier for crimes to be committed without the fear, the qualms of conscience or the danger of reprisals which there would be in a smaller group.

Africa contains examples of all the gradations in society mentioned here.[3] The pygmies in the Congo, the Bushmen of the Kalahari or the Maasai of eastern Africa with their rich traditions all represent different levels of complexity or stages of communities with inter-supporting legal, moral and social systems. There are Muslim communities in Nigeria or Mali with modern systems but laws still supported by moral precepts; and there are larger cities in West, Central and East Africa where conditions are beginning to approximate to the larger cities of Europe or America with their diverse collections of standards and systems.

Africa shares, then, the common problem; and the common problem is to explain why some people continue to observe established standards in our new mass societies and why others do not. We cannot pretend that, as yet, we have the full answer to this question. There may be one, many or a hundred reasons why people act contrary to the acceptable patterns of behaviour. Some may be in revolt against the system itself; others may be unthinking, negligent, careless or seeking short-cuts to profit. Some may be physically or mentally inadequate—incapable of meeting the complicated demands of a modern society. Some may have quite deliberately weighed the consequences and may believe the rewards to be well worth the risks of detection and punishment. Others may be taking an enterprising advantage of the borderline opportunities for gain which are so plentiful in a large urban community. Still other offenders may have been in such dire need that they felt impelled to take the risks involved in crime. There are people who have been weak and an easy prey to temptation. Then there are those who have been influenced by others or who were seeking notoriety at any cost. Some may have been deprived in early life of the training necessary to help them to understand their obligation to their neighbours; others have developed a psychopathic disregard for anyone's interests but their own.

The variations on this theme are legion. For in seeking the reasons for crime we are seeking the reasons for human behaviour generally. When we are able to say why people commit crime we will also be able to say why others do not. This is to say, we will be nearer to a general explanation of human nature and we are therefore inevitably involved in all kinds of deeper issues; philosophical questions of determinism and free-will, heredity and environment, biological constitution, physiology, psychology and the influence of culture.

This is why ethics are always difficult to exclude entirely, however clinical we try to be about crime and criminals. Morals and crime have finally been separated in modern legal systems and much literature has been devoted to the demonstration that crimes are not necessarily sins, and vice versa. In rural Africa, as we have seen, customary law, morals and conformity are often fused and distinctions are not easy to make. As society grows, the tendency is to purge the law of its moral overtones. But it all depends on what one means by morals. Immorality can arouse more public antagonism than many crimes and there appears to be a moral element in the public attitude to offenders which is difficult to avoid. Even those who deny any moral commitment may be inclined to self-righteousness in making the claim. It is not easy to maintain a completely objective approach to law-making or law-breaking and morals probably creep back under another name simply because it is difficult for the law to be its own justification. Certainly the public sentiment on offences and offenders does not always follow the legal pattern and, when the two get seriously out of line, both law and morals seem likely to suffer.

Another approach to the problem of crime is more sociological. It begins, with Durkheim, from the patent fact that crime is to be found in all known societies. Because of this it seems difficult to regard criminal behaviour in the general sense as being anything abnormal. On the contrary, its very prevalence makes it a normal feature of any society and it must therefore continue to exist because it has some useful social purpose to serve. It may be that crime is useful if only because it provokes people to organize against it and thereby promotes social order. It may be that crime is an outward expression of other social, economic or psychological problems and that its presence forces the authorities to focus attention on these. It could be that the protest, which is embodied in crime, against present restrictions and values is a subtle but dynamic factor in the whole process of social change and development. Aristotle regarded it as one of the factors in forcing the cycle of social change.

Again, political crime is sometimes distinguished from ordinary crime, the former being defensible, if not always tolerable, as a means of protesting against an existing régime. This difference is difficult to deal with in practice since an existing régime will appeal to law and order; and the creation of a disturbance or terrorist measures are all usually clearly illegal offences. Politicians may welcome arrest for publicity and criminals may seek political justification of their crimes. The line is never easy to draw legally, and in practice the questions of definition are resolved by events in the course of the political struggle.

Finally, there is the personal or psychological approach to our subject. This is to regard individual crime as merely one form of human maladjustment—a personal behaviour problem which may or may not be against the law. This it may be but, as yet, it has not been possible to treat all the effects of maladjustment equally or without reference to their social consequences. There is still a marked reluctance to treat all criminals as if they were sick and/or to treat non-offenders who are maladjusted in the same way as one treats offenders. Concepts of 'justice' complicate the medical categories.

Quite apart from the conceptual difficulties in crime there are also the complications of legislating for, preventing, or measuring crime. Criminologists have focused attention recently on 'dark crime'—undetected or unreported crime—and they have for some years been concerned with the idea of 'white collar' crime, that is crime committed by powerful commercial interests or 'respectable' people which often amounts to evasions of tax or excise laws but which may be no more than an exploitation of loopholes in the law. There are some 'crimes' which a state no longer prosecutes because public opinion no longer supports the laws concerned, for example Sunday Observance laws and, in some countries, adultery or abortion, or the homosexuality or attempted suicide already mentioned. Eventually, the laws in question are repealed; but there may be long periods during which the crime is defined (i.e. legally prohibited) but the law is not enforced.

Whatever approach or conceptual matrix we adopt, therefore we soon find ourselves confronted by the deeper questions of social growth and human conduct to which as yet we have but few real answers. Modern science has made greater headway in the present century than ever before; but, as most of us are painfully aware, its success has lain rather in discovering *how* we do things and not *why*. We know in minute detail how a man lives, but not why. We understand how a tree grows, but not why. We can explain how the sun gives light or how the weather changes, but not why. So too, with crime; we know how it is committed, we can sub-divide, calculate and plot the trends in crime; we can classify, label and psycho-analyse criminals, but paradoxically we are still a long way from any satisfactory knowledge as to *why* crimes are committed.

THE STUDY OF CRIME

Turning now from meaning to methods, it will be clear that the two are inter-related. The criminologist has to concern himself with the concept of crime in all its implications in order to formulate and interpret his methods. He usually has to be able to think of crime on several levels or in several contexts at once. Whilst appreciating its significance as legally defined illegality, he has to see it as a social event arising from a combination of community or individual circumstances; he must be alive to crime's psychological meaning and sensitive to the symbolism of behaviour; he can never disregard the emotional undertones of illegal conduct or of the collective reaction to it. Finally, the criminologist must be aware of the relativity of the concept, of its different meanings for different societies—even for sub-groups of people in the same society. Juridically, criminology is concerned not only with the laws which define offences but with the uniformity (or lack of it) in the application of these laws: it examines the moral standards and the social values which serve to determine the limits of toleration and which prescribe acceptable behaviour. It covers the procedures for collecting data on crime, the subtleties of interpretation and the statistical recording and measurement of crime.

The criminologist is interested in those physical and mental disabilities which make it more difficult for some people to conform to the demands of social life. He studies the economic conditions such as poverty, overcrowding, unemployment, and the interruption of earnings, and conversely the affluence, possessions, and material self-seeking, which may provide a background for crime. He considers the implications of delinquency being concentrated in certain age groups or being largely confined to particular districts of a town or being more prevalent within certain classes or income groups. He needs to understand the influence of biology and glandular structure on conduct, the psychology of normal and abnormal behaviour and to appreciate the profound interplay of heredity and environment in fostering, preventing or influencing conformity and non-conformity.

Criminology also implies an interest in the factors which lead to crime being hidden or reported, prosecuted or tolerated, resented or accepted. It connotes an examination of the principles of criminal investigation by the police and a concern with court procedure and the sentencing policy of magistrates and judges. It involves a study of the different types of crime and criminals and of their relative importance at different periods of social and economic development. It enjoins the tracing of criminal histories, case-studies of offenders and an inquiry into their diverse characters and characteristics. It examines social, political and economic policy with reference to behaviour tolerated or forbidden, and studies social change for its effects on these standards. It concerns itself with child care, education and training, both formal and informal, particularly with the defects in these which may have relevance for the production of frustration, maladjustment and delinquency. Finally, it implies an analysis and discussion of the various measures available to a state for the prevention of crime and the methods adopted to punish, deter or reform offenders of different types, ages and backgrounds.

CRIMINOLOGY AND PENOLOGY

Thus criminology is an immensely broad subject which knows few boundaries and becomes involved in all the sciences which deal with man and his social organization. The term 'criminology' seems to have been used first by Topinard, the French anthropologist, who was writing in the last quarter of the nineteenth century, and a great many of those renowned in the study of crime have been specialists in the related fields of medicine, anthropology, sociology, psychology, biology, law and statistics. The first writers like Beccaria, Bentham and Maconochie, were interested in the formulation of a logical system of legal administration. Others in the eighteenth and nineteenth centuries were penal reformers concerned with mitigating the severities in the administration of the criminal law. It may be argued therefore that criminology grew out of a prior interest in penology and legal reform.

In this book, the term 'criminology' is used to embrace penology as well as a variety of other subjects, but even today there are writers who make a distinction between criminology, the science of crime, and penology, the study of penal systems. The justification for using criminology as the umbrella term is that penology is not usually taught as a subject distinct from criminology and there are few, if any, criminologists who are not equally interested in measures to deal with crime. It would be odd if this were not so, if a criminologist interested in the problem of crime could be indifferent to the treatment of offenders. Obviously, the efficacy of penal measures tells us a great deal about the causes of crime just as the explanations of criminal behaviour determine the measures for dealing with delinquents.

A SEPARATE SCIENCE OR NOT?

The fact that criminology depends upon a variety of related social sciences cannot be avoided. This is because, with the other social sciences, criminology is involved in the study of human nature in its social setting, in the study of man amongst men. It is also because we can never say why men commit crime without saying why they don't. To explain criminal behaviour is to explain non-criminal behaviour. Criminology is therefore a dependent science; it has no separate techniques of its own. Hermann Mannheim, one of the greatest contemporary criminologists, has said: 'So far, criminology has developed no specific methodology of its own; its techniques of research are, on the whole, identical with those used in other social sciences.'[4] This eclecticism of criminology has sometimes evoked the opinion that it is not a separate science at all. It is true that many modern exponents of criminology are basically sociologists, psychologists, psychiatrists, statisticians, etc. One reason for this, however, is that criminology as a separate subject is relatively new in university teaching in the West. Until recently, a professional criminologist in England, for example, would have had difficulty earning his living by the study of crime alone. He had to have qualifications in related fields to obtain a teaching post—however much he might have wanted to specialize in the study of crime.

The dependence of criminology on the methods and findings of the other social sciences is no reason for denying its distinctiveness as a separate field of study. It has by now a literature of its own reaching back over some two centuries and it has a long history of research. Even the sociologist or psychologist interested in crime finds that he needs to devote so much time to mastering this subject that he tends to become, in effect, a sociological or psychological criminologist rather than a separate expert with only a passing interest in crime.[5] Certainly criminology is problem centred; it is concerned with one particular social problem which has roots in sociology, psychology, biology and a range of other subjects, but the linking and orientating of these various inquiries to the problem of crime, the correlation and application of what is known from a variety of sources and the conducting of independent research (albeit by borrowed methods) makes criminology a special field of study with a justifiable claim to separate treatment.

This whole question of criminology in relation to other sciences, and particularly to the social sciences, was examined by Ellenburger. He pointed out that even amongst the natural sciences there are some, like botany or zoology, which deal with the study of facts which are not strictly unique and individual and which are not dealing with general phenomena—as for example physics or mathematics. In the social sciences he concluded that criminology is like medicine. Criminology is based on other social sciences just as medicine is based on anatomy, physiology, physics, chemistry, etc. Neither medicine nor criminology are purely theoretical; they have a meaning which derives from their practical application. The justification for medicine lies in therapeutics and public health, that of criminology in penal reform, penology and the prevention of crime. Both have a series of value judgements with which to work, medicine with health, disease and healing, criminology with justice, responsibility, crime and punishment. Both partake of an element of human relationships which marks them off from more academic disciplines and each has its ethical purpose, expressed for medicine in the Hippocratic oath and for criminology in prevention being better than punishment and reform being better than deterrence.[6]

In 1938 Thorsten Sellin could say that the criminologist was a king without a kingdom,[7] but Szabo pointed out in 1964 that the situation had been changed by a quarter of a century of scientific progress.[8]

[1] However, one Caribbean country has only recently made incest illegal—showing that culture will determine the precise mixture of morals and law.

[2] This is not to resurrect the idea of natural law—although it is doubtful whether this ever died (see A. P. d'Entrèves, *Natural Law*, London: Hutchinson University Library, 1951, who would probably argue that it now emerges as civil or human rights; and in the racial morality of the United Nations). Our aim here is simply to show that a purely legal interpretation of public opinion or the notions of the party or group in power does not fully suffice.

[3] 'Gradations' as used here does not necessarily imply gradations in an evolutionary or time sequence; it could mean gradations of size, complexity, degree of organization or extent of contact with other societies. A range of differentiation exists, however, which justifies the use of 'gradations'.

[4] Hermann Mannheim, *Group Problems in Crime and Punishment*, London: Routledge and Kegan Paul, 1955, pp. 115-16.

[5] See N. Wolfgang, 'Criminology and Criminologist', *J. of Crim. Law, Criminology and Police Science*, Vol. 54, no 2, June 1963, pp. 155-62.

[6] H. Ellenburger, 'Recherche clinique et recherche expérimentale en criminologie' (mimeo.), 1962.

[7] T. Sellin, '*Culture Conflict and Crime*', New York: Social Science Research Council, 1938.

[8] D. Szabo, 'The Teaching of Criminology in Universities', *International Review of Criminal Policy*, No. 22, 1964.

2
CRIMINOLOGY IN AFRICA

If the study of crime is generally regarded as being in its infancy then it would be reasonable to suggest that the study of crime *in Africa* is conceived but still unborn. This is largely because the related social sciences are themselves underdeveloped in Africa and because some of the centres of higher education have only recently been established. Even in the countries where universities have been operating for some time, however, crime has only rarely been studied, attention having been given to the development of the basic social sciences, and to providing the emerging territories with the teachers, doctors, lawyers and other professional men which they need.[1]

All this is understandable but unfortunate for criminology itself. For, as we have noted, this section of the African continent is in rapid and significant transition and this process of change is important in itself for the study of the development of criminal conduct.

Since the Second World War there have been cultural contrasts, in both the urban and rural areas of Africa, of the greatest significance for any student of crime. To have been able to document over the past twenty or thirty years the changing concepts of crime in highly developed urban centres or in peri-urban areas, in simple pygmy or Bushmen societies, amongst the nomads and the lesser or more complex tribes, in the great historic kingdoms or in the emergent urban associations and organizations would have had inestimable value. To have been able to follow the changes in the patterns of behaviour in these contrasting settings over the past quarter of a century of industrial penetration would have constituted a great contribution to our understanding of crime anywhere in the world.

Whilst one may regret the lost opportunity, there is much that can still be done. For Africa south of the Sahara will remain, for a generation or more to come, one of the most promising areas of the world in which to investigate crime. There are few countries of this area without a variety of societies at different stages of social and economic development. There are few of these countries which can hope to eliminate cultural contrasts within the next generation. Moreover, these are developing countries in which the whole process of economic growth and social adaptation can still be followed in all its implications for crime.

It is for this reason that this book is concerned with the study of crime in Africa south of the Sahara. It is clear that criminology in Africa will follow a pattern of growth similar to that in other countries. As the social sciences develop so will the study of local crime become more precise and important. There will be a cross fertilization between the research which is done here and in other parts of the world. Hypotheses explored in the more developed countries can be tested in the less developed regions. Africa will gradually acquire similar methods for the collection and publication of data on crime.

It is necessary to distinguish here between the methods and the content of criminology. That the study of crime in Africa will follow the lines already established for the study of crime elsewhere means that the methods will tend to be the same, that is the tools of investigation will not differ in the foreseeable future however much the material may be computerized and however advanced the systems become for handling the data technologically. Whether, in the long run, Africa will devise new approaches of its own no one can now foresee, but since social groupings are universal it seems certain that any new methods developed in Africa would have an application outside the continent and would need to be regarded as contributions to the general science of criminology rather than something specifically African.

Content is a different matter and there are several reasons why criminology in sub-saharan Africa may already be regarded as something distinct from criminology elsewhere.[2] For one thing, the towns in Africa are nearly all less than a generation old. To this there are notable exceptions, such as the major urban centres of Nigeria, but the existence of these exceptions to the rule merely gives a greater opportunity for contrasting research. If, as seems true, crime is a specifically urban phenomenon it is particularly valuable to have such young towns to investigate. The fact that they are still developing rapidly provides many opportunities for ongoing research and for action studies designed especially to follow the process of growth in its effect on crime and on behaviour generally.

Secondly, Africa today offers a pattern of cultural differentiation the like of which is difficult to find in other regions. Certainly other continents provide examples of cultural contrasts but not usually the same range of contrasts. Moreover, the common history of varied societies in Africa links these smaller groupings at different levels or at different stages of development in a fashion of no small importance for the design of research. The common experience of food gathering, hunting, preserving traditions and struggling for survival; the groupings into kingdoms, nations and migrating herdsmen; the general inheritance of communal values and religious cults; exploitation by slave traders and subjection to colonial rule; and latterly the common experience of a rapidly acquired independence—all serve to weave a background of similarity to the foreground of contrasts.

The third significant characteristic of the African scene, from a criminological point of view, is to be found in the fact (already frequently mentioned) that there can be few areas of the world in which the transition from traditional to modern urban living has been accomplished with such speed: the cultural contrasts have often been carried over into the towns providing a situation which is different in its intensity, if not in its kind, from similar conditions on other continents. Most families, however sophisticated and intellectually advanced, in the towns of Africa still have one foot in the rural tribal village of their ancestors. The maintenance and application of some of the older values and traditions to modern political problems is topical. Concepts like the 'african personality' and 'african socialism' draw upon social and psychological principles which have survived the flood of modernization. The effects of rapid change can be studied very effectively in modern Africa with only two generations covering many stages.

Fourthly, and of considerable scientific importance, it may be said that the societies of Africa have been studied anthropologically to an extent comparable with any other part of the world. Thus, there is already a rich sociological background from which the studies of crime can begin. In Africa it is possible to follow through over the next generation the evolution and development of rural and urban behaviour in a way which is rare if not new. One can begin with the distinguished anthropological work which has been done and continue with the earlier studies of the towns and others which are beginning to appear. For the next few years it will be possible even to trace people who have been studied by anthropologists and to see what is happening to them, to their ideas, to their traditional standards and to their legal and illegal behaviour. This is an opportunity not often given to criminologists.

Fifthly, there is a very practical application of criminological work. For in studying the methods for dealing with crime there are still many areas of Africa where the services of modern penology may be developed from the beginning. This offers opportunities for experiment—for testing—for action research. It gives a chance to work out new ideas partly drawn from the rich cultural background and partly based upon the knowledge of mistakes made elsewhere. We have already seen that the geography and relatively limited means of this area demand a new, cheaper, and more effective approach to the prevention and treatment of crime. Planning and evaluating social defence (i.e. crime prevention and treatment) services for Africa can be an exciting experience in the next decade.

Sixthly, the people of Africa differ racially, culturally, sociologically, perhaps psychologically from people in other parts of the world. Much the same may be said, of course, of the varied peoples of Asia, of the Middle East or of Latin America, for each area of the world has something attractively different to offer in its people, its traditions and its outlook for the student of crime. This is an added reason to promote criminological research in areas not yet properly covered.

Finally, we may refer again to the fact that the population of Africa is predominantly young. This makes crime in Africa a particularly important problem since it is everywhere a problem of young people. This adds a note of urgency to the need to develop new ways of preventing and treating crime in Africa. If preventatives and remedies are not found in a relatively short space of time the crime rate may be expected to rise alarmingly—if only because of the greater numbers of young people available to be affected by the influences which produce illegal behaviour.

It seems not unreasonable then, to propose that the study of criminology in Africa is sufficiently important academically, and a sufficiently practical need for the newly developing nations, to merit very special attention (a) from criminologists, (b) from other social scientists in related fields and particularly (c) from administrators and developmental economists. Here, there are possibilities of reaching back to the earlier stages of development, of considering, by practical experiment and research, what might have happened elsewhere in the world if the modern knowledge of crime and criminals had been available much earlier. Here are prospects of working out some completely new approaches to crime and of reviewing the new concept within contrasting cultures and at different stages of economic and social development.

[1] Universities in Africa are sometimes criticized for not being sufficiently practical, but their original orientation to the professional, administrative and technical needs of the countries founding them is difficult to escape. For example the first university college in Kenya was in engineering, the first in Tanzania was in law, the first in Zambia was in social development, and medical faculties were quickly established in Salisbury, Kinshasa, etc. Agricultural and technical colleges have also had widespread support at various educational levels.

[2] cf. *Africa and Law*, T. W. Hutchinson *et al.* (eds.), Madison, Milwaukee: University of Wisconsin Press, 1968: especially A. A. Schiller's argument in the Introduction for a specifically 'African Law' based on a common experience of African countries in the first stages of their legal evolution—and on a common plurality of laws in African countries. But, if there is a specific African Law and law serves to define crime, then the argument for a specific African Criminology is strengthened.

3
CAUSATION

GENERAL

Everyone wants to know why people really commit crime; even some of the criminals themselves would like to know! It must be recorded, however, that after a century and a half of widespread research and a whole library of studies, the results are inconclusive. This is far from saying that we are no nearer an understanding of crime. On the contrary, our knowledge of crime and criminals has been greatly extended by the impressive work already done on the subject.[1] Methods of study have been refined over the years and the assumptions behind, or the superficialities of, a great many earlier generalizations have been exposed. We no longer regard criminals as necessarily evil, economically deprived, biologically inferior or always mere creatures of circumstance. We no longer devise punishments which are physically degrading or mentally oppressive in the hope that they will force offenders to see the error of their ways. (Such methods have not been abandoned by all countries of the world, however, and examples of recourse to cruel and inhuman treatment can still be found.)

Nevertheless, the fruitlessness of much of the earlier work on crime has to be recognized and even in some of the later work it needs to be acknowledged that older and cruder notions are being resurrected and clothed in more respectable technical language. However sophisticatedly and with whatever deeper understanding of the processes involved, we are occasionally saying what was said more bluntly before.[2]

It is not just that causation research has raised as many questions as it has answered, for this would be true of most research and it helps to advance knowledge. It is rather that the answers so far emerging from this wealth of studies have too often proved to be either specious, or subject to too many caveats, exceptions and qualifications. They have explained some crimes but not always as much as a majority of offences; certainly they have rarely, if ever, cast a light on all crimes. Moreover, when new lines of inquiry have seemed to be evolving the developments in the associated social sciences have had a habit of reviving older and frequently discarded notions. Biochemistry, for example, is resuscitating older constitutional theories of crime if not actually adding weight to Lombrosianism. As a result, our ability to control crime has not been conspicuous and there is more than just a feeling that the real reasons for crime are still eluding us.

A start is most appropriately made with the disenchantment which is growing with the time-honoured reasons for crime: economic, social, biological and sociological. People in the developed countries are no longer convinced that crime is due mainly to poverty, overcrowding, broken homes or educational failures. It is admitted that these are factors; but when affluence apparently produces even more crime than poverty, when it can be shown that the majority of people crippled by all kinds of social disadvantages manage nevertheless to keep out of trouble with the law, and when children with practically every material, emotional and educational advantage commit serious crime, then it is clear that the factors are not causes. Biological and psychological explanations have fared no better since people with some (or all) of the deeper conflicts and adjustment problems and/or with some (or all) of the significant mental or physical disabilities may still be divided into those who do and those who don't commit crime. In other words, the mental or physical condition is not really decisive. At times, there is a feeling of chasing a will-o'-the-wisp and one talks more in criminology of an 'aetiological impasse'.

As we have already seen, the problems with crime causation stem largely from the attempt to explain human behaviour in general. The concept of crime is so diversified that there can be no sufficient set of reasons for all illegal behaviour which is not at the same time a set of reasons for all legal behaviour, i.e. a general theory of human conduct. As this has so far eluded all the natural and social sciences we may conclude that whatever its shortcomings, criminology is not really as inept as it might at first appear.

Unfortunately, the dissatisfaction with the search for causes has aroused in some quarters a deep feeling that studies of this kind are doomed to failure before they begin because they are improperly conceived. It is held that 'cause' really has no effective meaning, that to look for causes is futile and that the quest for answers to questions which are really unanswerable should be abandoned. It is further argued that the control of crime in society does not necessarily require a knowledge of 'causes' and that even without such a knowledge it is possible to predict crime within certain limits.[3] We can plan for expected levels of crime—even for rises in certain types of crimes—as people concentrate in towns. More than this, we can now say, within limits, which children in a given group are more likely to become delinquent or which prisoners in a group are more prone to recidivism.[4] Why then do we need to pursue the seemingly barren search for causes?

Those who argue this way see in this something like the shift in the natural sciences from metaphysics to observable facts. In this case too, as Auguste Comte showed, one eventually stopped asking unanswerable philosophical questions and began to collect and record data to look for relationships and construct theories for testing. There are at least two good reasons, however, why this is no parallel and why we still need studies of factors in crime, whether or not we chose to call them 'causative'.

First of all, we now know that the shift from philosophic speculation to positivism, from *a priori* speculation to scientific objectivity did not mean any abandonment of theorizing. Nor did it mean that the new method of inquiry was inductive, i.e. a process of linking observed facts to attain general conclusions. On the contrary the new scientific approach was hypothetico-deductive: first, hypotheses were formed and then tested to achieve predictability. Applied to criminal science this means that studies of factors in crime (whether interpreted causatively or not) are at least needed to generate the variety of relevant hypotheses for testing. Secondly, however disappointing the so-called causative studies of crime may have been in eliciting information on the decisive elements in criminal conduct, they have not been discoursive or subjectively based in any sense comparable to the *a priori* metaphysical inquiries of the Middle Ages. On the contrary, they have usually been studies carefully designed to eliminate or reduce subjectivity in the observations or recordings; and the limitations of their conclusions have usually been clearly recognized and commented upon in some final chapter.

It is in any case rather naïve to believe that when man can control crime, he will cease to ask 'why crime?'. No generation has been more successful at controlling its own natural environment than our own; yet no generation has been more exercised than our own about its use of such controls, their impact on the life of man and the reasons (or lack of them) for essence and existence. We may expect therefore that, prediction studies or not, linear programming or not, the control of crime or not, there will always be a place left for those 'useless' but intriguing excursions into crime causation. We will still want to know why.

It has been necessary to cover this general ground to keep this book up-to-date on criminological issues but, as a matter of sober fact, a discussion of this type is largely irrelevant to criminology in Africa. Here, as we have seen, so much still remains to be done that there is ample scope for both the useful and 'useless' type of inquiry. In Africa, people are still prone to operate on some of the older notions of crime causation and to believe that improved economic and social conditions will in themselves reduce crime. There are still so many shanty towns and so many deleterious fringe effects of urban and industrial growth that it is easy to find crime concentrated in such areas and conditions and to draw the conclusion that they are related causatively.

There is sometimes an impatience with tribal conditions and an anxiety for political unity and rapid change which may obscure some of the benefits which tribal experience could confer on the new patterns of urban living. The problem is to know what to preserve and what to change, and in the case of crime too little is known yet about the factors 'associated with crime'. It is possible, of course, to make some very broad statements already—such as 'crime increases with the size of the town',[5] or 'most criminals come from the poorer urban districts'. One can even plot 'delinquency areas'.[6] But detailed studies have been few and far between and even such broad propositions as these need checking against other data in other countries of the continent.

We do not yet know whether the factors associated with crime in say Europe and America are associated with crime in Africa. Truancy, for example, has a different meaning in a region where universal primary education is not yet a reality, where many miss basic schooling and where education is for most people a kind of philosopher's stone to transform one's way of life. The 'broken home' has a great many possible meanings in Europe and America. Obviously, with polygamy, with Christian, legal, customary and Muslim marriages in conjunction, and with some people having experienced one or more of these, the 'broken home' is a concept not easily applicable in its European and American form. Where one adds the complications of a child being group-orientated and probably as closely linked emotionally to his uncles and cousins as to his immediate parents, it is clear that the 'broken home' needs wider interpretation for the rural born and tribally reared children who sometimes commit crime in Africa.

Similarly, mental illness and defectiveness and their connection with anti-social behaviour will have different interpretations where the level of toleration is greater and the compartmentalization of a machine or technological age has not advanced so far. There has, as yet, been no attempt to check the theory of biological defects or constitutional inferiorities amongst offenders in Africa. Here the factors of malnutrition and protein deficiency, counterbalanced by enhanced physical powers due to exercise where Africans have to live by hunting or to contend with the long distances to walk to town, are likely to have importance. Finally, the whole area of psychological development—intellectual and emotional—awaits exploration for its relevance to African conditions.

In this chapter therefore we try to look at work done or remaining to be done in Africa on the 'factors associated with crime'—or even on crime causation if one is prepared to explore the circumstances of illegal conduct with greater liberality than perhaps academic precision might normally allow. Inevitably, the references are to work still to be done, rather than to investigations already made; but that is simply the state of affairs in African criminology as one moves towards the last quarter of the twentieth century.

THE SUPERNATURAL

Man's undoubted capacity for unworthy conduct has always been as difficult to explain as his remarkable penchant for heroism, steadfastness and self-sacrifice. As long as he could be regarded as a creature of some supernatural process or cosmos, however, all such departures from the norm were amenable to explanation as (a) the outcome of the constant struggle within the individual between his better and lower nature—with the external powers of good and evil, grace and temptation—greatly influencing human decisions, or (b) the result of witchcraft or magic. When behaviour was so widely divergent from the norm as to be outrageous it was often believed that good or evil powers had actually taken possession of the person.

If one is looking for a first approach to crime causation it might be found here in this recourse to the supernatural or to demonology.

This readiness to attribute undesirable behaviour to the influence of malevolent spirits, to a fate about which man can do nothing or to some outside interference with the natural order of things, seems to have been ubiquitous.

In the pre-scientific era in Europe, crime could always be explained by demonology. A person might act out of character because he was possessed by some alien spirit. His punishment was for his own good because the evil presence was being beaten out of him. Similarly in Africa the earlier ideas of crime derived from religious beliefs, irrational fears and systems of magic, divination or witchcraft. In fact Marett writing on 'Primitive Law' in the Encyclopaedia Britannica suggested that the genesis of the very idea of crime is to be found along a line drawn between (a) offences which are irredeemable, i.e. for which a culprit must be eliminated (exiled or executed) because of the spiritual uncleanliness which makes him a danger to society and (b) offences redeemable by the payment of compensation.[7]

Where other continents (and even the north of Africa) have had the devil and original sin to rationalize crime and account for human proclivity to evil, Africa, below the Sahara, has had its world of spirits providing an extra dimension to life and giving meaning where this seemed to be lacking. This approach is too often disdained without being understood: it is not to be dismissed as unthinking or irrational however, for it is based on an inexorable logic. It usually follows from the fundamental premise that everything must have a cause, that nothing happens by pure chance.[8]

The extra plane of existence performs a useful function for man, explaining the inexplicable (including crime) and accounting for disease and misfortune, especially where these seem to afflict some more than others. In this integral cosmology of matter and spirit nothing ever happens fortuitously; hidden powers are subject to manipulation by the malevolent or by the initiated; departed spirits continue active in world affairs and have to be propitiated; everything is ultimately subject to a rigid logic or necessary cause and necessary effect. It is a way of looking at crime which, whatever its demerits, has at least the advantage of not classifying the offender as in any sense inferior or as a moral leper. Later, scientific classifications of offenders as 'recidivists' or 'delinquents', or even as 'maladjusted', carry a stigma of abnormality which was (and is) usually incongruous in so far as the supernatural approaches to crime are concerned. The possessed or bewitched might be unfortunate—they may be dealt with harshly for their own good—but their normality is not questioned. What has happened to them could just as easily have happened to anyone else. This of course, is only one of the positive social functions of religious or magical beliefs and practice.

How far do these beliefs still persist in Africa? The question is difficult—perhaps as difficult as to ask to what extent similar beliefs in the occult persist in America, Europe or Asia. Obviously in the depths of the Congo's Ituri Forest, in the far reaches of north-west Kenya or the waterless regions of the Niger, people in small communities relatively isolated from outside influences will live with such beliefs for a long time to come. But also enmeshed with the spread of education and the industrialization of Africa such ideas are still to be found. In 1956 Lord Hailey referred to the continuing influence of witchcraft in town and country.[9] Two years later Marwick thought that witchcraft and magic might be increasing in the process of industrialization because essentially, he argued, such beliefs have two social functions; to reflect the stresses and strains in society, and to provide occasions for vindicating the cherished values of a community. Thus, held Marwick, in circumstances of rivalry and competition in towns, accusations of witchcraft might come too readily to the tongue, but the recourse to witchcraft to relieve tensions or obtain supposed advantages in competition with others would also be frequent. As for values, the attributing of misfortune in towns to the neglect of traditional beliefs would be only too easy.[10]

Much of this is dated: towns in Africa have grown and become much more complex and sophisticated. Moreover, the angle of perspective has changed in social anthropology so that there is less the attitude of watching a society in evolution and much more of an appreciation that corresponding studies made in London, Amsterdam or Los Angeles would doubtless disclose similar survivals of traditional beliefs and practices.

'Readers' are in great demand in New York; fortune tellers flourish in Shinjuku in modern Tokyo; throughout the 'developed' countries there are still many different forms of spiritualism and occult beliefs which depend upon external interpretations of human conduct. Similarly, diviners still prosper in private practice in modern Accra, 'medicine-man' prescriptions are still on sale in the open markets of Kinshasa and the witch doctor in a lounge suit can still make a good living in Johannesburg. A few years ago a Zambian government magazine *Nshila* carried an illustrated article on a fifty-year old Zulu earning

£3,000 a year by his 'treatments', divination and sale of lucky charms in a Lusaka suburb. Apposite too is the spate of strange new religions beginning to attract those young people in modern cities who feel repelled and unfulfilled by the stark rationalism of an easeful technology and who are avid in their quest of new experiences. Horoscopes are still a popular feature of newspapers in Europe and America, computerized fortune telling is enjoying a boom in the most scientifically advanced countries and in the most unlikely quarters of modern business a routine care is still taken to avoid ladders, the breaking of mirrors and the number thirteen.[11]

Abstruse as it may at first appear, then, this recourse to the supernatural tends to bury its own undertakers, and in any scientific approach to crime it would be unwise to discount the influence of superstition and the supernatural. It is not just that these older ideas are preserved in modern society like fossilized species in geological strata—they are still very active and derive a great deal of strength from the uncertainties and frustrations of human life. Moreover, in addition to its own indigenous beliefs, Africa has for hundreds of years been a mission territory for Christianity and Islam in all their aspects and varieties; so that cosmology and crime may have interlinks and relationships fascinating to explore if not always amenable to objective research. Whether in Africa, the USA or the South Pacific, magic, spell casting or spirit intervention can be useful face savers—comfortable justifications for conduct otherwise embarrassing to explain. They can relieve a person of guilt or responsibility, and for offenders in any part of the world this kind of rationalization is at least subjectively important.

Whether one gives it objective credence or not, the very fact that such older refuges of occultism are being revived by a younger generation in the technologically advanced societies (even amongst students of technology or nuclear physics)[12] suggests that we could well have been in too great a hurry to deny this spiritual dimension.

Modernized or not, Africa should be careful, therefore, to treat this side of its social existence with more understanding. It may not explain crime but it may well explain a good deal of the self-conceptualization of offenders, their justifications, some of the exaggerated reactions to different forms of crime and, in general, it may have a relevance for the sense of security which lies at the basis of much of modern psychology and which has hitherto been far more described than it has been understood. In late 1973 the author heard of a case in Sierra Leone involving a previous Minister of Information and two companions found quilty of ritual murder and sentenced to execution by public shooting.

EARLY ATTEMPTS AT SYSTEMATIC STUDY

The question of why some people conform to social standards and others do not worried Aristotle, and it has been of concern to philosophers and men of learning from the earliest times. It is not difficult to understand that a child reared and educated in a criminal community will take to crime quite normally: this is the behaviour which he has been taught and it is the acceptable way of life in the group to which he belongs. More difficult to explain, however, is the obvious fact that many people act contrary to the values they cherish; sometimes they commit acts which they know to be wrong and they behave against their better judgement. To explain this deviation from all the earlier training and the usual pressures to conform is the crux of the problem.

It is, furthermore, a general problem. Despite the turmoil in certain of the modern permissive societies, the divergence from established values and principles may be much less than might be indicated by student demonstrators, the flow of anti-establishment literature and the more vociferous and publicized sections of public life. Recent studies of student radicals have suggested that they frequently come from radical or near radical backgrounds, or that they have parental sympathy if not encouragement for their conduct.[13] A survey of eighteen to twenty-four year olds sponsored by *Fortune* magazine in America showed some 80 per cent to be 'traditionalist' in their values.[14] The conformist trend was clear.

In Africa, of course, the pressure to conform has probably been much greater because of the predominantly rural conditions and the smallness of most communities. It is true that the pressure to modernize and innovate has also been very great in the past few decades. The advent of political independence and the wider spread of education in Africa have intensified the drive to change and have increased the incentives to break out of any traditional or customary strait-jackets on economic and social improvement. In nearly all the African countries there has been a surging revolution of hopes and expectations not always matched by the expansion of opportunities. There is nearly everywhere in modern Africa a conspicuous drive to change, to develop and to transform the established systems of living which have not provided incomes sufficient to meet the new needs and expectations.

The younger generation (especially in the urban areas) lives, moves and operates in a world which is far removed from that in which their parents were reared—and at a vast distance from the background of their grandparents with even more pronounced tribal roots. Nevertheless there are still majorities of the people in rural areas where the older values and systems still have vigour and it is interesting to see that in Africa, as elsewhere, even in areas of the greatest change the deeper rooted values often survive. There are some interesting studies of towns in Africa which show a carry-over of the older patterns of relationships and standards.[15] There are also studies of attitudes and opinions which confirm a continuity of ideas and values if not always of practice.[16]

Finally, the recent emphasis on sub-cultures in a complex society, demonstrating that deviates in terms of the larger community may be thoroughly adjusted and compliant to the norms of their own peer or neighbourhood groupings,[17] serves to confirm the general tendency to conform. And this is so even though the tendency to conform may not mean quite the same thing to all people in the larger and more complicated social structures.

To explain deviation is therefore still the central issue of criminology in Africa as it is elsewhere. However, the earliest academic interest appears to have been more concerned with the law and its administration than with the peculiarities of human nature and again this has been as true of Africa as it has been of Europe.

One of the earliest comments on crime, based on observation rather than introspection, was that of Montesquieu who, in his *Spirit of Laws* (1748) suggested that criminality increased in proportion as one approached the Equator whereas drunkenness increased in proportion as one approached the Poles. This was obviously a speculative generalization without any other data than personal observation; but it still remains to be confirmed or denied.

It was Montesquieu who is said, through his writings on politics and economics, to have influenced Cesare Bonesana, Marchese de Beccaria, whose very effective protest against existing legal systems included some important recommendations for the rationalization of the administration of criminal justice. His *Essay on Crimes and Punishment* (London, 1767) called *inter alia* for a systematic scale of crimes and corresponding penalties based essentially on the hedonistic principle of a human motivation inspired by rewards and punishments, pleasure and pain.

Beccaria is important because he was almost immediately effective. He was writing at an opportune time for criminal law reform in Europe, i.e. amidst the ferment of ideas on statecraft which preceded and naturally succeeded the French Revolution. Reform was in the air and Beccaria's recommendations were taken up in many countries. He made a special point of stressing the prevention of crime as being more important than its punishment, and this concept rose again in Bentham's 'criminal prophylaxis' and then again in Enrico Ferri's *sostitutivi penali*.[18]

This was, of course, the period when Africa was being colonized by the Dutch, the Portuguese, the Arabs and others. It was in 1652 that the Placaaten of the States of Holland were being introduced into the Cape, and we are told that the dividing line between criminal and civil wrongs only emerged clearly in Roman-Dutch law in the sixteenth century.[19] In any case these laws were originally for the settlers and customary law held sway for most of Africa at this time. It is difficult, therefore, to find the kinds of comments on crime and its treatment which might match those of the European settlers, but it may be noted that the *Fetha Nagast* or 'Law of the Kings' which was introduced into Ethiopia in the seventeenth century had its moral injunctions and observation on crime as well as provision for punishment.[20] There is doubtless a wealth of material just waiting to be developed from the minutes, reports and drafts of model penal codes which relate to the early years of colonization and which would at least indicate the attitudes to crime and its punishment of the first administrators. The *Blue Book* issued in Ghana in 1859 held that 'the lash is the only real deterrent'; but the *Blue Book* of 1903 recorded only 35 whippings in 3,942 convictions.[21] The Penal Code of the Portuguese territories of Africa was formally extended to these countries from Portugal by decrees of 1869 and 1880 and provision was made for respecting local usages and customs. Article 84 enjoins the judge to 'take into account the seriousness of the offence, its results, the degree of deceit or of guilt, the motives of the offender and his personality'.[22]

But it is really not easy to trace the kind of early observations on crime which parallel those of Europe. In Africa the eighteenth and nineteenth centuries were the years of tribal hostilities and slave trading. So much went unwritten and unrecorded. Crime could mean very different things in the several parts of the continent, or it could depend on power or social status and the punishments could be incredibly light by European standards (e.g. payment of compensation for rape or murder) or severe in the extreme. However, in what is known, there are some telling comparisons with Europe not only in the legal concepts implicit in African customary law,[23] but also in the use of exile, the ordeal, imprisonment and compensation.

Yet, as is well known, there is a treasury of anthropological research in Africa. These systematic descriptions of rural, tribal (and occasionally urban) life in Africa usually outline the law and its administration in a tribal setting.[24] In some cases the judicial procedure is the main theme of the study and there have been attempts by colonial government anthropologists to codify customary law.[25] Other works have analysed the processes of conflict or cohesion in a society, the effects on tribal life of a crisis (e.g. caused by a government order to transplant the village,[26] or more gradually, by the loss of effective manpower through urbanization), or the principles of political structure and change.

Whilst nearly all of this is of criminological interest, it is a great pity that anthropologists have not focused attention until very recently on specific social problems in a simple society and on the procedures adopted to solve them. It has usually been the normal rather than the abnormal which has attracted anthropological attention—and the attachment to social classifications and structural typologies has frequently excluded any detailed study of a phenomenon such as crime.

The various studies of conflict, for example, have given little direct attention to deviant behaviour. Schapera discussed incest amongst the Tswana[27] and Seligman considered its relation to social structure and descent;[28] but incest as a crime, its incidence and the types of persons involved or the kinds of families in which it occurs remain to be fully investigated. The picture is changing, of course, and more interest is being shown by social anthropologists in such aspects of social life, but it can be said of Africa, as of Europe, that early attention of an academic nature tended to concentrate on legal, social or administrative systems or problems—or on studies of controls and the elements of customary law—rather than on crime and criminals.

To return to Europe, a more objective approach was that of Adolph Quetelet (1796-1874), the Belgian astronomer and mathematician sometimes called the 'father of statistics'. Quetelet, working on the then grossly inadequate figures for crime, found a certain regularity in the statistical pattern from which he deduced that each age-group had a fixed proclivity for crime which remained more or less constant throughout the ages (provided that the basic economic, political and social conditions did not change). In a more sophisticated form this theory is not without its supporters in modern times—notably in the writing of the Dutch expert Professor van Bemmelin.[29]

Quetelet also suggested that crimes against the person were prevalent in the south and in warm weather whilst crimes against property were concentrated in the north or in the colder seasons. This he called his 'thermic law of delinquency'. Though some exceptions have been found (especially in respect of murder) there have been more recent criminological studies which go some way towards supporting this unusual proposition. As a social explanation of this phenomenon, it has been suggested that in Mediterranean areas, or in countries with warmer weather, there is more social intercourse with people spending most of their time outside their houses. This additional social contact means more opportunities for quarrels and assaults. In colder seasons or colder countries people spend more time at home with less opportunity for the social gatherings where quarrelling and personal offences like assault are likely to arise. On the other hand, inclement weather has often, in the past at least, meant greater economic stress and therefore more economic crime. It is worth noting that Lombroso suggested at the turn of the nineteenth century that extremes of temperature, hot or cold, sap the individual's energy and leave little time or inclination for deviations such as crime.[30] There have been few statistical approaches to crime in either the early or later studies made in Africa, partly because the procedures for data collection are only just being developed, and also because the expertise for any serious statistical analysis has been lacking.

Before we knew as much as we do now about mental illness and mental defect, before we made the allowances which we do now for the considerable force of circumstances, it was usual to equate crime with sin and to consider such behaviour as always being the result of a conscious and responsible choice by the person concerned. This might be the result of the battle for the soul being waged between God and Satan, but in the last analysis the choice was made by the individual between the promptings of his lower and better nature.

Immoral or unethical behaviour was considered as much the province of law as the more overt public misdemeanours. Today, we clearly distinguish between sin and crime, partly because we appreciate the difficulty of making any human judge a judge of conscience, partly because of the difficulty of trying to enforce any law dealing with private morality, and partly (perhaps most significantly) because we are no longer agreed amongst ourselves as to the meaning of sin. But although we separate the immoral and illegal, they obviously overlap and some forms of immoral behaviour which are clearly definable and capable of legal check and proof are also crimes, for example sexual offences, perjury, theft, etc. Other forms of immorality are not usually illegal, for example private drunkenness, prostitution on private premises, and adultery.[31]

It would be an over-simplification to say that our ancestors in Europe or Africa did not appreciate the distinction between sin and crime. Elias has shown that a distinction was clearly made between public and private offences in African customary law and that the overlap remaining could be compared to the overlap in the development of Western law.[32] The fact that spiritual danger to the community often entered into this distinction does not exclude the understanding that all spiritual offences were not crimes or that all crimes were not sins.[33]

In the medieval West they even provided separate ecclesiastical courts for moral offences. The point was, however, that no type of anti-social or undesirable public or private behaviour was thought to be outside the scope of the law. Crime or sin, the action was held to spring from the same source—the perverse free will of man himself. In these earlier times, crime was explained simply by man's fallen nature as affected by Satan playing upon it with a variety of temptations.[34] The courts, lay or ecclesiastical, enforced the law, not only to keep order but to help man himself to resist such temptation.

In Africa there was apparently little concept of man's 'fallen nature' and often guilt or intention was less important than remedying the consequence of the act, actual or spiritual. The Nuer did not think in terms of guilt in cases of homicide: the killer himself had to be cleansed of his blood-spilling so that the fixing of guilt did not arise.[35] The Barotse were strictly enjoined to observe custom and taboo, and intention did not enter into it.[36] There was, however, a spiritual dimension to much of the wrongdoing which, as we have seen, served to differentiate crimes from torts to a considerable extent. This is an area of study which is still only partially explored and much more is needed to make any positive pronouncements of a general nature for Africa. Probably sin and crime were equated on the earlier European pattern in some societies even when the basic cosmologies differed.

In other societies there may have been greater reliance on restoring balances without too much concern for sinfulness as this was understood in the West.

There is a belief amongst some people today that the divorce between law and morals may have gone too far and that the higher rate of crime in developed countries may be traced in part to the decline of morals land the negative quality of an objective law unsupported by moral precept. There are still ethical questions about law enforcement and justice which cannot be eliminated. For instance, it might be possible to prevent crime by paying pensions to criminals. This, however practical, is still excluded because of the 'just' or ethical arguments against it. The subtle if no longer violent methods used by the police to induce confessions may sometimes be considered 'unethical', and the use of electronic 'bugging' devices or the administration of drugs to obtain evidence or control offenders introduce issues of human rights which may be said to be ethical in the last analysis. Again there are circumstances investing offences which the law cannot always take into account but which morally aggravate the crime, for example stealing from people who can ill afford to lose the money, assaulting the weak, taking unfair advantage of a lack of education. Law and morals are therefore related in a way which sometimes makes it difficult to maintain the distinction.

Nevertheless a change has taken place in our attitude to crime which does not permit us to ignore the fact that, however much they overlap, morals and law are not the same thing. Situational ethics and the recent emphasis on the relativity of morals have effectively deprived the concept of morality of much of its practical value for law-making.

Much of the change in attitudes and thinking may be ascribed to the size and complexity of the social organization and to the time sequence in development. It has already been suggested that where societies are small and relatively uncomplicated the fusion between morals and law is necessarily more pronounced. The need for distinction in practice is not so pressing even if the differences are perceived. In tribal Africa, for example, customary law, whilst exhibiting many of the essential characteristics of a more developed law, is essentially a mixture of law, custom and morals. Behaviour is regulated by custom, and custom not only covers accepted conduct towards political authority but also behaviour towards the elders, towards relatives, or within the family. In such societies immoral behaviour such as adultery might be serious for the society as a whole since it could lead to disputes and quarrels or to people seeking redress in a way which would promote public disorder. It therefore has to be treated as a public offence. The smaller the social group, the more likely it is that there will be no distinction between law and morals. The large number of traditional societies in Africa with customary law to regulate all conduct, legal or moral, reminds us again that the explanation of crime is a part of the explanation of human behaviour generally.

Our scientific studies both in Europe and Africa have taken us in a rather different direction from that which holds man wholly and entirely responsible for his own behaviour. When we enumerate today the subtle and profound influences of inherited defects, of the handicaps which emerge from faulty child care or the outright neglect of children, of physical disabilities such as epilepsy or glandular disorders, of the powerful impact of environment, we may well wonder whether man is a free agent or whether he is not a victim of endowment and circumstance—hardly, if at all, to blame for his indiscretions. Genetics, psychology, physiology, sociology and anthropology all provide us with explanations of behaviour which tend to shift the responsibility for crime from the individual to the conditions of his nature, nurture, and social situation.

Furthermore, there is a new interest in the areas of human conduct which the law should or should not be seeking to cover. The flood of legislation regulates behaviour to an extent not previously known and creates crimes out of actions and omissions which no longer outrage the public conscience. There is a growing tendency therefore to review criminal justice systems with a view to reducing the risks which people run of appearing before the criminal courts.

Yet, whatever the branch of modern science, we are still left without a full explanation of crime if we omit entirely the natural perversity of human beings. If man is not fully the master of his fate, he still cannot be fully explained as an automaton, reacting in a fixed way to his instincts and to the stimuli about him. It is not adequate in the light of our modern knowledge to think of him as being entirely free to act or react as he thinks fit or to pretend that he always rationally counts the consequences and then makes a calculated choice or decision. These myriad influences are there and they undoubtedly affect his action; but some element of personal choice is there too and it is the balance of these which makes us human.

The early explanations of crime showed little appreciation of such niceties. They were simpler, more direct and less complicated because the knowledge was more limited. Crime was an aberration to be dealt with by measured and 'just' deterrents. Nowadays we are not too sure that crime is an aberration and, being pragmatic, we are more concerned to know whether deterrence really works. Today we appreciate more the observation of Dr Johnson, 'As I know more of mankind I expect less of them and am ready to call a man a "good man" upon easier terms than I was formerly.'

MORE RECENT THEORIES

The first modern studies of the criminal were studies of prison populations and they suffered from the tendency to generalize about criminals from the recorded characteristics of offenders who had been caught. We cannot forget that not all criminals are caught. In fact a detection percentage of 50 per cent is considered today to indicate a creditable degree of police efficiency. There are therefore as many offenders uncaught as caught and generalizations about prison populations have probably more reference to the reasons why these people have been unable to escape capture than they have to the reasons for crime.

(a) Heredity—Physical Constitution

Without doubt, the credit for directing modern scientific attention to the offender himself must go to Lombroso (1836-1909). Lombroso was an Italian Army physician who therefore had a professional bias towards biological inquiry. Towards the end of the nineteenth century he became interested in the physical differences between well disciplined soldiers and those soldiers who were insubordinate, badly behaved and troublesome. He noted not only that they appeared to differ physically but also that the offenders had a marked weakness for lurid tattoos. Later he investigated groups of convicts and eventually emerged from his studies convinced that criminals were born and not made. He demonstrated the physical inferiority of convicts as compared with people generally and he suggested that there was a definite criminal type which could usually be identified by such features as high cheek-bones, a flattened nose, handle-shaped or sessile ears, a long lower jaw, excessive hairiness or the abnormal lack of hair.[37]

Lombroso explained crime therefore as an atavism, a pathological regression towards our animal nature. If this seems rather far-fetched today we should note that as recently as 1939 an American anthropologist named Hooton went out of his way to confirm it. He did tremendous work measuring and comparing 14,000 convicts in America with 3,000 non-convicts including firemen, swimmers and hospital out-patients. From his work he concluded that crime could be almost entirely explained by physical or racial inferiority. 'Criminals', he said, 'present a united front of biological inferiority.'[38]

Both Lombroso and Hooton were trying, of course, to emphasize the importance of heredity as an explanation of crime. But, as usually presented, the conclusions over-reach the evidence. Just because we find that people in prison are physically and mentally inferior to the population generally, does not mean either that criminal tendencies are inborn, or that crime springs from such physical or mental disabilities. We have already pointed out that there may be criminals outside prison and within the group which we are comparing with prisoners. This, in itself, invalidates the conclusion that criminals are necessarily different. Even more important, however, is the fact that there are a greater number of people outside prison with the same physical and mental handicaps who do not commit crime. They are the proof that defects or deficiencies alone are an inadequate explanation of crime. Criminality does not invariably go with inferiority—nor is it absent in many well developed and intelligent people.

Nevertheless, the more general argument that behaviour is influenced, if not governed, by our physical constitution is not so easily dismissed. Modern schools of crimino-biology have refined and modernized the Lombroso approach, especially in Europe. Kurt-Kells in Germany, Macauliffe and Segaud in France, Villa and Nicole Pende in Italy, have all held it to be the morphological and consequent psychological tendencies of the individual which must be examined to really understand criminal behaviour. They have sought evidence of inherited dispositions or inclinations, still in the belief that heredity is the most decisive of the various factors in crime.

There have also been attempts to prove the influence of physical factors or heredity, particularly the studies of single families like the Jukes or the Johnsons (a family of counterfeitors).[39] In these studies, the families were traced through several generations to show how the anti-social characters persisted over time. This was advanced as a proof of the influence of heredity; but it could equally be argued as a proof of environmental influence since children born to such parents are subjected to definite and very similar external pressures which may have nothing to do with heredity but which may induce conformity to the family pattern of behaviour. The fact that a family is consistently delinquent from generation to generation does not prove that criminality is inherited for we cannot be sure in such families how much is acquired during the upbringing. Clearly nutritional habits, poverty, occupational grouping and religion are all aspects of a family's environment which may persist from generation to generation.[40]

Only about five or six years ago the heredity theory of crime received stimulation from the discovery in prison hospitals of a significant number of tall males with an extra Y chromosome. Since then the number of studies of this XYY karyotype have multiplied and XYY genetical constitutions have been advanced in court to substantiate pleas of diminished responsibility. This new concept of the 'born criminal' has been described by Mergen as:

> Karyotype XYY; conspicuous height (over 180 cm) due especially to the extraordinary length of the leg; tendency towards juvenile acne, eczema, varices and ulcers of the leg; conspicuous early delinquency (first offence at 10-12 years of age); EEG changes suggestive of minimum brain damage; a conspicuous ECG; an obviously dysregulated sex life; sporadic impulsive actions; indulgence and lack of inhibitions; egocentricity; lack of a sense of values; sporadic aggression against individuals or objects; pathological affective features.[41]

However, the case is by no means proved. Mergen points out that the characteristics he enumerates can claim neither general validity nor exclusiveness and it is clear that a comprehensive analysis is required by all the disciplines concerned. In calling for this Mergen also made the point that a 'born criminal' is not necessarily an offender: he merely has more criminogenic qualifications than others.

Surveys of several thousands of newborn infants have shown the XYY karyotype to be far more common than was suspected. Sergovich, a geneticist, suggests that his surveys cast doubt on the theory of an inherited predisposition since they make it likely that a great many well-adjusted persons may possess the extra Y.[42] In 1966 the Elwyn Institute, Pennsylvania, began a study of tall males in a variety of Pennsylvanian institutions which, although 'a more extensive and thorough study' is needed, suggests again that the XYY male has been falsely stigmatized. The frequency of his involvement in anti-social behaviour and crime may not be very different from that of the average citizen.[43]

On the other hand, a procedure developed for the rapid breeding of XYY killfish and observing them in competition with other males (XY), demonstrates that the XYY fish emerges victorious from nearly every physical combat with normal males and that it wins competitions for female's favours 88 per cent of the time. The conclusion is that if not more aggressive they are certainly more competitive.[44] Some dramatic cases are being reported of persistent criminals or violent murderers with the extra Y,[45] and considerable public interest has been aroused.

With samples still small and control groups inadequate, it would be unwise to pontificate on genetic predispositions of this kind. Large-scale testing of both criminal and non-criminal populations is required. There have been indications that the additional Y does not exercise its influence via the intelligence[46] and a suggestion that a supernumerary Y does not result in any clear-cut, phenotypic features.[47] There are many angles to the social interpretation of the extra Y, therefore, but its significance could be very great for criminology and may be expected to absorb a great deal of attention during the next decade or two.[48]

Along with the extra Y chromosome should go many more studies of the genetic complex known as the Klinefelter Syndrome (XXY) which results in hypogonadism and sometimes intellectual defect. The typical individual with this genetic make-up finds it difficult to adapt and has low social drive. He is emotionally unstable and may manifest a variety of neurotic, psychotic and sociopathic types of behaviour.[49] Once again the question is: to what extent is the Klinefelter Syndrome distributed in the criminal and non-criminal groups—and of course what is meant by 'criminal' and 'non-criminal' in this context?

Other factors currently being probed in the search for inherited traits with significance for criminology but which suffer equally from the inadequacy of data on distribution, include the incidence of congenital dyslexia and dysgraphia (reading and writing defects),[50] and the predisposition to the affective illnesses.[51]

Still on the theme of genetic heritage, there have been some interesting studies of twins. Ashley-Montague, Lange, Rosanoff and Hardy[52] have all shown that the behaviour of monozygotic or identical twins is very similar. If one is criminal, then, as a rule, so is the other. Lange's study was of thirty pairs of adult male twins. Of this group thirteen were monozygotic and seventeen dizygotic or fraternal. He found that 77 per cent of the identical twins and 12 per cent of the fraternal twins showed similar behaviour—if one was criminal so was the other. Other studies by similar methods have given results showing the same tendency amongst identical twins but with differences from fraternal twins which are not nearly so striking as Lange's.

It has to be remembered, however, that such twins do not only inherit similar traits and characteristics—they are subjected from birth to very similar environmental influences. It is also clear that in many cases one monozygotic twin acquires dominance over the other which accounts for similar behaviour as readily as does the notion of heredity. Furthermore from these studies themselves we have ample evidence of the behaviour differences in dizygotic pairs.

In 1925, the English translation of Kretschmer's work *Physique and Character* was published. In this Kretschmer divided mankind into four physical types, the asthenic, athletic, pyknic and dysplastic, and he suggested that each physical type had its corresponding temperament. Very briefly, he was arguing that everyone may be classified as being of either slight build, muscular build or fat and round. He thought that one's physical build determined one's personality or mental illness—schizophrenia or manic-depression depended upon one's physical type. Thus, the pyknic or rounded person would tend to be jovial and extroverted and more likely, if he suffered mentally, to be a manic-depressive; whereas, the lean angular figure would be more likely to be reserved, asthenic, or moody and, if he suffered at all mentally, would be more prone to schizophrenia. Criminologists like Mezger and Aschaffenburg quickly saw the implications of this. Aschaffenburg suggested that most habitual offenders were physically of the athletic or asthenic types whilst most occasional criminals were pyknics. In other words, one was less likely to be criminal if one were fat and round than if one were long and thin.

A more sophisticated version of this theory has been developed in America in recent years by Sheldon and his colleagues.[53] Using three 'somatotypes'—the ectomorph (leptosome—long, thin, delicate), the endomorph (pyknic—round, short, pouchy and flabby) and the mesomorph (athletic, muscled, broad, big boned), he showed differences in physical type corresponding to differences in temperament and disposition as between delinquents and non-delinquents. This difference he believed to be a form of inferiority which criminals inherited. Sutherland and Cressey consider that his evidence did not warrant such conclusions.[54] Freed in South Africa used the classification of Sheldon along with the Kretschmer dysplastic in a study of eighty-nine delinquents. Though he found that ectomorphs and mesomorphs were more persistent in crime than the other two types—and that mesomorphs were prone to personal offences, like assault, whilst ectomorphs went in more for theft—he refused to draw any general conclusions because of the smallness of his sample.[55]

It appears to be fairly well established today that our physical build or constitution does have some influence upon our personality or character and that it may, in part at least, explain our inclinations, attitudes, interests, impulses and the general trend of our behaviour. However, since pure specimens of the three or four constitution types are rare and most people are a mixture of these various physical categories, there is still ground for believing each individual to be unique in his physical and mental make-up. It appears rather extravagant of Sheldon, therefore, to have supposed that eventually, with accurate physical measurement, we might be able to predict a person's conduct.

Other developments in the biological approach to crime have been in the realm of endocrinology or the study of glands. Since people can be made more or less active, more or less nervous, more or less alert or relaxed by gland treatment, it seems reasonable to believe that the condition of the glands in the body may be the clue to certain types of behaviour.

Schlapp and Smith were hopeful in 1928 that a study of crime based on endocrinology would solve most of the problems.[56] Others like Berman[57] and Cobb[58] regarded the glands as the real determinants of conduct, legal and illegal. Later writers were less confident, however, and in 1941 Hoskins warned that there is 'more to be done before psychology, sociology and criminology can be convincingly rewritten as aspects of endocrinology'.[59]

The very inconclusive study of physical types by Freed is the one example known to the writer of a study of heredity and crime in Africa south of the Sahara at the time of writing. For reasons already given it is still rather too early to expect work at this level—but the indications are that it will not be long before the first probes in this direction begin to be made.[60]

Common sense would lead us to expect that age and sex would affect rates of crime. Early in the century, Goring found maximum crime rates in the fifteen to twenty age range.[61] He suggested that where heredity gave criminal inclinations offences could be expected at a very young age. English figures show that the age of maximum convictions for indictable offences is twelve or thirteen for boys and sixteen or seventeen for girls, whilst American figures place this age between eighteen and twenty-four.[62] Crime, then, seems to decline with age in most countries. Moreover Fox found that as offenders aged, the offences they committed shifted from the more violent and physical (kidnapping, burglary, robbery) to fraud, forgery, embezzlement and sex.[63] This seems reasonable—vigorous crimes being committed when offenders are young and strong, more deceitful offences being preferred with age.

In Africa south of the Sahara any analysis of ages is hampered by the general lack of comprehensive registrations of births. At the time of writing there are still large numbers of people who do not know their own ages and only where the births were locally registered at administrative or mission centres can age be known with any certainty. It is significant that a recently published work, *African Penal Systems* (op. cit.), covering thirteen countries and giving many figures for crimes and criminals makes no reference to the ages of offenders. Nevertheless studies of the offenders' age groupings have already begun especially relating to young people. Clifford found twelve to sixteen years of age to be the group into which most of the juvenile offenders in Zambia fell[64] and there are other studies now being undertaken but as yet unreported.

As regards sex, it seems everywhere true that women commit less crime than men. All kinds of reasons have been advanced to account for this. It is often held that prostitution is the real form of female crime and that most of this goes unrecorded—but so does male immorality which is probably no less. Clark, in an early study, found a stronger sense of honour amongst girls.[65] Grünhut spoke of greater leniency shown to women and girls, who are less likely to be prosecuted and more likely to be acquitted.[66] Other explanations include the degree of emancipation, female crime rates being higher where women are more free;[67] the biological differences between men and women, the latter being more passive and less aggressive;[68] the dependence of women on men, the former instigating rather than committing crime; the greater protection and supervision of girls to avoid early pregnancy; the different social position of women. It has even been suggested that women are more deceitful and do not get caught so frequently. No doubt both social and biological differences are important, but for the time being it remains very much a mystery why the differences between male and female crime should be so great. It seems that Africa shares this common world experience of having far fewer women than men brought before the courts.[69] However, the proportion of female to male crime has risen dramatically in Europe and the USA since 1969. In some areas a rate of one woman to ten men has become one in five.

Finally, on the biological determinants of behaviour there is the information becoming available from the experience of prefrontal leucotomy (a surgical operation on the lobes of the brain which changes personality and conduct), the biochemical research on the molecules of ribonucleic acid (RNA) or the antibiotic puromycin which promotes or retards memory, and the drugs like sodium-amytal, promazine, frenquel, etc., used in the treatment of mental illness to tranquillize patients or relieve depression. There is also the controversy about LSD (lysergic acid diethylamide) the 'consciousness-changing' agent which is held by some to be capable of giving greater concentration and insight without being habit forming. There are drugs not normally regarded as 'psychotropic' (e.g. anticholinergic drugs and diphenylhydamtoin) which are centrally acting and decrease or occasionally increase aggression, but most of the published experiments have been with animals. These all have a profound effect on behaviour, but it is difficult to keep track of the biochemical developments in this area. By the time this book has gone to press all the above drugs could well be out of date. Moreover, there is, at the time of writing, a considerable campaign in America to legalize drug-taking—especially of the soft type (marijuana, hashish or hemp) so that the question becomes one not only of the effects on behaviour but also of the extent to which that behaviour is criminal. However, in a radio discussion in New York whilst this was being written it was being estimated that in some areas nearly 80 per cent of the crimes could be traced to drug-taking and that a 'junkie' needed as much as US $150 a week to keep up his habit.

The development of encephalography suggests that epileptics and psychopaths have similar graphs of mental activity when their 'thought waves' are traced electrically. This brings us back to Lombroso and his 'epileptoid' basis for criminals. It has also been thought that abnormal electro-encephalographs might correlate with criminal behaviour, but the results have been conflicting. In a study of EEGs of 1,250 persons in custody for crimes of aggression extending over twenty years, an attempt was made recently to compare the habitually aggressive offenders and those, who, although they had been placed in custody for a major violent crime were not habitually aggressive. It was found that there were abnormalities in the EEGs of 65 per cent of the habitually aggressive offenders but in only 24 per cent of the other group. These may be compared with an estimated 12 per cent abnormal EEGs for the population as a whole. When the prisoners known to be mentally retarded or who had epilepsy or a major head injury were excluded the figures for abnormal EEGs were still 57 per cent of the habitually aggressive but only 12 per cent of the apparently normal people who had committed a solitary crime of violence.[70]

A great deal of this work is, as yet, unco-ordinated and few writers suggest that it excludes the element of personal responsibility or the effects which training or contact with other people may have on behaviour. It is obvious, however, that the Lombroso approach to a constitutional explanation of crime has found greater and more scientific support over the years. It is no less clear that future work on the biological influences on behaviour will be of great interest to criminologists.

(b) Social Explanations

The early deficiencies of the biological school led criminologists, especially American criminologists, to move towards the other extreme and to argue that crime is the result of the social and economic environment. This preference for a sociological or economic interpretation derived much of its force from two social attitudes of the time. It accorded well with the American desire to believe that men are born equal and their destiny is in their own hands. There was a pride in self-help, personal achievement, inventiveness and adaptability in America which did not sit easily with any predestination which might flow from the rigid view of heredity as a determinant of behaviour. Secondly, the preference for a social explanation of crime was deeply influenced by the prevailing climate of social or economic reform. The social structure should be changed to solve society's deeper problems—including crime.

It would have been surprising if the twentieth century preoccupation with socialism and the Marxist struggle against capitalism had not found its echo in the writings of criminologists. Early in the century, Bonger, a Dutchman, wrote a doctoral thesis, which in 1916 was translated into English as 'Criminality and Economic Conditions', showing the statistical correlation between crime and poverty or under-privilege. He contended that crime was a feature of the capitalist system: thus the debilitating leisure of the upper classes, on the one hand, and the widespread misery of the masses in the lower classes, gave rise to crime. The only solution was a transformation of the total economy.[71]

Bonger has achieved fame less by the significance of his analysis than by the attention he attracted from those who have sought to expose his errors and refute his theory. He could certainly have argued that crime resulted from industrialization and urban growth—this was in line with common experience and may have been what he was really implying in his denunciation of capitalism. To go further and blame capitalism itself for crime was to invite not only economic and social, but also political refutation. It was to imply that socialism would eliminate or significantly reduce crime.

The Third United Nations Congress on the Prevention of Crime and the Treatment of Offenders held at Stockholm in August 1965 saw delegates from certain socialist countries maintaining that crime in their nations was declining in importance. This was so contradictory—nearly all other developing countries experiencing growing rates of crime as their towns grew—that some delegates asked whether indeed East and West were talking about the same thing. It is possible they were not since 'crime' is always re-interpreted when revolutionary, and particularly communist, governments come to power. In so far as general news is available it would seem that socialist countries have a problem of 'wayward youth' familiar in the West. In 1964 a symposium on the control of juvenile delinquency was held in East Berlin where papers dealt *inter alia* with juvenile gang delinquency and the liability of parents for their children's misbehaviour.[72] And in Poland it has been shown that despite falling crime rates in the years 1961-6, the crime rate in the largest cities is particularly high.[73]

This pattern of serious urban delinquency but generally improving rates of crime prevention in socialist countries may reflect less the effect of socialism as a doctrine than the effect of an authoritarian rule with a unifying ideology. This has an obvious range of advantages over any permissive society. The writer's travels in Eastern Europe in 1970 left him with the impression that these countries were certainly not experiencing the rise of crime, and especially of violent and organized crime, which was currently troubling a number of the Western nations. Urban disruptions were having their effects but mobility was relatively controlled. There was no apparent dissent on fundamental values, and sub-cultures on the American pattern were a great deal more difficult to form.

It is interesting to see that there have been some moves in this political direction in Africa due to the development of African socialism. Zanzibar has favoured a system of 'Comrades Courts' to deal with gangs and robbers in particular, and 'Operation Vijana' launched by the Tanu Youth League in 1970 had norm-enforcing implications.[74] No doubt parallels could be found in the other African countries especially those favouring single parties and a nationalistic ideology, and it seems reasonable to expect that there will be some crime-reducing effects.

Whatever the influence of socialism on crime, Bonger's approach was too general for validity. He seems to have followed too readily his own socialist leanings. He does not seem to have allowed for the fact that more people who are underprivileged do not commit crime than those who do. He appears to have accepted too the oversimplified concept of capitalism which was in vogue at the time. On the other hand, he produced an interesting classification of crimes according to motives and he found much support for his view that selfishness was at the base of most criminal conduct. Behind this, of course, was his implication that selfishness was especially characteristic of capitalism. One can agree without going so far as to imply that selfishness is a monopoly of capitalism.

It would have been interesting to have had Bonger's observations on the modern situation in developed countries where, although the rigours of classical capitalism have been greatly modified to the extent that workers are frequently shareholders, and people are better housed, better educated, better paid and fed than previously, there is more crime than ever before. Crime by the affluent does not fall into Marx's category of the dissolute rich when the condition of relative comfort is so widely spread. On the other hand, it could be argued that expectations have increased so that 'poverty' is really more widely spread.

The argument that a reform of the politico-economic system could eliminate crime, or—to put it another way—that crime is caused by a particular economic structure, is rather outmoded and hardly accords with the Durkheim view that we can expect crime in all societies. This is not to say, however, that some politico-economic structures may not be more productive of some types of crime or that changes in the patterns could not radically change the incidence of crime. We have observed that a uniform ideology and an ordered society probably provides less incentive or opportunity for crime and provided a society is prepared to meet the political, social and economic costs of such a change it could reduce its crime rate. There may be mid-positions, however, which are probably best observed in modern Africa. More to the point, it has long been obvious that economic circumstances will exercise some influence on individual behaviour. It is, in fact, well established that the bulk of all the crime reported and prosecuted is concentrated within the lower income groups; that is to say amongst the unskilled, the less well educated, the poor and the badly housed sections of the population.[75]

Apart from the pressure of material need being a reason for crime, it has been questioned whether such evidence is really reliable. The discussion of white collar crime initiated by Sutherland[76] suggests that there is probably a range of delinquent behaviour amongst 'respectable' and socially powerful classes which is handled by civil courts or administrative tribunals and which does not find recognition in police statistics. Again, police policy may lead to the underprivileged being prosecuted more frequently. Finally, it has always to be remembered that many more poor people are law-abiding than criminal. Immigrant groups like the Japanese in Seattle,[77] the Jews or the Chinese, have been observed to have low crime rates even when economically they were no better off than neighbours with high crime rates. Similar low rates of crime were observed by the writer amongst the Armenians in Cyprus and the Asians in East and Central Africa. Many of them were no better off than the people of other communities but they lived in integrated groups with standards of their own. Sheldon also found that there was no significant link between juvenile crime and economic position when other factors were held constant. By contrast, holding the economic factor constant there was a marked degree of social disorganization amongst delinquents.[78] It may be agreed that if physical hardship and material deprivation were the basic instigators of crime, then Africa with its millions at subsistence level would be crime-ridden, and this is the reverse of the facts. The relatively low crime rate in rural Africa, and in Africa generally, suggests that other factors are more influential and underline the relativity of the concept of poverty.

It seems, therefore, that material penury alone is not responsible for crime but a *feeling* of poverty combined with a variety of other social factors probably is more criminogenic. Certainly the difference between the classes in society is still with us and later studies have suggested more subtle reasons for crime due to difference of class or race standards.

The fact that in the large towns crime tends to be concentrated in particular areas or districts also attracted the attention of earlier investigators. Clifford Shaw and his collaborators were busy on this from 1929. They showed that delinquents lived usually in central districts alongside warehouses and factories. These were the slum areas, marked by dilapidated dwellings, overcrowding, poverty, unemployment, the lack of recreational facilities and a variety of other social problems. They found districts in Chicago where the crime rate had remained high despite changes in the population over the years.[79]

Other towns have been studied since, in both America and England, and whilst the existence of delinquency areas is confirmed, there have been important modifications in the presentation of the theory For. example, such areas need not be central and need not be slums. Thus Sutherland and Cressey quote a study of criminal residence in Peiping showing a concentration of crime in the slums near the city gates.[80] Or again, studies of new suburban housing estates have sometimes shown them to have concentrations of crime. Slum populations moved to new and better housing on the outskirts of towns have not always been less delinquent as a result. More recent work on this subject, in England particularly,[81] has shifted the emphasis from the purely physical and material conditions in such areas to the local climates of thought and opinion about the kind of behaviour which is acceptable and non-acceptable. It is fascinating to speculate that the newer 'affluent' offenders in Europe and America may be inhabiting areas within which people from former delinquency areas were settled; but there has been no definitive work on this yet. In Africa, shanty towns, 'Bidonvilles', 'unauthorized locations' and the like, have usually been recognized as centres of crime and refuges for offenders. These slum areas, which usually are on the outskirts of large towns, housing people who have newly arrived, who are too poor to pay municipal rents or who do not qualify for municipal housing, often represent new urban sub-cultures in Africa with a considerable effect on the shaping of enforcement policy.

The many and diverse studies of the geographical distribution of crime and criminals are of obvious importance, and far more data of this type needs to be collected for Africa. Yet the simple collection of data available on crime distribution in each country and in each province or town would do much to enable Africa to assess the importance of the environment for criminal behaviour. It should be recognized, however, that the problem would still remain that considerably more of the people submitted to the severest of such conditions and the worst of such influences do not commit crime than those who do.

In 1938 Thorsten Sellin, one of the most highly respected international figures in criminology, directed attention to the considerable influence of culture on crime. Citing cases of peasant immigrants who had taken the law into their own hands (when, for example, their daughters had been dishonoured) he pointed out that America had not one but a collection of different cultures, values and standards which the immigrants had imported with them. These really belonged to other lands and to other circumstances but they still motivated individual conduct so that what the law of America now required of its new citizens might sometimes be at variance with more time-honoured standards and practices; and, from this conflict of cultural values, crime could arise.[82]

It would be impossible to enumerate the studies of cultural conflict which have flowed from this early work by Sellin, but it is clear that 'culture' has not always meant the same thing.[83] High delinquency rates amongst new immigrants are perhaps to be expected in the process of acculturation, but the phenomena are by no means uniform or always comparable. Shoham gives figures showing that the probation officers for Tel Aviv and Haifa reported their highest rates of delinquency in areas inhabited by 'new' immigrants and he says that the highest rate of delinquency in the whole country was recorded in the rural region of Jerusalem 'whose population is composed entirely of "new" immigrants'.[84] But he quotes the Agranat Committee on Juvenile Delinquency for a 'great preponderance of delinquency amongst the Oriental Jews over the delinquency amongst the European Jews'.[85]

More recently the culture conflict 'hypothesis' has been subjected to critical analysis by Kaiser in its relation to European immigrant labour. He concludes that whilst there is a culture conflict, this is no more than the ubiquitous conflict of standards which is tautology and that it is too vague a frame of reference for crime among foreign labourers. Moreover, he points out that an analysis of offences committed by foreign labourers supplies no indication that crime increases if the culture conflict increases. Finally, the relative delinquency amongst foreign labourers is currently low, with the rates for only a few offences exceeding the mean and there is no evidence of a more serious culture conflict in the early part of the stay of these people in the host country.[86]

The concept of culture conflict has been modified, refined and restated in the past twenty-five years. Thus in 1958 Miller, although very much in the Sellin tradition, underlined class differences and ascribed crime to lower class youths reacting unfavourably to what were essentially middle class standards.[87] Gradually, therefore, the idea of cultural influences was giving way to the more detailed concept of sub-cultural influences. It is argued that any large town consists of a variety of different levels of living, of different standards and local ideas about what conduct, dress or interests are acceptable or unacceptable, what is fashionable and what is outmoded. Sometimes these different values and standards are institutionalized so that clubs, trade unions or professional associations set patterns of behaviour for their members. More informally every district or group of people can be found to have a locally dictated frame of reference for behaviour which may not always accord with the patterns which are set for the larger society. We have already seen this emerge from the studies of opinion climates in delinquency areas.

Sub-cultures, like cultures, indicate, to those who belong to them, the kind of behaviour, dress and ideas which are prestigeful, fashionable and acceptable, and those types of conduct which are frowned upon. Acceptance in the group depends upon conformity to these ideas. These local standards impose an array of expectations to which all the members are expected to submit and these expectations are more powerfully enforced by the local face-to-face groups than could be any legal rules for people generally. To ignore them is to risk ridicule, ostracism and perhaps physical assault.

Cohen maintains that sub-cultures in a complex society are formed for people with similar problems.[88] But it seems equally possible that they emerge as a collective response to the larger and vaguer situations by people who have similar interests and beliefs which they wish to advance or to protect. Cloward and Ohlin have classified all deviant sub-cultures in one generic group which covers: 'all subculturally supported behaviour that violates some conventionally sanctioned set social expectations or rules of conduct',[89] and then within this genus the *delinquent sub-culture* is identified as one in which the central position is accorded to specifically delinquent activity—one has to be delinquent to retain membership and to rise in the hierarchy of the group.

This is the pith of the sociological theory of sub-cultures—the idea that in a mass society people operate within influential sub-groups so that delinquency may often be explained as the result of differences between the values of these sub-groups and the laws or expectations of the wider society. The concept has considerable relevance to the cultural conditions obtaining in Africa, as we shall see.[90]

It has been suggested, however, that the idea of conflicting standards between sub-groups or sub-cultures and the wider society is too simple. What has been taken as different value systems may be rationalizations of the failures to live up to accepted standards. For instance, the views of Redl and Wineman[91], as developed by Sykes and Matza,[92] seem to indicate that the members of delinquent sub-cultures do not necessarily have opposed standards of their own but merely modify the general rules to suit their own circumstances. Thus, they point out that delinquents will generally agree that stealing is wrong but will excuse their own stealing on various grounds such as 'everyone is doing it', or 'I was forced into it', or 'I was getting my own back'.

We may connect the sub-cultural approach with another sociological concept of value for understanding delinquent behaviour. Merton and Kitt[93] coined the phrase 'reference group theory' defining it as the fact that men frequently orientate themselves, and shape their behaviour, not with reference to their own group or culture, but with reference to a group outside their own to which they like to think of themselves as belonging. This is exemplified by the working man who dresses and behaves as if he belonged to the managerial class, by the student who behaves much older than his years because his reference group is the age group older than his own,[94] by the uneducated who mould their behaviour to imitate that of the students. We see it at play when children mould their behaviour on that of favoured adult groups; but it can have more serious consequences. Thus, Bettelheim[95] has shown how the long-term prisoners in Nazi concentration camps began to behave in accordance with the values of the camp authorities, identifying with the guards and adopting their attitudes towards other prisoners.

Not infrequently crime may be explained either by young people following the example of older and more experienced delinquents or by the fact that the offenders have been led into crime by trying to keep up with a group to which they wanted to belong but for which they did not have the means.

Connected too, is the idea of the roles which people play in their contacts with others. Shakespeare said that all the world is a stage and we are the actors. Sociologists have made use of this idea to show that each one of us has a number of roles to play. Thus, a man may be at any one time a husband, a father, a workman, a taxpayer, a member of a social club, a gardener, a house owner or tenant, a tourist, a trade unionist, a politician or member of a political group, a voter, a shareholder, a medical patient, etc. The more complex the society, the more roles a person must fill and the demands of one role may be in conflict with the demands of another. The theory is outlined by Sarbin[96] who defines a role as 'a pattern of behaviour associated with a distinctive social position'. This concept of social roles, the demands which they make on the individual, the obligations they impose, the strains they create and the conflicts they generate, both for the individual and society, offers an opportunity to explain social behaviour in terms of a person's position within the social structure. The concept is useful therefore in the study of deviant behaviour.[97] The diversity of roles arising, as we have seen, from sub-cultures, groups, classes and urbanization generally, often means that deviant and delinquent behaviour can be explained as the acting out of roles proffered to individuals by the particular social situation. Thus, a man trying to live beyond his means may eventually write a false cheque to keep up appearances; a student given to wearing 'far out' or 'trendy' clothes might feel impelled to reinforce his role by radical action; the leader of a gang may feel obliged to be delinquent to maintain his position; a person torn between his economic role as an unskilled labourer and a social role he may have developed as a club leader, great drinker or local politician may find the conflict too much and resort to stealing from his place of work; an assault may be to maintain one's position in the eyes of others; even sadism, rape or indecency may follow from the kind of role one believes one should be filling in relation to the opposite sex.

It is important to observe that all these sociological constructs of sub-cultures, reference groups, role playing or the self-image are inter-related. No one excludes the others and in any explanation of a total situation all three have a place. They are like three different angles or aspects of any event or set of circumstances: we can interpret any such situation in terms of cultures, roles or reference groups.

Nor do these three exhaust the possibilities. We may also interpret behaviour in terms of the classes in society. Merton[98] has introduced a modification of Durkheim's 'anomie' (the theory that man in modern urban society becomes uprooted from his traditions and values) to explain all deviant behaviour as a consequence of a social structure which holds forth success goals widely and enticingly but distributes the legitimate means of reaching them very unevenly throughout society and especially unevenly as between the social classes.

Education, success in business, the prestige of high positions in the public service, are the generally approved goals in a modern community. But, obviously, such goals are much more easily attained by the upper classes. In these higher grades of society the recognized success goals are not difficult to attain by legitimate means. Moreover, since the places at the top are limited it is the upper classes with all their financial, educational and social advantages which tend to monopolize them. However, these success goals are equally the approved objectives for the middle and lower classes. The lower a person descends in the social scale the less chance he has of reaching these success positions by the ordinary legitimate means. Only the rare individual from the lower classes can plough through the many difficulties to reach the prominent positions in a legally approved way. For the vast majority of people in the lower income groups there is just no chance of attaining this much-sought status by legitimate means.

Illegitimate action is therefore a back-door method by which some people attain the prestige, status or at least the public attention to which they aspire; and it is particularly attractive if one can avoid detection. Individually it is a means of satisfying a frustrated desire or fulfilling a need which cannot be fulfilled legitimately. Collectively it may be regarded as a kind of passive or indirect protest or revolt against the system.

Unfortunately, in a large, complex and impersonal industrial society, prestige often follows outward appearances and the fruits of success may be accorded to those who 'arrive' (i.e. have adequate funds and influence), *whatever may be the means by which these have been acquired*, providing only, that, where illegitimate methods have been used, they have not resulted in a criminal prosecution.[99] It is often said—and not always humourously—that one should not ask a millionaire how he made his first million, the implication being that he probably did so in ways which would not be approved of, if they were known. A gangster's methods may be deplored but if he can manage to avoid prosecution and conviction, the funds he has illegally accumulated will allow him to enjoy all the benefits of prestige and success. In those places, not far from home, where he is not known, he may be well respected because of his affluence and there will be no close scrutiny of the methods by which he has achieved his position of financial power.

The result is a great temptation for many frustrated in the race to the top to seek the back door—to get there by any means available, legal or illegal. In a community large enough to create personal anonymity, where people keep to themselves and do not know each other's business, it seems that only failure is really penalized. Success in illegal activity (i.e. obtaining what is wanted whilst evading detection or arrest) brings its own very real rewards. In the larger and more complicated urban communities it has often been realized that the rewards might be greater and the chances of evading capture more effective if such illegal activity is organized and systematic. Extreme violence has been used to suppress evidence or terrorize those likely to help the police.

As we have already seen, the concentration of crime in the lower classes of a society has been confirmed by most studies. Examples have been given but these could be multiplied. Thus Burt declared in 1925 that 'over one-half of the total amount of juvenile delinquency is found in homes that are poor or very poor'.[100] He quoted with approval Breckinridge and Abbot who had previously concluded in America that 'in round numbers, nine-tenths of the delinquent girls and three-fourths of the delinquent boys come from the homes of the poor'.[101]

So too Bagot found in his Liverpool study that one-half of the families of juvenile offenders were below the poverty datum line which had been drawn up for the University of Liverpool's 'Survey of Merseyside'.[102] More recently Morris has underlined the incidence of juvenile delinquency among the lower classes.[103] The question of poverty being a determining factor in crime was considered above. But membership of the lower classes of the less influential groups in society has other implications. Merton's approach led to a wider view of crime as something created by the social as opposed to the economic structure of society. The two are not really separable in fact but conceptually there is an important difference. Frustration of expectations rather than penury is the theme.

Cloward and Ohlin decided that young people were vulnerable to deviant behaviour where there was a disparity between aspirations and the opportunities for achievement.[104] Cohen found gang behaviour to be a group solution to the needs and frustrations of the American lower class boy in a world of predominantly middle class standards,[105] and Miller has carried this further with his view that gang delinquency is a product of sub-cultural norms of the lower classes.[106]

Thus there is a tendency in recent years (which has been greatly reinforced by the student protest and the emergence of militant revolutionary groups in the US and Europe) for criminology to become concerned less with crime as an individual disorder or as a form of social disorganization and to regard it more as a creation of (perhaps a natural part of) the kind of society which has been developed especially in urbanization.

In popular discussions of crime in 'developed' countries, the cinema, the radio, television and the press have often been blamed for the growing incidence of juvenile crime. It is, of course, very difficult to gauge the effect of these various methods of mass communication. Obviously, far more people subjected to such influences do not commit crime than those who do—which may cause us to doubt the criminogenic effect of mass media. At the same time, it is clear that for many who may be more highly sensitive, mentally disturbed, less emotionally stable or very impressionable these media of communications may have a considerable influence. The difficulty of carrying out effective tests probably explains why most specialized studies have failed to be conclusive about this. However, Burt attributed very little importance to the cinema in England[107] and in America, Blumer and Hauser concluded that: 'motion pictures were a factor of importance in the delinquent careers of about 10 per cent of the male . . . offenders studied.'[108]

It seems that what people actually see or hear—the meaning of it—varies according to their economic, social, racial, religious or cultural backgrounds.[109] It seems possible that children who live in areas of high delinquency or who are in touch with offenders are more likely to imitate what they see of crime on the screen or to follow what they hear on the radio.[110]

It is therefore very difficult to generalize about the effect of books, the cinema, radio or television on crime. It seems substantiated that the effect will differ with personality, temperament and the kind of social contacts and background of the hearer, reader or viewer. It is possible, however, that insufficient work has been done on this subject. There is at least a possibility that values and standards are propagated by mass communications. It seems possible that frustration is increased by the insight given of the comforts and satisfactions of life at levels beyond the attainment of those who receive such information. Perhaps the real influence of mass communications is to spread a type of philosophy of life with indirect significance for crime rather than being responsible for any immediately imitative behaviour.[111]

This section on the social or environmental background to criminal behaviour illustrates the inter-relatedness of all the factors in the study of crime. Probing in any one direction eventually connects with the others. One gets the impression of looking at the same thing from several angles but never being in a position to see them all at once. Some sociological criminologists have shown an inclination, therefore, to stand further back to get a better look at the whole picture. This is not easy to do, but the tendency is indicated by the gradual inclusion of white collar crime, the nature of the 'underworld' structure, racial discrimination, political pressure groupings, organized rackets and the institutions and values of society itself, in the studies of crime. There is a distinct attempt to study not merely the world of the offender and the ways in which it conflicts with the more general order—but to study and question the general order itself.[112]

In Africa, it is advantageous to begin here—at the point which the sociologists appear to have reached; that is to relate and combine the social factors in the attempt to achieve an overview. Of course the lack of data will force the examination of separate and combined social elements in crime in Africa for many years ahead but the 'whole' view could well be the most effective construct for practical studies of crime on the continent of Africa.

One consideration which makes this necessary is the duality of most economic and social life in the majority of African states. This juxtapositioning of the older and newer, the modern and the less modern, the custom-derived and colonial-derived systems of law, economics and social affairs, enjoins a constant view of a diverse world which is, in effect, a fusion of two worlds. The situation is changing as nationalism develops and education with the help of mass media exercises its value-unifying influences. Tribalism, in its older form at least, is receding; but, at the time this is being written at any rate, it would be grossly misleading to suggest that tribal life and tribal influence are either dead or dying. In the politics of many modern African states, tribal backgrounds and affiliations exert a pressure which is frequently decisive. True, the tribal way of life is being transformed and is incorporating modern styles and values; but there are still large areas of Africa comparatively untainted by education and untouched by modern technology. The drive to modernize has made great headway and political independence has given it the impetus which it required; but a synthesis between modern and traditional values prevails and there is still a very long way to go before the two worlds can be reduced to one.

It is for this reason that this section on the social factors in crime in Africa is in two parts—one dealing with the effects or possible effects of some of the older tribal conditions and concepts (and which for want of a better shorthand we term 'traditional' without intending that the title should denote a time sequence or stage of development), and the second part dealing with modern conditions and concepts which, again for want of a better term, we call 'contemporary'. These are purely conceptual devices: the traditional is not intended to be non-contemporary or the contemporary devoid of the traditional. As indicated above, there is really only one world when the factors in crime are under consideration. There will be many regions of the continent where the division, which is made here only for convenience, could be fairly interpreted as 'rural' and 'urban' and others where it could mean the older and younger generations. Everywhere it will require local modification because generalizations are dangerous where there is such known diversity. And everywhere there will be an obvious merging and overlap of the two outlines. However, a start has to be made somewhere—if only to provide something to be criticized.

i. Traditional

Where traditional living persists in Africa, life makes sense only in terms of the past and the future. Because the three basic relationships of kin are descent, filiation and marriage, the present generation is linked and obligated both to ancestors and children unborn; lineages are continued and often names will pass from the deceased or grandparents to a newly-born child;[113] contemporary existence is often conceived as only one segment of a wider process covering a timeless span and a wider universe.[114] In traditional life (where this can still be found) the spirits are as real as parents: land, animals and other property are held in trust from those clan members who went before for those who will come after. A Nigerian chief told the West African Lands Committee in 1912 '. . . land belongs to a vast family of which many are dead, few yet living and countless numbers are unborn'. Custom descends by word of mouth from older generation to younger generation and those with the longest memories are the more respected as founts of knowledge.[115] Behaviour has to be related therefore to its significance for the spirits still hovering with the family or clan;[116] and a prime responsibility of all concerned is to keep this social group united.

This last point is of the utmost importance for it links not only the worlds of spirit and nature, but also the traditional world, with some modern concepts of crime in Africa. To explain this, it is necessary to begin at the beginning when people in small tribal groups in Africa were extremely vulnerable to the wild beasts, disease and the extreme climate. To stay united as a clan, or tribe was a *sine qua non* for human survival. Not surprisingly, all rules of conduct, moral, religious or secular, were designed to promote social unity and to avoid divisions. Spirits of departed ancestors were often thought to be no less concerned to keep their families, clans or tribes together,[117] and the emphasis on immemorial custom—on doing things as they had always been done before, on preserving harmony and discouraging novelty and innovation—was explainable as a relentless unending campaign to assert corporate identity. It was a public vigilance to avoid dissension and those causes of difference which might lead to quarrels, rivalries or fights resulting in a break up of the unity essential to life.[118]

Either the conflicting interests and loyalties or the fear of losing the unity and understanding essential to community survival can be discerned in the desire for normality and social harmony illustrated by the Abaluyia prayer 'Let things take their normal courses . . . let the sun rise and shine as usual'.[119] Fortes dealing with ancestor worship amongst the Tallensi concluded that 'It is not a question of morality in the sense of righteous conduct. It is not a matter of, say, dealing honestly with one's neighbours, refraining from adultery, never committing a murder. Virtue in these matters does not earn the blessings of the ancestors and a wrongdoer will escape their wrath unless his actions are also transgressions of the rule of kinship amity. It is a question of moral relationships, not of good deeds.' [120] This may lead to what in modern terms might be considered injustice but its justification is its final objective—the preservation of peace and order. Expediency is often resorted to in order to maintain the system. Amongst the Venda, for instance, a court (i.e. tribal council) will never support an individual against his own group. On the contrary, it seems that the fact of his being alone against the majority is itself good evidence that he is in the wrong.[121] Again, it has been said that the Bunyoro tribunals have a primary aim of restoring good relations rather than punishing the offender. His position as host when he has been ordered to pay for the meat and beer for a reconciliation feast is an honourable one.[122] Gluckman in his study of the Barotse of Zambia was careful to add that this regard for the preservation of good relationships did not go so far as to sacrifice legal or moral rules 'since wrong-doers are upbraided and punished';[123] but Meek writing of the Nigerian Ibo said that elders were in most cases referees and mediators rather than prosecutors and judges and their decisions were 'judicious rather than judicial'.[124] The process is probably more complex than can be summed up in these few phrases and quotations.[125] Moreover, the relative complexity of a society and the development of its authority structure introduce variations on the theme, but the desire to preserve order at most, if not all, costs remains clear. Gluckman was looking at a relatively developed kingdom and at a 'later' stage in judicial growth.

Crime, then, for a great many rural Africans, is (and was) behaviour which can be clearly and unmistakably defined in their terms as something physically or spiritually detrimental to social relationships, and likely to affect the ties of kith and kin adversely. It will be contrary to customary law if it threatens this harmony and it may or may not be offensive to the spirits: in everything it is the social context which really matters most. The expulsion or killing of a witch may now be seen in this social perspective: whether the person be a witch or not, he or she is a menace to the harmony of the tribe.[126] The serious view taken of incest, marriage within forbidden degrees or behaviour considered sexually indecent is again not only a morally or religiously conditioned attitude but one which derives from a long tribal memory of the harm inflicted on the community by the conflicts, enmity, secession and disruption resulting from the breach of the sometimes far-reaching exogamous marriage prohibitions.[127] One attitude to offences inherited from this earlier situation and conditioning by modern Africa is the continuing abhorrence of insulting language—a loathing which is very widespread in Africa south of the Sahara and which has in the recent past often led to strikes or demonstrations and occasionally embittered relations with foreigners. Both in studies carried out by the writer in Zambia and the Congo and in independent inquiries made by the Project for the Reinstatement of African Law in East Africa of the London University School of Oriental and African Studies in the period 1964-5, it was found that tribal elders and a wide variety of other people thought that the penal code was far too lenient with those who used insulting language. This, to them, was a crime almost equal to a serious assault. The reason might be, of course, that it once was a serious matter when it could lead to fights and feuds which might break up the tribe. Children were taught to avoid and detest it and it seems that this habit of mind could have persisted. A magical or near magical efficacy was attributed to the spoken word.

Conversely, the widespread use of discussion, prolonged negotiations and compensation to settle disputes and to expiate many crimes such as theft, abduction and murder is adequate testimony of its effectiveness in resolving conflict, restoring order and smoothing ruffled feelings. It is interesting to note incidentally, that practically all that has been said here about customary attitudes and crime, and the importance of maintaining the balance rather than assigning guilt, can be applied equally to international law and to the operations of international bodies like the United Nations or the inter-governmental bodies which try to keep the peace and restore order. In essence international law is still largely customary law.

Generally, in these simple conditions, behaviour and its consequences are not regarded as being purely individual. This could be the background to (or perhaps a logical development of) the traditional African preoccupation with crime as a social peril. Either way, it seems to be easier in simple societies to think in terms of communal or collective, rather than individual responsibility. A person attacked is his kin attacked: a person stealing means an act of stealing by his kin. '. . . If he be slain it is the blood of the kin that has been shed and the kin is entitled to compensation or vengeance. If he commit a wrong the whole kin is involved and every member is liable, not as an individual but as part of the kin.'[128] Religion and family, law and morality, then, fit naturally into this general social context and the identity of community beliefs and practices lead to a concord of ideas of sin, crime and anti-social behaviour. We have observed that at this level there is usually no abstract concept of justice or morality to which the courts try to conform. They are dealing with concrete situations not higher principles. Indigenous beliefs generally have a very practical application to the social ties and thus accord with customary law. Practice rather than conscience, the action rather than the guilty mind is important. Where magic, divination or ancestor worship prevail these are expressed in rites and procedures which are used to affect daily events and to preserve or ensure health and material success.

An obvious consequence of this stable, integrated way of living with social, moral and legal laws supporting each other, is that it not only discourages self-centred or subversive activity, but also serves to reduce to a minimum the emotional conflicts so familiar to us in industrial societies and which seem to breed deviates and criminals. Such tribes in Africa are untroubled by juvenile delinquency and undisturbed by teen-aged gangs responding to sub-cultures of their own (there is no adolescence—just children before initiation and adults afterwards). There is indeed no room in most situations for sub-divisions typical of larger and more complex societies and no real scope for a criminal underworld. Even less is there an equivalent to 'white collar' or economic exploitation. The group is usually too small to carry such social disorganization whilst maintaining its separate identity.[129] This is not to say that conflicts, clashes of interests, antagonism and revolutionary tendencies do not exist. It is merely to agree with Gluckman that these are reconciled, ritually accommodated or institutionalized to the extent that they contribute to, rather than detract from, the social order.

It should be pointed out that all this clan affinity, internal loyalty, shared responsibility and consistency of organization and conduct ends abruptly at the tribal limits. No similar obligations are felt towards other tribes or other peoples. To steal from outsiders may even be rather creditable—it is certainly no recognized offence unless it brings disaster or misfortune on the tribe of the thief. Stock theft is a great problem in many parts of rural Africa for this reason. The Maasai believe that in some earlier era they were the only people in the world to own cattle so that, although it is against the modern law and may have unfortunate penal consequences if they are caught, there is, for the Maasai people, nothing morally wrong about stealing other people's cattle—it is only taking back what should rightfully be theirs. Actually, with the far-reaching effects of radio and tourism, this may be an over-simplification and this older belief may not now be held—but it is at least still doubtful whether the Maasai would feel any moral wrong in taking the cattle of alien tribesmen if this did not bring down upon them the power of the government. Similarly, their neighbours, the Kipsigis, have a reputation for cattle theft which is not really discreditable in their own traditions.[130]

This admittedly over-simplified outline of prevalent traditional attitudes to crime and its causes has been provided at some length because it has obvious and far reaching implications for the social explanations of crime in modern Africa. With so many 'crimes' conceived as offences to be dealt with by compensation and reconciliation there is, in tribal conditions, a concept of crime somewhat different from that of the modern sector. Sometimes tribes really cannot understand why imprisonment is used or a fine imposed for an offence which could well be dealt with by compensation. The act has not made the offender so unacceptable to society that he cannot go about his normal life, once he has made restitution; and what does the victim get out of the offender being imprisoned or fined? It is doubtful whether the resettled cattle thieves in Tanzania understand or accept the logic of their resettlement. An interesting example of a customary court dealing with a case of bestiality as damage to property so as to ensure compensation is given by Beidelman.[131]

On the other hand, a difference of view as to the ways of handling an offence is not the same as a fundamental difference in concepts of anti-social behaviour. The concept of juvenile 'delinquency' does not appear to differ fundamentally as between modern and traditional systems in Africa.[132] And the London University Project for the Restatement of African Law found only six or seven differences between the traditional view of punishable behaviour and the largely imported penal code. The difficulty here, however, is to determine the extent to which these common concepts are a genuine coincidence of traditional and African concepts and the extent to which they derive from the colonial overlay of Western laws and legal typologies. Some people would argue that even 'tribes' are an invention of colonial administrators and it is indisputable that their life style is a product of their chequered history.

From the above account, it is obvious that the very fact of living among people to whom one felt none of the basic ties could constitute a kind of release from traditional inhibitions and social controls. It is known, of course, that the majority of those whose tribal lives have been transformed by industrialization, urbanization or modernization did not commit crimes. The point for consideration here is that many of those who did would probably suffer none of the pangs of remorse, conscience or feelings of shame if discovered, which they would certainly have felt by behaving in this way amongst their own people. Nor should one minimize the stress and complications of living with people of so many other diverse cultural backgrounds. Culture conflicts, role confusion and frustrated aspirations are only a few of the social factors in crime which could be expected to have full play in most of Africa's urban areas. There is ample confirmation of this in the literature on African towns.

Secondly, the use of money puts many significant relationships and negotiations, which are open and publicly celebrated in a rural setting, into a novel privacy—with far-reaching effects. Where there was no registration of marriages and no written records in the tribe, the ceremony, and especially the public transfer of property as dowry or as bride wealth (according to tribe), acted as a public registration: it fixed the event in people's minds. Years afterwards there would always be some people to testify to the customary legality of the marriage. In towns (i.e. before any comprehensive registration system is introduced) the dowry or bride wealth paid in cash is not always seen to be handed over and it therefore provides no such protective mental registration in the public mind; and it has often been difficult to determine the legal wife in a case of bigamy or divorce. It is very important to know whether the price was paid and how much, but this transaction in money is not usually open and sufficiently public in the towns, and even if it is, the people witnessing it may have left the area.

Thirdly, the money-economy itself introduces alien values of accumulated wealth rather than sharing. On the one hand there is the desire for possession of goods—bicycles, radios, cars, etc., and on the other hand, the weekly wage introduces an insecurity about housing and clothing which could not have existed in rural areas where both such commodities were easily obtainable for the trouble of creating or making them.

Fourthly, housing, separation from relatives on whom one has been accustomed to rely, budgeting for specific time periods, controlling children without the help of traditional sanctions and guides, providing for the aged, and generally handling daily affairs in which all the older beliefs and supports have a decreasing relevance, are all new complications of change in modern Africa which await more detailed study.

Finally, the new ambitions, the striving for education, prestige and higher earnings, the intoxication of political independence with its opening of vast new prospects and the wave of frustration where expectations may have been too high—all these are social elements which have significance for criminal behaviour but about which far too little is yet known in detail.

ii. Contemporary

Turning now to the 'contemporary' aspects of the social situation in Africa, there are several important factors competing for the attention of any criminologist. Undoubtedly the first of these is the widespread phenomenon of urban unemployment and rural under-employment. It would be difficult to look at the crime situation on the continent without taking into account the widespread idleness and growing frustration of thousands of urban youth across the face of Africa. This must be an obvious factor in deviant or delinquent behaviour and indeed the low-income unemployment factor has shown up in nearly all the limited studies of delinquent groups which have been carried out so far.

In 1952 Mr E. W. T. Keiser, Principal of the Diepkloof Reformatory in South Africa, in an M.Ed. thesis which he produced for the University of Potschefstroom on 'Native Juvenile Delinquency', showed that about 120,000 'native' children of school-going age were idling their time away on the streets. They were not in school and were without employment.

A study of juvenile delinquency in Elizabethville (now Lubumbashi) also showed that in 1959 over 40 per cent of all juvenile offenders were unemployed (and not at school).[133] In Leopoldville (now Kinshasa), Raymaekers estimated that in 1960, 63 per cent of the population was under twenty-five years of age. He calculated that in May 1961 the city had some 50,000 unemployed of which 20,000 were under twenty-five. More significant, however, was the fact that these figures were already double those which he had arrived at by an identical procedure only two years before. In 1971 it was estimated that Kinshasa had some 200,000 unemployed with 120,000 under twenty-five. Raymaekers went on to describe predelinquency and delinquency amongst these young people, including gang activity, drug taking and general law-lessness.[134]

Much the same emerged from a study of juvenile crime in Zambia in 1964. Of forty-nine offenders at the Approved School there, only two had been employed and only thirteen had been at school at the time of arrest.[135]

On the other hand, it is distinctly unwise to deduce a simple functional association between the two phenomena—crime and unemployment. Far more likely is it that the connexion is indirect and comes via the boredom and aimlessness on the one side reinforced by the opportunities for illegal conduct which unemployment creates, on the other side.

Once again it has to be remembered that thousands of unemployed and school-deprived young people do not commit crime. Thus one must look to the differentials of external pressure and internal tolerance to understand why some but not others commit crime.

A second factor is the progressive growth of the towns themselves. This is no modern phenomenon in Africa except perhaps in its magnitude, its pace, and the variety of cultures which it encompasses. People have been moving from rural to urban areas in Africa for many years. Migrant labour has been an economic necessity both for the host and the home countries in many parts of South, Central and East Africa;

and the quest of education has brought millions of young people to town. But in recent years the flow to the towns has greatly accelerated. The radio and the opening up of roads to the interior as well as the opportunities created by political independence have all enhanced the urban pull and despite large sums spent on rural development the movement goes on. Africa, is thus, like the rest of the world, experiencing urbanization on a considerable scale[136] with all that this means in terms of family disintegration and the heavy pressures on the traditional ways of living.

In 1942 the Minister of Justice and Native Affairs for the Union of South Africa appointed a Committee to study the position of crime on the Witwatersrand and in Pretoria. In this area there had already been considerable industrial and urban growth over the previous thirty years. In its report, the Committee blamed the general process of industrialization and the squalid conditions of life in the African 'locations' (i.e. in the segregated African suburbs usually on the outskirts of the towns). Crime, according to this report, was rooted in adverse social and economic conditions as expressed in the inadequacies of home life, educational opportunity and facilities for recreation. The committee was not unnaturally affected by prevailing preconceptions and some of the conclusions reached by the studies of crime then available from Europe and America. It considered crime to be associated with a fall in moral standards, abject poverty or to broken homes. And as there was ample evidence for all of these in the locations, the Committee believed them to be at the root of the problem. Industrialization, said the committee, had led to thousands of 'native' men and women living in locations under conditions which were: 'lacking in any moral standards, either African or European'.

On disrupted family life it pointed out that:

> Cohabitation without any form of civilized or Native marriage is the manner of life adopted by a high percentage of inhabitants of these locations. The conditions under which thousands of Native women live with no marital rights or security for themselves or their offspring produces an environment in which the propagation of a criminal environment is inevitable.[137]

If one discounts the unfortunate use of value terms such as 'civilized' and 'native' and the evident lack of comparative data on local custom, this passage finds an echo in many other urban centres of Africa troubled with crime. Thus:

> We find in Leopoldville all the signs of a strikingly brutal discordance in urban development: demographic explosion: urban drift [of people]: unemployment . . . : juvenile delinquency: sentiments of frustration: material and moral misery expressing itself in revolt.[138]

So too, in a study of urban acculturation in the Katanga province of Zaïre, we read:

> . . . with the specific aspects of urban growth such as promiscuity, alcoholism, unemployment, the lack of educational institutions . . . with the growing exasperation of tensions between races and tribes. It is to be feared that the new generations which rise more divorced from the traditional morals of their ancestors and which are faced with conditions of existence progressively more complex will provide more delinquents than those [generations] which have preceded them in the urban milieu.[139]

Similarly of Dakar we are told:

> There one finds shanty towns, over-populated districts where the housing, put up haphazardly, consists of hovels where promiscuity is rife. Water is scarce and polluted, sanitary arrangements non-existent, and the air is foul with the accumulation of refuse on the ground. All the factors favouring the transmission of infections and parasitical diseases are combined there. Naturally, it is there above all, that children in moral danger, juvenile delinquency, dope addicts and prostitutes are to be found . . . . In short, one shanty town is like another, a place where one sees the decline of family authority and the disintegration of traditional family links and values.[140]

Examples could be multiplied showing comparable situations in Nairobi, Dar es Salaam, Lagos, Accra and other major towns.

Where all this is associated with industrialization it means for Africa a new spirit of competitiveness and self-seeking to displace the older values of co-operation and group solidarity. These are areas for considerable research in the future in order to show the relationship between the changes which have taken place and the rise of crime in the countries concerned.

The formation of towns, the way in which slums and overcrowding have sometimes been concentrated near the centres of the urban areas (as in Western Europe) and the contrasting spectacle (mainly in the white-settled countries of Africa) of shanty towns huddling around the city limits to provide for those people unable to afford the official housing area rents and not qualifying by employment for subsidized housing, is a phenomenon worth further study. This differential conurbation has not been sufficiently investigated for its sociological, economic, anthropological and medical significance to be fully available to the town planners. It is clear that the delinquency area studies which have been done in other parts of the world are replicable here.

The contrast is perhaps greatest between the towns which began as mining settlements in Zambia and Zaïre, and those like Lomé in Togo, Accra in Ghana or Lagos in Nigeria which began as coastal settlements in more direct touch with other countries. Then there are artificial creations like Lusaka and Pretoria, Entebbe and Zomba —and perhaps Nairobi, which grew out of a halt in railway building to become one of Africa's most modern capitals.

Thirdly, the rate of urbanization combined with industrialization needs more consideration. Later studies of urbanization have been dissatisfied with descriptions of the overcrowding and general collapse of standards of behaviour. They have looked for some of the key factors at work in seemingly disrupting and converting standards rather than more gradually evolving, declining or transforming them. Naturally, the *speed* of urbanization has attracted attention—for instance, Mitchell has pointed out that the towns of Zambia are barely thirty years old and still have few inhabitants over fifty.[141] It has been supposed that there might be an understandable limit to the extent to which individuals can adjust to rapid change without, so to speak, losing social balance.

Apart from this pace of growth there is the disruptive effect of increasing mobility. McCullock studying Livingstone in 1956 noted that 405 of his sample of the inhabitants had shifted at least twice from one town to another and although nearly two thirds of the men were married, only 46 per cent had their wives in town with them.[142]

Others have drawn attention to the preponderant demands made by the new money economy. Thus in 1961 Southall observed:

> The reason why kinship obligations can be more easily evaded in town is not merely the frequently high mobility, as a result of which particular kin are constantly disappearing from the urban scene, but restriction in the scope of kinship [in the economic field].[143]

The type of housing, work opportunities and living conditions in the towns hardly favoured large families. And the unevenness of age and sex ratios in the early days of urban growth obviously complicated normal settlement.

Earlier, Laura Longmore had underlined the role of money in the process of behaviour change:

> Money had provided the impulse for urban African individualization . . . . Financial independence has caused a rapid dissolution so marked that some of the fundamental elements of traditional life seem to have vanished . . . . There is a decay of a sense of responsibility . . . a breakdown of authority within the family group and inevitable increase in general lawlessness and juvenile crime.[144]

The towns then, as we forewarned, have absorbed much of the attention both officially and academically. This is not to say that the countryside has been over-neglected. Most governments have rural development policies and in colonial times priority was often given to rural schemes in the hope of slowing down the drift to the towns—yet the rural depopulation went on.[145] In fact, the reality is that without rural development it may be quite impossible for African countries to feed their people. The rural areas have therefore attracted a number of sociological and related studies of value for the criminologist and we may expect more attention to be given to them in the years to come—despite the competing interest of the urban areas.

The behavioural changes in modernization have been related on the one hand to the early stages of economic growth and on the other hand to new cultural perspectives provided by radio, television and other means of mass communication. The felt needs and demands of Africa today are far less 'insular' than the modernizing needs were in, say, the nineteenth or the early twentieth centuries in Europe and America. These countries are not separated from and are not cut off from the outside as were so many other nations, either by circumstances or design, in an earlier age and at earlier stages of this development. This is an important aspect of the new international styles and the cosmopolitan social life which influences profoundly all the youthful aspirations, fashions and values. It is reflected in the types of crimes and in the modern cult of notoriety. The modern display of large numbers of imported articles of a prestige or status significance has its effect on the conduct of people generally, and particularly young people. More and more, the benefits of possession are untrammelled by the niceties of legal acquisition so that temptations are great.

With so little documentation of names, ages or the earlier family history, a person does not find it too difficult to move to a new urban area and to a new life when this becomes attractive or necessary.

iii. The social scene as a whole

The great presumption of offering any generalized picture of the social background to crime in Africa has been freely acknowledged above. Yet, there exists a real need to maintain at some level a general conception of crime and its problems in Africa just as this has been maintained in African law and, to a great extent, in anthropology. This means *inter alia* not ignoring the differences but keeping an overview of the social scene. Of course, there are so many aspects of the sociological study of crime which will require any number of specialized, micro-criminological studies, but for any effective planning in countries which are ethnically and socially complicated and to achieve the perspectives necessary for the prevention and control of crime to be organized, the broad view is essential. As we have seen, the wider concept is equally important if one wishes to avoid the limitations of studying only certain social factors or certain social processes which seem to have relevance for criminal behaviour. The general approach, for all its own shortcomings, tries to keep the variables and their interaction in constant view and to escape any possible complacency of a preoccupation with multivariate analysis.

The habit has somehow to be acquired of looking not only at crime but at its setting—not only at its negative side but at its positive contribution to the social structure. We are not necessarily back here at Durkheim and his view of crime as normal, because the basic tenets which made this analysis possible for Durkheim may no longer apply in a period when total economic and social change would probably be accounted as 'abnormal'. We are back at his conceptualization, however. The criminal has to be seen not only as a social drop-out (with which phenomenon one connects low income, lack of education, housing, frustrated aspirations and the decline of social controls) but as part of what the system really is.

In this total system the 'traditional' and 'contemporary' types of society not only co-exist but positively cohabit. There is always a need to look for the new ethnic or tribal sub-cultures which are developing in the towns and to probe the structure of the even newer inter-tribal sub-groupings which are becoming typical as nationalism becomes the ideal in many areas. Correspondingly, there will be distinctive urban roles, styles, ideas and adopted values to be noted in the villages as these become grafted on the older patterns of life in rural areas. Group loyalties are changing—some enduring, others falling into desuetude, and new, wider affiliations being made.

The social scene in Africa can be appreciated only if there is a ready understanding of the effects of world comparisons which many people are making for the first time—comparisons of life in other countries with life in one's own country. The social scene is dominated by politics in many areas but by education everywhere. The provision of schools and the extension of opportunities for schooling at all levels is a political issue in most countries and provides a very distinct orientation of traditional and contemporary social life. Thus crime is affected by the disdain many young educated people feel for the older customary controls maintained by customary courts, even when in some cases these have been improved and incorporated into a new state system of criminal justice.

There are so many deeper implications—most of which are waiting to be explored—of an African culture or range of different cultures being thrust, torn or self-propelled at varying rates and paces into a fast technological and kaleidoscopic modernism. Crime will derive from the interaction of all these, so that even when circumstances limit the area or the scope of a particular research project, its results should always be interpreted in the wider context. For instance, delinquency areas must be seen not only as concentrations of the worst physical conditions but in terms of their (very frequent) community cohesion, their important role in the process of urbanization and their service to the newcomer to town. They must be viewed not only alongside the population, migration and housing problems but as being permeated with the older and newer habits of social living which have often complicated the planning of municipal areas or led to their neglect. It is obvious, for example, that the towns are quite unable to provide the accommodation required by the increasing numbers flowing to the towns; and even the modest provisions usually made are often inappropriate for a family which is in behavioural and domestic transition from rural to urban life and from 'traditional' to 'contemporary' conditions.

The differences which exist between the regions in Africa provide opportunities for comparative studies. To illustrate, youth behaviour problems probably show more differences than similarities when Kinshasa is placed alongside Cotonou or Ouagadougou; and the youth problems of South Africa and the urban youth along the line of rail into Katanga are likely to differ substantially from those experienced in

Bukavu, Moshi or Niger. Comparative studies would provide, amongst other things, a great deal of information about the extent to which generalizations are valid.

It would be a mistake to overlook the vast differences between Africa and the rest of the world in the roles of women. In many parts of Africa women are the family providers because, in the past, men were the hunters. Women are not only vital, as is well understood, in the organization of the family and the care of children, but in Africa they are crucial to the economic life of the family. Yet, it has been shown above that female rates of crime are lower than those of men, that is, their different roles do not seem to affect this common attribute of women, namely that they appear to commit less crime. We may have more opportunity here of getting to the root causes of this difference in delinquency between sexes. It follows that the role of girls is also significant and their preparation for their broad function either in primary production or in commerce must be taken into account in interpreting the factors which give rise to modern crime.

African countries share with other countries a problem of intoxication—with its local peculiarities and special forms. There is a widespread use of hemp (see p. 143 below) but the use of beer in traditional style has been greatly modified in its social setting by the overlay of Western influence—producing interesting differences between the English-speaking, French-speaking and other parts of Africa.

The different cultures brought together by economic, political or other pressures will not always intermesh and adjust easily. Sellin's examples in the United States were trivial compared to the tremendous differences in styles of life and expectations which jostle in a modern African suburb. There are inevitable clashes of expectations, principle and practices: there have been very interesting forms of institutionalization of the apparently irreconcilable. In some countries there has been a widespread probing by families and officials for the kind of day-to-day accommodation and adjustment considered necessary to achieve new heights of modernization without losing all that is best from the customary past. This is perhaps most dramatically exemplified by Tanzania's quest for an African socialism which seeks to combine the best traditions with modern techniques in order to reach new levels of economic and social improvement.

Community development, family planning, social welfare services, health, labour and educational services of all kinds have been introduced in many countries in the effort to transform the old ways of life; but there is still concern about losing, in this process, the good and valuable as well as the old and outmoded. Crime is frequently ascribed to this failure to retain the most important qualities of the older styles of living. We cannot ignore the possibility that crime itself may be a form of adjustment.

The intermingling of individualism and group action, of private initiative and corporate allegiance is everywhere apparent in modern Africa. It could be a powerful combination for future growth and development but there are still many circumstances within which they do not mix easily. The philosophical collectivism to which Asante refers emerges, for instance, when people flocking to the towns form their own mutual security or mutual help societies (often along tribal lines). Whilst these are similar to the friendly societies which grew up amongst the workers in an earlier phase of industrialization in Britain—and whilst they frequently began in the same way as societies to prevent a pauper burial—they have very different cultural roots and have far more communal qualities than any usual urban collection of individuals united for a common purpose. This kind of spontaneous sub-grouping can often be traced too in what might be reasonably called delinquent sub-groups in the shanty towns or peri-urban settlements: again they may look like their Western counterparts but there are probably subtle and significant differences.

Change has swept over Africa so quickly that many of the stages or time periods logically associated with the economic and social progress of a country from subsistence levels to industrialization have been telescoped or thrust into a complicated juxtaposition or partially fused. Historical stages of economic and social growth derived from other regions of the world do not suit therefore what is happening in Africa, for this kind of economic and social advance is a new experience in many respects.

The application of Western-derived constructs of a sociological nature to the social situation in Africa has therefore to be undertaken with no little caution. Role playing, self-images, reference group theory, sub-cultures and attitude or opinion constructs all have an obvious and fascinating application to the situation which has been described in this chapter, but the danger of superficial similarities is great. Even when the fit seems perfect there will always be the possibility of an undercurrent to confuse decisions based upon outward signs and the risks of too shallow an analysis are great.

(c) Psychological Approaches to Crime

The law has from ancient times recognized *mens rea* or 'evil intent' as a distinctive element in crime: in many cases the intention with which an act is committed makes all the difference to whether it is a crime or not. Most seriously illegal actions therefore presuppose a prior state of mind, i.e. a preceding decision, inclination or neglect. In this sense, it is possible to suggest that there is always the psychological aspect of a crime. If one includes the fears, latent aggression and other principles of unconscious motivation which help to determine public policy, there is an important psychological dimension to the criminal justice system itself.

Some of those who commit acts forbidden by the law are manifestly insane or abnormal and are therefore exempt from all criminal responsibility. On the other hand, though they are not liable, not being responsible for their behaviour, they may be committed to mental institutions for treatment, for their own benefit or for the protection of the public.

We need not linger over the crime committed by those of 'unsound mind'. It is understandable that a person who is hallucinated may murder, steal or commit rape in the firm belief that it is right in the circumstances. Schizophrenics have been responsible for many cases of violence; manic-depressives may commit suicide or assault those who get in their way and, of course, paranoics are always likely to attack those they believe to be responsible for persecuting them. On the other hand, there are again a great many people suffering from such mental illnesses who do not commit offences and who are often treated outside closed institutions.[146]

Even so, mental abnormality or normality is a matter of degree, and difficulties arise as we come down the scale to consider offenders who are less obviously afflicted. Defects of temperament, neuroses and emotional conflicts are to be found amongst offenders and non-offenders alike and it is not always easy for the courts, even with the help of specialists, to assign the measure of responsibility for a crime. The question is just how far deficiencies of intelligence, personality disorders, emotional disturbances and related conditions are 'causes' of crime. We cannot in these cases have recourse to the more extreme detachments from reality which characterize some of the more serious mental afflictions.

The significance of lower than average intelligence in crime has been frequently stated. Lombroso had referred to the mental inferiority of offenders. A little later Goring, on the basis of a 1908 Royal Commission survey and the evidence which he himself had gathered, discovered a high correlation between criminality and defective intelligence.[147] He concluded that 'the one vital mental constitutional factor in the etiology of crime' is defective intelligence.[148] Soon afterwards appeared the work of Goddard at the New Jersey Training School for the Feeble-minded in America. His book included a number of studies of the intelligence of prisoners and offenders with percentages regarded as feeble-minded ranging from 28 per cent to 89 per cent.[149] He came to the conclusion that: 'It is no longer to be denied that the greatest single cause of delinquency and crime is low grade mentality much of it within the limits of feeble-mindedness'.[150]

This conclusion, however, arose from his application of tests to the inmates of the training school for the feeble-minded and from his unwarranted assumption that all those admitted there *must* be feeble-minded. This led him to regard anyone with a mental age of twelve or less to be feeble-minded. This hypothesis when tested for army drafting in the First World War gave such a high proportion as feeble-minded that it was obviously impossible. Thus in 1927 Goddard himself accepted that 'most of the twelve and even of the ten and the nine are not defective'.[151]

The effect was that feeble-mindedness as a general explanation for crime tended to disappear[152] and more recent studies have shown that the difference between the intelligences of offenders and the population generally are not so great. Thus Stott, using the Raven Progressive Matrices test based on a logic of spatial relations, found that his sample group of delinquents at an Approved School obtained an average score of forty which indicated that on the average they could be counted as more intelligent than 36 per cent of their groups and less intelligent than 64 per cent of their age group in the population generally. This, he maintained, did 'not support the view that the bulk of delinquents are found among the mentally dull'.[153] Bowman has suggested that the feeble-minded as a group are not more likely to commit sex offences than are others,[154] and still in connexion with sex offending, Frosch and Bromberg found that mental deficiency played a minor role.[155]

For crime generally, Sutherland, after reviewing 350 studies which had been made up to 1929, thought that the intelligence test scores of offenders were not dissimilar to those for the population as a whole,[156] and Gittins in England obtained an average score of 89.5 per cent

(100 regarded as normal average) for the 1000 Approved School boys he studied.[157] Mary Woodward after a study of low intelligence and crime concluded that 'low intelligence plays little or no part in delinquency'.[158] This does not mean that the level of intelligence does not play an important role in crime or that mentally backward people do not commit crime. Of course they do—as do the other intelligence levels of the population. Indeed, on a common-sense appraisal, one would expect to find more people of less than average intelligence amongst offenders who are caught since these may not be so clever at evading detection and arrest. Moreover, a limited intelligence makes it more difficult to avoid tangles with the law. A person who is mentally backward has less success in school and may find it difficult to keep regular employment: he is subjected therefore to much greater temptations to shine in other ways and he is likely to lack the foresight to appreciate fully the possible consequences of taking the attractive but more questionable short-cuts to the satisfactions he seeks. But, if mental retardment is one of the factors in the causation of crimes it is by no means the important factor it was once supposed to be. Not only are there more mentally backward people who do not commit crime than those who do, but the backwardness itself may merely accentuate emotional difficulties which are the more immediate cause of delinquent behaviour.[159]

In recent years psychologists have evolved a variety of tests to measure personality and temperament. These are sometimes based on inter-related questionnaires like the Minnesota Multiphasic Personality Inventory (MMPI) which includes 550 items, and sometimes they are less specific like the Rorschach Ink Blot Test by which people are asked to say what different shaped ink blots suggest to them, or the Thematic Aperception Test (TAT) which provides a picture of an event and leaves the observer to supply an appropriate story. All these have been applied to delinquents.

In 1950, a survey was made of such tests of delinquents and non-delinquents over the past quarter of a century. Taking 113 studies which compared offenders and non-offenders the authors of the survey decided that 42 per cent showed differences in favour of the non-offenders whilst the rest were indeterminate.[160]

Indeterminate too were the results of Rorschach tests applied in the famous Glueck study of delinquency. Five hundred young delinquents matched with five hundred non-delinquents as to age, intelligence, nativity and residence in under-privileged areas were given the same tests. Certainly there were more 'poorly adjusted' and 'unstable' amongst the delinquents, but anxiety and insecurity, resignation and introversion appeared more frequently amongst non-delinquents.[161]

Similarities between delinquents and non-delinquents were also more marked than differences in Monachesis' MMPI study[162] in which he compared forty-nine delinquent boys with fifty-six non-delinquent boys. This, he said, confirmed the hypothesis that 'non-delinquents living in such areas [areas of high delinquency] are not significantly different from delinquents in many personality characteristics'.

There have been suggestions, however, that delinquents differ from non-delinquents in temperament. One of the best known and earliest formulations was proposed by Sir Cyril Burt in his 1925 study. He argued that each person is endowed with a fund of 'general emotionality' which lies behind the different instincts. Briefly, some had an excess of emotionality and as a result were essentially extroverted, quick tempered, impulsive, unpredictable and lacking in consistency: at the other extreme were those with a 'temperamental defectiveness' inclined to be reserved, withdrawn, introverted. In his comparison of delinquents with non-delinquents he found both extremes more prominent in delinquents but especially were the delinquents marked off from the non-delinquents by an excess of emotionality.[163]

We may compare this with the Gluecks' general impressions of the Rorschach test results which we have seen to have been largely inconclusive. They said: 'On the whole, delinquents are more extroverted, vivacious, impulsive and less self-controlled than the non-delinquents . . . they are, as a group, more socially assertive.'[164]

In the same context comes Bowlby's well known study of maternal deprivation. He pointed out that a child needs a close secure relationship with its mother and where this is lacking, there may be personality problems in later life. Partial deprivation of the mother or a mother substitute may lead to insecurity, anxiety, an excessive demand for affection. In a study of juvenile thieves he described a type of young delinquent which he called 'the affectionless character',[165] and later linked this with maternal deprivation—the result of protracted separation from the mother.[166] Similarly, Burlingham and Freud studied children separated from their parents when they were evacuated during the Second World War, concluding that this resulted in psychological damage to the children and a disruption of normal personality formation.[167] Balancing all this, there appeared, in 1960, Andry's study of the role of parents in delinquency from which he concluded that: 'The prime differentiating feature between delinquents and non-delinquents, as far as parental role playing is concerned is the delinquents' perception of their fathers' role as being negative'.[168]

This would indicate that in the development of personality both parents play an important role and the absence or indifference of either to their children's needs may have unfortunate consequences for normal emotional growth. Thus, it seems possible—though it can by no means be taken as proved—that temperamental differences, in so far as these can be shown to exist between delinquents and non-delinquents may be due to faulty upbringing due to a disruption in normal family care.[169]

The effects of inadequate child care, the failure to socialize children, leaves them with inadequate control of their impulses so that many of them have to learn life's lessons the hard way and perhaps only when they have been in conflict with adult society. It can leave children aggressive, immature or inadequate and in some cases the results can be very serious indeed. Thus Bowlby's reference to 'the affectionless character' has much in common with other work which has been done on the 'psychopathic personality'. These are persons who whilst not insane or mentally ill in the usual sense of the word, appear to be conscienceless, cold-hearted, unsocialized, devoted to their own selfish interests and apparently incapable of postponing their needs for physical or emotional gratification for very long.[170]

The best known work on psychopaths is that of Henderson.[171] He describes the psychopathic state as applying to those who from an early age have 'exhibited disorders of conduct of an anti-social or a social nature' and who do not respond to ordinary treatment. They may be of high, low or average intelligence. However, the use of this name for offenders or patients who do not fit into other known groups has been indiscriminate. It has been too convenient. So many different types of offenders have been labelled psychopathic simply because the more regular classifications did not apply, that the late Sir Norwood East warned, some years ago, that 'some observers consider it to be little more than a wastebasket nomenclature'.[172]

Yet psychiatrists continue to study this clinical type which may be difficult to define adequately but which is well known to most people concerned with delinquency. Psychopaths are responsible for some of the most cold-blooded and heartless crimes. Frequently of high intelligence,[173] they may exhibit no little ingenuity and their selfishness and lack of sentiment or feeling renders them at once capable of the worst excesses whilst being impervious to most of the usual forms of treatment. Sir Norwood East who had considerable experience in the British prison medical service recognized the type whilst, as we have seen, he was aware of the problem of describing it. His own tentative approach to a definition was: 'A person who, although not insane, psychoneurotic or mentally defective is persistently unable to adapt himself to social requirements on account of abnormal peculiarities of impulse, temperament or character.'[174]

The British Royal Commission on Mental Illness and Mental Deficiency recommended a new classification of patients as (1) the mentally ill, (2) the psychopathic and (3) the severely subnormal personalities. It enlarged the second category to include: 'any type of aggressive or inadequate personality which does not render the patient severely subnormal . . . but which is recognized medically as a pathological condition.'[175]

The question for the courts has always been the extent to which such individuals should be held responsible for their behaviour. The psychopath knows the difference between right and wrong in an intellectual sense but he does not have the normal feelings for the differences between the two types of behaviour. He is completely amoral and at one time he was described in law as being 'morally defective' for want of a better description. Many of the battles between psychiatrists and lawyers on the concept of legal responsibility have been fought over the psychopath.

Treatment is also a problem because the psychopath does not respond to the usual reformative measures. Punishment appears to be ineffective. Henderson has shown the results of electro-convulsive therapy and insulin to have been disappointing.[176] In Denmark, a special colony has been created for psychopaths to which they are sentenced indeterminately. Recently Denmark has abandoned the indeterminate sentence and in the interests of human rights has discontinued this specialized form of treatment. The institution is now a more general psychiatric hospital for offenders. They fit oddly into both prisons and hospitals so that the recourse to special institutions where they can be segregated for the protection of the public seems to be the only answer. Cavanagh and McGoldrick suggest that time may be effective and that some psychopaths begin to change in middle age.[177]

The problem of the psychopath, the affectionless character, the person who is weak-willed or inadequate, may be the result of faulty upbringing or defective child care. This introduces the much-used concept of the 'broken home'. Obviously these kind of problems in the care and training of children could arise from the death of either parent, from parental separation or divorce. Carr Saunders, Mannheim and Rhodes in a broad survey of young offenders which they conducted in England just before the Second World War found that broken homes in this sense were to be found in 25.6 per cent of the cases of delinquents in London but in only 13 per cent of the cases of non-delinquents and in 31.5 per cent of the delinquency cases in certain other English towns as against 18.6 per cent of the non-delinquent cases.[178] Much earlier, Burt had found that 'defective family relationships' occurred more frequently amongst delinquents,[179] and in Stotts account of 102 youths between 15 and 18 years of age committed to an Approved School, the broken home appeared as 'a powerful predisposing factor'.[180] Bonner studying sexual psychopaths noted that their life histories often revealed broken homes, lack of supervision or too little discipline.[181] Keiser records that of 936 juvenile delinquents committed to the Diepkloof Reformatory in South Africa only 305, that is less than one in three, came from a home which contained their biological mother and father.[182] The instances could be multiplied for the broken home has been cited in many studies as being a causative factor in delinquency.

The evidence is not all one-sided, however, and Howard Jones quotes three studies which seem to show that the significance of the broken home has been over-rated. Thus Ferguson in Glasgow found that homes from which one parent was absent produced only slightly more delinquency; Shaw and Mackay in one of their delinquency area studies found only 25.8 per cent of broken homes amongst delinquents as against 26.4 per cent amongst non-delinquents; and Hughes following up a group of Coventry probationers obtained follow-up results for delinquents from broken homes which were quite as good as from homes with both parents.[183]

As Howard Jones points out, it all really depends upon what is meant by 'broken home'. This is an umbrella term covering a variety of situations some of which are probably not comparable. It may be, for example, that in using the term we are referring to defective parental relationships which might equally exist even when the parents are together but are indifferent, negligent or in constant conflict with each other and unable to provide the kind of background which a child needs to grow up normally. For this reason the Gluecks in their monumental study of juvenile delinquency in America concentrated more upon the nature of the relationships with parents. Where these were defective there was more likely to be delinquency—so much so that such relationships were construed as an integral part of a prediction table by which the Gluecks considered that delinquency could be forecast. Where home relationships or adequate supervision or discipline were absent it was highly likely that the child would become delinquent.[184]

The importance of home life and early training brings us to the clinical studies of psychiatrists from which generalizations have been made about total behaviour and frequently about delinquent behaviour in particular. No account of the psychological theories of crime would be complete without a reference to psycho-analysis and to Freud who created it. This can receive but sketchy treatment here,[185] but the Freudian system seeks to explain crime as only a part of a more general background for all behaviour. Freud and his early school were preoccupied with the deeper inner emotional conflicts aroused by man being obliged to inhibit his natural animal impulses, instincts or urges in order to meet the demands of society for conventional behaviour or conformity. For Freud this basic instinctive nature of man derived its force from libido, a kind of suffused and diffused sex appetite. According to Freud the psychic life of man is in three layers:

1. The *Conscious* mind—which is aware of what is happening at any given moment;
2. The *Preconscious* mind—which preserves the memories and complexes and is capable of becoming conscious at any time;
3. The *Unconscious* mind—which contains our original racial experiences, instincts and basic impulses as well as any repressed feelings which were previously conscious.

We learn that in the course of life a child growing up has certain unpleasant experiences which he often represses into the unconscious. There they remain with the deeper instincts as complexes which have a force of their own and seek a masked symbolical expression in dreams or other kinds of behaviour which the conscious mind does not fully understand. This accounts for us sometimes acting in ways which seem to us to be out of character.

This deeper side of our nature which is often the real motivation for our behaviour can only be reached by protracted psycho-analysis, by free association which allows us clues to the deeper feelings when we speak without thinking, or by the analysis of dreams which properly interpreted as wish fulfillment tell us a great deal about ourselves which we could not learn otherwise.

In the process of growing up and becoming socialized our instinctive desires have to be curbed to meet social expectations. One very special example of this is the Oedipus situation. A child of two or three years of age has a natural desire for closer intimacy with the parent of the opposite sex and natural feelings of hatred towards the other parent. It is socially unacceptable that such sexual desires should be satisfied or that the hatred should be expressed. There is indeed a fear that the hated parent who is more powerful will punish the child for such thoughts. As a result they are repressed to the unconscious where in later life they may govern the person's attitudes to sex, his choice of a marriage partner or his reaction to authority. This is the Oedipus situation, but there are many other circumstances in which the obligation of conformity obliges the child to repress basic desires.[186]

Such repression is normal and natural and if the situation is handled maturely there is adequate satisfaction in sublimation and a normal character and personality formation. If repression occurs too early, too forcibly, if the home situation is unbalanced by an over-affectionate mother, an over-severe father or by the absence of one or other parent or if there are other defects in normal up-bringing then the repression of innate desires creates complexes and frustrations which the individual might later act out on society either consciously or (more commonly) symbolically—in a way which even he himself cannot fully understand if he has not had recourse to psycho-analysis to explain his hidden urges, feelings and frustrations. Thus certain types of criminal behaviour might well be a substitute for the more direct release of the fundamental urges or may be the result of repressed complexes. It could be a form of substitute satisfaction.

Aichhorn, an Austrian psycho-analyst applied these ideas to his study of young delinquents. He concluded that a great deal of crime was the result of faulty child care and the child not being adequately socialized. He reasoned that the child controls his animal desires in return for affection but where he is starved of love or given affection too easily by an over-indulgent parent the control of innate impulses does not take place and he grows up aggressive, difficult and unsocialized.[187]

The conflicts which are repressed in the unconscious side of our nature may give rise to insecurity, anxiety and especially to unwarranted guilt feelings. These latter might even create an unconscious desire for punishment to redress the inner feelings and assuage the guilt. The criminal, according to this theory, may actually commit an offence ostensibly for gain or satisfaction but in reality because he wants to be punished, and therefore in the act he will quite thoughtlessly leave clues behind him which lead to his arrest and prosecution. The punishment which follows has then a cathartic effect making it easier for the offender to live with himself.[188]

Whilst not all offenders are actually seeking punishment, the crime they commit is usually interpretable by the Freudian approach as a substitute satisfaction for deeper unconscious conflicts resolved by being acted out. Thus, in a well-known study of seven cases Alexander and Healy in America drew conclusions of this type. By psycho-analytic procedures and dream analysis for example these authors concluded about one case of persistent theft that the stealing was not for gain at all but a reaction to a strong sense of inferiority as well as being a means of getting rid of guilt feelings towards his brother and being a spite reaction against his mother.[189]

It is, of course, difficult to either substantiate or refute this kind of formulation of crime. In the psycho-analytic relationship between the analyst and the patient from which such conclusions are drawn, there is a considerable element of subjectivity. It is also difficult to believe that a good deal of selectivity does not intrude into the apparently detached delving amongst forgotten incidents, old rancours and repressed urges.

The great question still remaining in psychiatry is whether the theory follows from the objective study of cases or whether the theory precedes investigation and in the process of study the case-evidence is fitted to the theory.

Of course, with clinical practice growing, the Freudian-oriented psychiatrists claim a gradual accumulation of more and more evidence to substantiate their basic concepts and in America especially the id and ego constructs of Freud have permeated much of the social work with offenders. On the other hand, there has been a distinct drift away from the cruder principles of Freud by many modern psychiatrists. It has been realized that there was a degree of question begging in some of the earlier work and that far-fetched symbolical interpretations were often preferred even when the reasons for a crime were more obvious and fully understandable in terms of gain, selfishness or opportunism.

We have seen that the basis for the Freudian conception of the id and unconscious was essentially sexual. But the sex instinct is only one of man's powerful and primitive urges. Therefore, not all psycho-analysts who are prepared to accept the general outline of a conflict between repressed desires and social demands have been able to follow Freud in his preoccupation with sex. Adler, also of the Vienna school, preferred a more directly perceived theory of an innate will to power. The wish to obtain satisfaction by dominating is at the basis of our physical and mental development and we tend to compensate for defects in a variety of ways. Thus, a little man might develop a loud voice and an aggressive manner and a man with a speech defect like Demosthenes might be impelled to become a public orator. Thus, crime might be explainable by a desire to shine in ways otherwise denied. For example, juvenile delinquency might sometimes be due to a boy being backward at school and finding the appreciation he needs as a gang leader after school hours. A loud-mouthed aggressive bully given to violence might be obtaining respect and the feeling of domination he needs because he is incapable by education and mental ability of shining in other ways. Even secretive theft may give the satisfaction of being cleverer than others to someone who is otherwise frustrated. Adler's method became known as Individual Psychology and had considerable vogue in educational circles.

Another colleague of Freud who differed with him on the issue of sex was Jung who eventually founded a rival approach to psychoanalysis which he termed 'analytical psychology'. Jung preferred to generalize the concept of the unconscious, finding there not only the individual urges but also the collective impulses and images which we share with all other human beings. This was the basis of much of our culture and religion and for the development of different value systems. For Jung the unconscious had a more abstract, collective significance which did not exclude the notion of God as had materialistic Freud. For Jung too, each person had a second side to himself. All men had an anima as well as an animus—a female and male set of characteristics. In males of course the animus predominated just as in females it was the anima: but every woman had some male inclinations just as every man had female inclinations. When this got out of balance we had an explanation of transvestism, homosexuality and other sex deviations. Jung also proposed that each person had a mask which he presented to the outside world and behind which his real self moved. In this role playing it is not difficult to see how some crime might be explained as the result of trying to keep up appearances or preserving a self-image. For years Jung found more acceptance than Freud in religious circles where his ideas could take account of the soul, the Revelation and the older collective ideas of God.

This is not the place for a full discussion of psycho-analytic theory and its various alternatives. We should note, however, that Freud and many who follow him are avowedly materialistic, deterministic and opposed to the notion of personal responsibility for behaviour. There are a great many other psycho-analysts who are not wholly Freudians and do not share this materialistic or deterministic orientation.

Freud, whatever his limitations, gave a new impetus and direction to the study of the human mind and behaviour. The psychiatrists of all shades of opinion have given us new insights into emotional problems, neurosis and psychosis—all of which are undeniably responsible for a great deal of criminal conduct. Nor have their efforts been without success in the courts for today the 'irresistible impulse' is recognized in a number of countries as reducing liability for crime—notably in England and certain American states. Psychiatric treatment is available to offenders both inside and outside prisons and psychiatric examinations are often requested by the courts—especially where the 'common sense' interpretations of behaviour appear to be inadequate.

However, it would be a mistake to accept that the concept of mental health which has developed over the past seventy years or so is now so firmly established that it cannot be fundamentally changed. As one moves to the last quarter of the twentieth century there are signs of a challenge to the widespread diagnosis and labelling which has become a part of social existence and more particularly a part of the correctional pattern of work. At the Eighth Congress of the International Society of Social Defence held in Paris in November 1971 one Scandinavian group argued that a society really had no right to correct or reform or rehabilitate offenders and it even objected to individualized forms of treatment. Each individual had a right to his own values and if in his behaviour he clashed with society at large then he could be expected to pay compensation or suffer a retributive punishment but the idea of considering him as in need of treatment—unless he be suffering from some physical ailment—was rejected. Similarly, Dr Thomas Szasz, a psychiatrist and psycho-analyst in private practice and a professor of psychiatry at the Upstate Medical Center of the State University of New York, has published several books which claim that mental disease does not exist—only that kind of mental disorder which can be traced to physical ailment. Behavioural problems certainly exist according to Dr Szasz but it is wrong to treat them as illnesses. There is a great deal of unhappiness and misery but this is because of the complications of living in a society with its own difficulties of relationships and communications and there is no call to treat these 'problems in living' as diseases.[190] These kind of ideas could transform the whole psychology of criminal and delinquent behaviour within a decade or two.

Perhaps, of all the social sciences, psychology has, as yet, received the least attention in Africa and there are still few universities in Africa with separate departments of psychology. Yet, as early as 1943, the Rhodes/Livingstone Institute published a study, by the Principal of the Barotse National School, of African development and thinking resulting from the local patterns of child care.[191] In this, Ritchie sought to apply Freudian psychology to his experience of African nursing and adult behaviour. Although the data obtained permitted of only limited conclusions, his work was a notable exploration of a new field. Much later, Carothers attempted a very broad and provocative interpretation of African thinking for the World Health Organization which was necessarily highly generalized.[192] More detailed experiments in personnel assessment and aptitude testing have been pioneered by the National Institute of Personnel Research in Johannesburg and this early work has been followed up in other parts of Africa. Even so, the field is relatively undeveloped. We have still no suitable tests which can be standardized for the measurement of African intelligence and personality studies are lacking.

The psychology of crime in Africa—indeed the psychology of behaviour generally in this part of the world—might be characterized, not unfairly, as an unopened book. Too little groundwork has yet been done for there to be the kind of informational structure on which psychological interpretations of conduct depend. What is being attempted now is a cautious probing of the unknown with occasional sorties into reasonable speculation.

We have seen that intelligence tests have not yet been standardized and although there are a few examples of the application of European tests—or of assessments according to the degree of 'modernization'—it remains true that valid intelligence tests on any wide scale, are, for the time being, ruled out. Even more so with such personality assessing devices as the Thematic Aperception Tests, the Rorschach Blot Tests or the Multiple Personality Inventories. None of these can have reliable meaning if the interpretations of responses are to be according to Western stereotypes. Nor is there any guarantee that the Freudian-based concepts of human growth and emotional development (based on a typically nuclear European family) have necessary relevance for Africa's extended family system, for surviving tribal conditions or even for the new forms of urban living which have evolved on this continent. It is possible that even Pavlovian and purely behaviourist explanations of conduct would also require modification to be readily applicable to African conditions. And it is certain that the categories of mental illness used elsewhere in the world cannot yet be applied to Africans with any real confidence.

Thus, it is seen that here, as elsewhere, mental deficiency, mental illness and a great many other psychological factors enter into the amount of crime which is committed. There are cases of abnormality involving mental defect or retardation, and instances of outrageous behaviour due to insanity which is so conspicuous and socially dangerous as to need no precise testing or careful diagnosis for the existence of such disorders to be established to the satisfaction of the authorities. When persons like these clash with the law the psychological factor is easy to identify even if it cannot be properly measured or conveniently classified.

We will come later to the problem of treatment, but we shall note here, however, some of the complications which go beyond diagnosis. Most countries in Africa have at least one large reference hospital for mental illness which also admits cases committed by the courts. Very rarely there will be two such hospitals but more generally the services of psychiatrists and/or psychiatrically trained nurses has been extended by means of out-patient services (and perhaps a few short term beds) for the mentally ill at the other general hospitals or local health clinics.[193]

In this work, it has become customary to use a number of the Western labels in the diagnosis of disorders. Thus, one refers to manic-depressed states, to paranoia, anxiety neuroses and schizophrenia. But 'schizophrenia' being such a 'dustbin' term in the developed countries (i.e. a convenient appellation for anything not otherwise classifiable) is probably even more so in Africa. There was a time in Malawi just before independence when people under pressure were being treated at the Zomba Mental Hospital for what the psychiatrist liked to call 'political neurosis'. If the external behaviour seemed to fit the group, the person was classified.[194] However, the tendency is to use psychiatric appellations in Africa which we used elsewhere and perhaps only Lambo has referred to a possibly distinctive African syndrome: 'malignant anxiety.'[195] Milner and Asuni refer to the cultural effect of local ideas of sexual potency and fertility and the intensive influence of witchcraft and the supernatural.[196] Diagnosis frequently has to depend mainly upon the external behaviour because the communication channels between doctor and patient are likely to be treacherous to understanding where there are so many hundreds of languages and dialects. Even if all the problems of applying intelligence, emotion or personality tests had been solved and an African Psychology had become clinically applicable, it would still be true that only the really polyglot psychiatrist—or a team of psychiatrists covering all languages used—would be able to diagnose effectively and offer adequate psycho-therapy. For language reasons alone, it is often difficult to contemplate any deep psycho-analysis or to hope to obtain more than a superficial understanding of the emotional reactions of a patient. Thus, there tends to be a strong dependence on the physical forms of mental treatment, for example electric or insulin shock therapy, tranquillizers or other drugs which modify or control behaviour.

Of course, as biochemistry discovers more varied and effective ways of treating mental illness by pills, medicines and injections, the difficulty of recourse to psycho-therapy in Africa may become much less serious. It does not alter the fact, however, that in both diagnosis and treatment the gap between doctor and patient is still much too wide for either comfort or security. In some of the larger hospitals, hundreds of patients are kept as long as their behaviour seems troublesome but without very much in the way of treatment. Releases or discharges from hospital can still be purely on the basis of external conduct and without an intimate understanding of the thinking, the prejudices, the syndromes of concern or the abnormal conceptualizations of the patient. These will be beyond grasp very often either because of the language complications or because of all the difficulties flowing from the problem of being frequently without adequate and determinable norms from which to judge or assess future prospects.

There is certainly a vast field of extraordinary—sometimes harmful—human conduct due to mental illness or defect but which is not abnormal enough to qualify for recognition as mental illness or defect, and which remains interpretable therefore as fully responsible behaviour. As we have seen, the norms are not usually sufficiently established to allow diagnosis any sound foundation from which to proceed: but even if they were, the psychological and psychiatric services in Africa at present just do not extend in either sufficient quality or quantity to allow us to present this kind of conduct in its true light.[197]

Thus, a very considerable amount of crime in Africa is probably attributable to psychological factors which are never disclosed, or, if disclosed, are not understood. High grade mental defectives, to take only one example, may well pass for people of average intelligence—especially if they have good verbal abilities—even in developed countries. How much more must this be true of Africa? So too, there are varieties of emotional disturbance likely to pass as normal. Moreover, with psychiatric services as restricted as they are, it is not easy for African countries to indulge in such legal niceties as 'irresistible impulse' which requires psychiatric evidence.

In so far as investigations have been made or evidence exists, the link between obvious insanity and/or mental illness and crime in Africa is not very pronounced. The number of criminally convicted patients in the mental hospitals is very small, just as the number of criminals committed by the courts as insane or not responsible for their actions, remains relatively insignificant. For instance, over a three year study period in Zambia, between 130 and 166 patients were admitted to the mental hospital annually and of these the number of 'criminal lunatics' (i.e. found guilty but insane) varied between eight and ten a year. In residence at the end of 1959 for all previous years, there were thirty-two 'criminal lunatics'.[198]

This general pattern is in line with experience elsewhere. Thus in 1954 the Medical Research Council in England sponsored a survey which showed that of 12,000 mental defectives in institutions only 5 per cent had a record of sexual perversion, pregnancy or venereal disease and only 2 per cent had been charged with stealing. In Africa the mentally defectives are usually cared for by some member of the family and only when the extended family has dispersed and the responsible relative has died, does trouble arise from a defective left to fend for himself. It is then that hut-firing, public disturbance, stealing or other forms of anti-social behaviour might occur—often as a form of protest or means of claiming attention. The writer has experience of this happening in the case of a defective albino who was something of an outcast—and who reacted accordingly. He will be controlled or tolerated whilst cared for by a relative—and will clash with authority or the local community when left to his own devices.

It should be observed, however, that the level of tolerance is high in Africa. Thus on a recent visit to Togo the writer stayed in the best beach hotel—round the corner from which a middle-aged woman, naked to the waist, talking to herself and obviously abnormal was living on a piece of waste ground, cooking for herself the things she had gathered during the day and sleeping in the sand. Along the sea front each day walked a young man with a beard, naked, but keeping one hand hovering over his genitals. These odd individuals were not interfered with by the people around them who 'accepted' their eccentric behaviour. No doubt there was a law forbidding their conduct, but, if so, it was apparently not invoked in these cases.[199]

Although it is undoubtedly true that the amount of crime due to mental abnormality in Africa is small—and whilst there is good reason to believe that the psychopathic offender is relatively scarce—it must be acknowledged that with services as inadequate as they still are in most countries south of the Sahara, and with so few courts served by psychiatric services at all, the few figures and sparce information existing cannot be taken as being either representative or conclusive.

It will be clear from all this that notions like 'adequate child care' or 'socialization', 'broken homes' or 'maladjustment', and indeed the total relevance of early experiences to later adult conduct and adaptation, will need re-interpretation to become applicable in an African context—that is to say, re-interpretation as soon as the necessary basic (and subsequent) research has been instigated into the psychology and sociology of the African family in the many cultures and countries which are our concern.

This was specially emphasized at the First Pan-African Psychiatric Conference held in Nigeria in 1961, where Professor Lambo, in his paper on the Growth of African Children (Psychological Aspects) complained of the lack of data. He mentioned especially the effect not only of socio-cultural factors in the psychological sphere, but also chronic protein and vitamin deficiencies. He said that whatever the Nigerian child's fears, hates and uncertainties, they had failed to trace the genesis of neurotic behaviour excessively to any form of unhealthy relationship in childhood. Childhood in the traditional African setting is, on the whole, a happy uncomplicated period with nostalgic memories of love and consideration. Yet, says Lambo: 'In spite of this warm, emotionally stable and happy childhood, we still find that frank anxiety underlies his adult dealings and relations with others.'

Professor Lambo then deals with the problem of diminished maternal affection and the importance of ridicule in the process of socialization of African children. He confirms the views expressed here that the Oedipus complex must look very different where there is polygamy and many 'fathers' in the total kinship group. He shows that toilet training is lax and flexible, that breast-feeding is irregular and liberal and adds: 'I have no evidence, however flimsy, to say that weaning is traumatic.' Here he is referring to the long period of breast feeding typical of African life (where substitute baby foods are not readily obtainable) and the sudden weaning of children at about the age of two when the next child is expected. It is arguable that despite this shock of sudden separation from maternal care the sharing of roles which a child experiences in an extended family could more than compensate for any incipient feelings of deprivation resulting from the weaning. The sharing of roles, the development of a group-centred mentality and a sense of co-responsibility could all be valuable to personality development. All of which firmly underlines the need for a deeper study of many aspects of child development in Africa before one begins to apply Western categories and classifications. Human nature may be the same all over but there is a world of difference between the cultures in their moulding of behaviour.

The very fact that there are significant similarities between delinquency in developed and developing countries suggests that the conception of delinquency itself may be a stereotype apt or prone to produce the pattern of behaviour which it describes in whatever culture this occurs. In other words, just to use the term 'delinquency' may be to institute a search for the kind of predisposing circumstances to which this word refers in Western society. In this case, it will always be found, and when found it will be exhibiting all those characteristics which have been sought simply because they were associated with the concept elsewhere; for example child neglect, backwardness, emotional hostility, insecurity, etc.

It should not be overlooked that cultural change, urbanization and the conceptual transformation taking place in Africa heighten the possibility of mental or emotional disturbance. The Cornell-Aro Mental Health Research Project in Western Nigeria studied twenty-five villages and eight parts of a town, classifying them as 'disintegrated' and 'integrated' on the basis of poverty, breakdown of lineage or family solidarity and ineffective leadership. It found one and a half times as many people were potentially psychiatric cases in the disintegrated areas as in the integrated places. Women were particularly affected. However, the disintegration or integration was not a straight 'traditional' or 'modernized' system. Many traditional and many modernized places were found to be 'integrated' so that the process of change was not itself wholly responsible: a good deal depended on how it was received. Moreover, the question of cause and effect is apposite: was it the cultural problems which affected mental health or the mental condition which made cultural changes difficult to accommodate?

GENERAL OBSERVATIONS ON THE CAUSES OF CRIME

We have reviewed the greater part of the work which has been done on the causes of crime, and in each general area it has been possible to give only a few examples of the vast amount of work which has been done, especially over the past thirty or forty years.

It will be seen that interest has veered from time to time. First, there was a concern with crime generally, then a concentration on the individual offender, later a preoccupation with social and environmental conditions followed by a swing to psychological differences, reverting later to genetic influence. Lately the criminal justice system itself has come under scrutiny.

Most attempts to show differences, either physical or psychological, between offenders and non-offenders have had very limited value. The techniques for measuring the differences may have been faulty—as with Lombroso, Goddard or even Goring; the sampling might have been inadequate, as with Hooton; and in the last analysis our scanty knowledge about the distribution of such characteristics in the population generally leaves even the best work in this direction as being suggestive only. This is the problem now besetting those who are trying to show that an additional Y chromosome is a source of aggression.[200]

The explanation of crime as individual disorder is no more satisfactory. As we have seen, not only is there a good deal of subjectivity in this work but again we do not know that there are not just as many, if not more, people with similar or worse disorders who do not commit crime. The most we can say about clinical work in psychology is that it helps us to understand those who have committed crime, even if it does not adequately distinguish them from those who have not been brought before the courts.

Environmental studies have served to show the correlation of crime with particular economic or social conditions. Their main defect is that they fail to explain why more people submitted to such influences do not commit crime than those who do. To decide this we are forced back to studies of individual differences. Not surprisingly, then, Burt concluded that: 'Crime is assignable to no single universal source nor yet to two or three: it springs from a wide variety and usually from a multiplicity of alternative and converging influences.'[201]

This has led to the team approach to criminological investigation including a number of different specialists, the classical example of which has been the Glueck study of juvenile delinquency in America.[202] But eclectism of this kind has its own limitations. Thus Vold has said: 'Eclectism tends to reject and deny the possibility of making valid generalizations out of the assorted information at hand. Logically, this can only mean the impossibility of formulating any consistent scientific theory in the field.'[203]

One of the very few attempts at a general theory of crime came from Sutherland who argued that crime is really no more than learned behaviour depending upon the frequency, intensity and quality of influences flowing from a person's association with those about him. This theory of 'differential association' states that criminality results from an excess of 'definitions favourable to violation of the law over definitions unfavourable to violations of the law' learned by the prospective offender in social interaction with existing criminals.[204] Thus, the theory is based upon the idea of learning by association. He who associates with delinquents will become a delinquent. It is another way of saying 'show me your friends and I will tell you what you are'.

It is obvious that not everyone who associates with thieves is a thief, but Sutherland would explain this by saying that in that person's case the frequency, intensity or quality of the influences were rather different from those impinging upon the others who became criminal. The problem is that this is arguing *post hoc propter hoc*, that is, simply because the person does not succumb, therefore his complex of associations *must* have been different. This *may* be so, but it could also be a sheer assumption and it does not help us to validate the theory.

In an article which he published in the *British Journal of Delinquency* in 1956, Sheldon Glueck attacked Sutherland's theory calling it 'a superficial and superfluous generalization'.[205] He pointed out that proponents of the theory stress the *numerical* superiority of 'definitions favourable to violations of the law' on the basis of which it would be reasonable to suppose that the biggest criminals would be professors of criminology, prison guards and prison chaplains. When faced with this they refer to the quantitative differences of the definitions saying that they vary in frequency, duration, priority and intensity. But if this is the case then the numerical significance falls away. It will probably be impossible to validate Sutherland's theory anyway because it is going to be impossible for anyone to count such 'definitions' or measure their frequency and intensity in any individual case. Nevertheless it remains as a brave attempt to reach out to a general theory of crime.

A second general theory, as we have seen, flows from the Freudian attempt to explain all behaviour in terms of his psychological concepts and behaviour being determined by up-bringing, repression and symbolic behaviour. This stands or falls on the validity of the basic principles, and most behaviour interpreted in accordance with Freudian constructs may be interpreted in several other ways. It has been pointed out that the repressed unconscious of Freud cannot account for the motivation required for conduct since by definition it is removed from awareness.[206] More important, the validation of the Freudian theory awaits a more objective attitude by the psycho-analysts themselves. As long as they maintain that only one who has himself been psycho-analysed is competent to judge and since psycho-analysis is only possible with someone who has accepted the basic suppositions, it is obvious that there is a closed shop excluding objective validation. As it stands, objections to the principles of psycho-analysis are held to derive from the critic's own unconscious conflicts; open discussion is therefore excluded.

What is at least clear in our survey of the different studies of crime, is that the constitutional, psychological and social factors are inter-dependent. Thus, whatever body form or gland structure is inherited its effect on behaviour will be affected:

(a) by the social situation in which the individual finds himself, and
(b) by the training in socialization which he receives and which constitute his eventual character or personality.

Similarly, the effects of bad housing or economic depression will differ according to the heredity and psychology of those subjected to such pressures. And in the same way the psychology of a person is influenced by the family or social group into which he is born and the effects of the environment which make demands upon him.

Moreover, we can detect a drawing together of some of the different approaches to crime. We saw, for instance, that original studies of delinquency areas led to a preoccupation with climates of opinion, attitudes and ideas, that is social psychological concepts. The idea of role playing is as psychological as it is social and Jung's psychology finds much common ground with cultural explanations of crime.

There is an increasing awareness that all the approaches to, and all the factors in, crime are inter-related, inter-connected and form part of a total complex of which crime is itself only one aspect. As Reckless pointed out in 1940, 'a social phenomenon such as criminal behaviour is so involved that it may even be a cause of some of the causes which are supposed to cause it'.[207]

If then we are still a long way from explaining crime the work which has been and is being done is by no means wasted. To explain crime, as we have seen, is to explain human behaviour and this is a very tall order—even in an age when we look forward to a landing on Venus.

[1] For example, we have a much deeper knowledge now of the sociology and psychology of criminal behaviour, the inter-relationships of norms, the biology of behaviour, the chemical control of impulses, the limitations of law and the internal structure of law enforcement institutions.

[2] Sutherland's 'differential association' was essentially expressed in the old saying 'show me your friends and I will tell you what you are' and reflected in the courts' frequent emphasis on 'bad companions'. Also the old 'underworld' is back in vogue with 'sub-cultures', however much more we may now understand its facets and complications. See fn. 204, p. 103 below.

[3] W. K. Clifford in a lecture 'On the Aims and Instruments of Scientific Thought' delivered to the British Association for the Advancement of Science in 1872 pointed out that the word representing 'cause' had sixty-four meanings in Plato and forty-eight in Aristotle! See W. K. Clifford, *The Common Sense of the Exact Sciences*, New York: Dover Publications, 1955.

[4] See below (pp. 107ff.) for an account of prediction studies.

[5] W. Clifford, *Juvenile Delinquency in Zambia*, United Nations Trends Study SOA/SD/CS.5, 30 April 1967.

[6] ibid.

[7] This could only be a surmise—the factual evidence for such a *process* being scanty—but there is ample confirmation for there being a distinction in African tribes between offences redeemable by compensation and others not being so redeemable because of their 'morally' or 'spiritually' reprehensible character. cf. Matson on the Akan, Penwill on the Kamba, Wagner on the Bantu of North Kavirondo. Also T. O. Elias on *The Nature of African Customary Law* (Manchester University Press, 1956), quotes Matson for the Akan distinction of offences dangerous to the community (usually spiritual) and offences against individuals.

[8] There is a whole literature in anthropology which substantiates this kind of philosophy as it emerges in indigenous African belief. In particular the studies of African conceptualization in Zaïre and in other parts of francophone Africa are relevant. In English an apposite reference is in M. Fortes, *Oedipus and Job*, Cambridge University Press, 1959.

For a summary of the situation in Africa as revealed by anthropological studies and legal inquiries, see Hilda and Leo Kuper (eds.), *African Law Adaptation and Development*, Berkeley and Los Angeles: University of California Press. The Kupers at p.10 summarize the religious context of the legal systems in a number of African countries as shown by the contributors. Forde's essay on the Ibo system and Vansina's article on the Kuba are especially relevant.

[9] Lord Hailey, *An African Survey*, Oxford University Press, 1956, revised 1957, p. 625.

[10] Max Marwick, 'The Continuance of Witchcraft Beliefs' in Prudence Smith (ed.), *Africa in Transition*, London: Max Reinhardt, 1958.

In a minute written to the Chief Secretary of the Nyasaland Government at Zomba in 1928, Judge Haythorn Reed said '. . . the District Commissioner of Milanje reports that he knows of 28 deaths from poisoning and witchcraft during 9 months of 1927' (16 July 1928). See also *Sunday Mail* (Central African paper), 11 February 1962, for increase of murders near Blantyre due to witchcraft.

[11] On 10 January 1971, the *New York Times* reported the Agence France-Press for the news that President Jomo Kenyatta of Kenya, opening the Kinango Catholic Hospital near Mombasa, warned against witchcraft hampering efforts to introduce modern medicine.

[12] See article by A. M. Greeley, 'There's a New-Time Religion on the Campus', *New York Times Magazine*, 1 June 1969.

For a police view of the significance of the criminogenic role of 'soothsayers, spiritualists, fortune-tellers and other "pythonesses" ', see 'Indictable Witchcraft', *Brujeria delincuente*, Esc. Gen de Pol., Madrid, 1967.

Raybin has recently traced the influence of magical thinking on the creation and maintenance of family myths and curses in America (J. B. Raybin, 'The Curse: A Study in Family Communication', *American Journal of Psychiatry*, vol. 127: no. 5., November 1970). See also Selma Fraiberg, *The Magic Years*, New York: Charles Scribner's Sons, 1959, pp. 107-45 in which she describes this type of thinking in young children. So too S. Rado 'Obsessive Behaviour' in S. Arieti (ed.), *American Handbook of Psychiatry*, New York: Basic Books, 1959, suggests that magic's deepest root is in the infant's belief in his own omnipotence and in magic as a universal phenomenon. Similarly Piaget emphasizes the origin of magical thinking in the young person's inability to use an adult's sense of causality. Among adult psychiatric syndromes magical thinking has long been described for the obsessive-compulsive where it takes on a coercive aspect (see Rado above); for the hysteric where there is performance magic of illusory fulfilment (again see Rado); and the schizophrenic who uses ritualistic and mysterious gestures and symbols to attempt to exert control over a hostile universe.

Alan Milner and Tolani Asuni, 'Psychiatry and the Criminal Offender' in *African Penal Systems* (A. Milner (ed.), London: Routledge and Kegan Paul, 1969) say *inter alia* that it is clear that there is a strong cultural emphasis on sexual ability in the male and child-bearing capacity in the female and 'intensive belief, in witchcraft and supernatural powers are powerful anxiety inducing agents' (p. 322).

[13] See Joseph Alelson, 'What Generation Gap' in the *New York Times Magazine*, 18 January 1970.

[14] ibid.

[15] See W. Bascom, 'Urbanization Among the Yoruba', *American Journal of Sociology*, 1955, **60**, pp. 446-54. See also Ellen Hellman, 'Life in a Johannesburg Slum Yard' in S. Ottenberg and P. Ottenberg (eds.), *Cultures and Societies of Africa*, New York: Random House, 1960, pp. 546 ff. Also, by the same author, *Rooiyard*, Rhodes/Livingstone Papers, no. 13, Oxford University Press, 1948.

[16] W. Clifford, *Juvenile Delinquency in Zambia*, op. cit.; also *African Profiles in Crime*, Social Welfare Research monograph, no. 3, Lusaka, 1964.

[17] This concept of sub-cultures has a special relevance for urban areas in Africa where peoples of different tribes, of different mores, with varying patrilineal, bilateral or matrilineal lines of descent, different marriage and bride wealth systems, etc., are all thrown together.

[18] See L. Radzinowicz, *In Search of Criminology*, London: Heinemann, 1961, p. 142.

[19] J. W. Wessels, *History of Roman-Dutch Law* (1908), p. 700.

[20] See S. Lowenstein, 'Ethiopia' in A. Milner (ed.), *African Penal Systems*, London: Routledge and Kegan Paul, 1969.

[21] R. B. Seidman and J. D. Abaka Eyison, 'Ghana' in *African Penal Systems*, op. cit.

[22] F. O. Gouveia da Veiga, 'Portuguese Africa' in *African Penal Systems*, op. cit.

[23] See Gluckman and Elias, op. cit.

[24] cf. the series published for the International African Institute by Oxford University Press.

[25] Max Gluckman on the Barotse, Bohannan on the Tiv, Meek on the Ibo, below; and for attempts at codification see the work of Cory in Tanzania or Howell in the Sudan.

[26] See Colson on the Tonga, fn. 113, p. 98 below.

[27] I. Schapera, 'The Tswana Conception of Incest' in E. M. Fortes (ed.), *Social Structure*, studies presented to A. R. Radcliffe Brown, Oxford: The Clarendon Press, 1949.

[28] B. Z. Seligman, 'Incest and Descent', *Journal of Royal Africa Institute*, London, vol. LIX, 1929.

[29] J. M. van Bemmelin, 'The Constancy of Crime', *Brit. J. of Criminology*, volume 2, no. 3, 1952.

[30] Caesare Lombroso, *Crime: Its Causes and Remedies*, Boston: Little Brown and Co., 1913.

[31] Though nowadays only rarely enforced, some of the US states still have laws against adultery: see N. Morris, and G. Hawkins, *The Honest Politicians Guide to Crime Control*, University of Chicago Press, 1969, p. 16. Adultery is also an offence in African customary law.

[32] T. O. Elias, *The Nature of African Customary Law*, op. cit.

[33] M. Gluckman, *Custom and Conflict in Africa*, Oxford: Blackwell, 1955. Gluckman has persistently argued that basic legal concepts like 'the reasonable man' and gradations of liability, are to be found when African customary law is examined closely enough (see his 'African Jurisprudence' in *Advancement of Science* XVIII, January 1962; also *The Ideas in Barotse Jurisprudence*, New Haven: Yale University Press, 1965). See also P. Bohannan, *Justice and Judgement Among the Tiv*, London: Oxford University Press, 1957, and P. Howell, *Manual of Nuer Law*, London: Oxford University Press, 1954.

Similarly, it should not be imagined that supernatural interpretations exclude a distinction being made between crime and sin: that the two are separate but sometimes overlap was doubtless understood if not always expressed.

[34] The English indictment used even in the nineteenth century spoke of the defendant 'being prompted and instigated by the devil' and the Supreme Court of North Carolina said in 1862, 'To know the right and still the wrong pursue proceeds from a perverse will brought about by the seductions of the evil one' (quoted by Sutherland and Cressey, *Principles of Criminology*, Philadelphia: J. B. Lippincott Co., 1952, p. 51—quoting H. Shepard, *Journal of Criminal Law and Criminology*, **13**, 486, January/February 1927.

[35] P. Howell, *Manual of Nuer Law*, London: Oxford University Press, 1954.

[36] M. Gluckman, 'Reasonableness and Responsibility in the Law of Segmentary Societies' in H. and L. Kuper (eds.), *African Law, Adaptation and Development*, Berkeley: University of California Press, 1965, p. 132.

[37] C. Lombroso, *L'Uomo Delinquente*, Milan: Hoepli, 1876.

[38] E. A. Hooton, *The American Criminal*, Cambridge, Mass.: Harvard University Press, 1939.

[39] R. Dugdale, *The Jukes: a Study in Crime, Pauperism and Heredity*, New York: Putnam, 1877; A. H. Estabrook, *The Jukes in 1915*, Washington: Carnegie-Institute, 1916; H. H. Goddard, *The Kallikak Family*, New York: Macmillan, 1912.

[40] For a more recent study of family influence see H. J. Grogan and R. C. Grogan 'The Criminogenic Family', *J. of Crime and Criminology*, 14/3, 1968, pp. 220-5.

[41] A. Mergen, *Der geborene Verbrecher* (Ein Bericht über Chromosomenforschung und Kriminologie), Kriminalistik Verlag, Hamburg: 1968, quoted *Abstracts on Criminology and Penology*, vol. 9, no. 5, 1969.

[42] F. Sergovich of Victoria Hospital (London, Ontario) reporting in the *New England Journal of Medicine*, 17 April 1969.

[43] G. R. Clark, M. A. Telfer, D. Baker and M. Rosen, 'Sex Chromosomes, Crime and Psychosis', *Amer. J. Psychiatry*, 1970, 126/11 (1659-1663).

[44] See Robert W. Stock, 'The XYY and the Criminal', *New York Times Magazine*, 20 October 1968, describing the experiments of Dr. James B. Hamilton of Brooklyn, New York.

[45] cf. S. Wiener, G. Sutherland and A. A. Bartholomew, 'A murderer with 47, XYY and an additional autosomal abnormality', *Aust. N.Z. Journal of Criminology*, 2/1, 1969.

[46] J. P. Leff and P. D. Scott, 'XYY and Intelligence', *Lancet*, 1968, 1/7543 (645).

[47] S. Gilgenkrantz, J. Beurey, M. Weber and H. Gurecki, 'The YY Syndrome', *Ann. Méd., Nancy*, 1968, 7/1 (26-37).

[48] See R. G. Fox, 'XYY Chromosomes and Crime', *Aust. N. Z. Journal of Criminology*, 1969, 2/1 (5-9).

[49] D. W. Swanson and A. H. Stipes, 'Psychiatric Aspects of Klinefelter's Syndrome', *Amer. J. of Psychiatry*, 1969, 126/6 (814-22).

[50] C. Weinschenk and I. Sambach, 'Die Häufigkeit der Erblichen Lese-Rechtschreibeschwäche bei weiblichen Strafgefangenen', *Mschr. Kriminal Strafrechtsreform*, 1970, 53/1-2 (13-20).

[51] J. S. Price, 'Genetics of the Affective Illnesses', *Hosp. Med.*, 1968, 2/10 (1172-9)

[52] Rosanoff *et al. Journal of Criminal Law and Criminology*, 24, 1934; Lange Johannes, *Verbrechen als stricksal: Studien an Kriminellen Zwillingen*, Leipsig: Georg Thieme, 1929.

[53] W. H. Sheldon with E. M. Hartl and E. McDermott, *Varieties of Delinquent Youth*, New York: Harpers, 1949.

[54] Sutherland and Cressey, op. cit., p. 105.

[55] L. F. Freed, *Crime in South Africa*, Cape Town: Juta and Co., 1963, pp. 170-71.

[56] M. G. Schlapp and E. H. Smith, *The New Criminology*, New York: Boni, 1928.

[57] L. Berman, *The Glands Regulating Personality*, New York: Macmillan, 1931.

[58] I. G. Cobb, *The Glands of Destiny*, London: Heinemann, 1927.

[59] R. G. Hoskins, *Endocrinology*, New York: Norton, 1941.

[60] Studies of African physical constitutions are being made for other purposes, cf. studies of the apparent heart disease immunity of the Maasai.

[61] C. Goring, *The English Convict*, London: HMSO, 1913, p. 201.

[62] Sutherland and Cressey, op. cit., p. 108.

[63] V. Fox in *Journal of Criminal Law and Criminology*, 37, 1946, quoted by Howard and Jones, *Crime and the Penal System*, London: University Tutorial Press, 1956, p. 109.

[64] W. Clifford, *Crime in Northern Rhodesia*, Lusaka Rhodes/Livingstone Communication no. 18, 1960, p. 64. This he confirmed in a later study for the United Nations, *Juvenile Delinquency in Zambia*, op. cit.

[65] R. Clark, 'A Direct Study of the Child's Sentiment of Honour', *International Journal of Ethics*, **42**, pp. 454-61, July 1932—quoted by Sutherland and Cressey, op. cit.

[66] Max Grünhut, *Penal Reform*, Oxford University Press, 1948, pp. 411-2.

[67] E. Hacker, *Kriminal statistische und kriminalaetiologische Berichte*, Miskolc, Ludwig, 1941.

[68] e.g. S. Schafer, 'On the Proportions of the Criminality of Women', *Journal of Criminal Law and Criminology*, **39**, 77-8, May/June 1948—quoted by Sutherland and Cressey, op. cit., p. 112.

[69] W. Clifford, 'Crime in Zambia', *New Society*, 13 August 1964; also *Crime in Northern Rhodesia*, op. cit. Clifford later substantiated this conclusion by examining 3,127 cases (i.e. the total crime reported in the City of Lusaka in the years 1958/9) and finding only 62 female cases. See *Female Crime in Lusaka*, paper presented to the First Central Africa Scientific and Medical Congress, Lusaka, 26-30 August 1963, London: Pergamon Press, 1964.

[70] D. Williams, 'Neural factors related to habitual aggression: considerations of differences between those habitual aggressives and others who have committed crimes of violence', *Brain*, 1969, 92/3 (503-20).

[71] W. A. Bonger, *Criminality and Economic Conditions*, thesis, (Amsterdam University), English translation, Boston, 1916.

[72] M. Lupke and D. Seidel, 'International Symposium on the Control of Juvenile Delinquency in Socialist Society', East Berlin, 24-27 September 1964, *Excerpta Criminologica*, vol. 5, no. 2, March-April 1965, pp. 125-34.

[73] S. Walczak, 'Planning Crime Prevention and Control in Poland', *International Review of Criminal Policy*, United Nations publication sales no. E.70.IV.1, no. 26, 1968, pp. 43-55.

[74] G. H. Boehringer; see fn. 130, below.

[75] See M. G. Caldwell, 'The Economic Status of Families of Delinquent Boys in Wisconsin', *American Journal of Sociology*, **37**, pp. 231-9, September 1931; higher proportion of unskilled workers among parents of delinquents than in employed population generally. Sheldon and Eleanor Glueck, *One Thousand Juvenile Delinquents*, Cambridge: Harvard University Press, 1934; economic status of parental families of delinquents over 70% below 'comfortable' level. W. F. Ogburn, 'Factors in the Variation of Crime Among Cities', *Journal of the American Statistical Association*, 30, pp. 12-34, March 1935; important correlation between poverty and crime in 62 cities.

[76] E. H. Sutherland, *White Collar Crime*, New York: Dryden, 1949.

[77] Quoted by Sutherland and Cressey, op. cit., pp. 194-5.

[78] H. D. Sheldon, 'Problems in the Statistical Study of Juvenile Delinquency', *Merton*, **12**, pp. 201-23, 1934.

[79] C. R. Shaw and H. D. McKay, *Juvenile Delinquency and Urban Areas* University of Chicago Press, 1942.

[80] Sutherland and Cressey, op. cit., p. 159.

[81] cf. P. Jephcott and H. P. Carter, *The Social Background of Delinquency*, University of Nottingham, 1954; J. B. Mary, *Growing Up in a City*, University of Liverpool, 1955; T. P. Morris, *The Criminal Area*, London: Routledge and Kegan Paul, 1958.

[82] T. Sellin, *Culture Conflict and Crime*, New York: Social Science Research Bulletin, No. 41.

[83] W. B. Miller, 'Lower Class Culture as a Generating Milieu of Gang Delinquency', *J. of Social Issues*, **14**, no. 3, pp. 15-19.

[84] S. Shoham, *Crime and Social Deviation*, Chicago: Henry Regnery Company, 1966, p. 73.

[85] ibid., p. 82.

[86] G. Kaiser, 'Die Kriminalität der Gastarbeiter und ihre Erklärung als Kulturkonflikt, III', Uberprüfung de Hypothese des Kulturkonflikt, Tübingen: *Kriminalistik*', 1969, 23/7 (363-9).

[87] W. B. Miller, op. cit., pp. 15-19.

[88] A. K. Cohen, *Delinquent Boys*, Glencoe, Illinois: The Free Press, 1955.

[89] R. A. Cloward and L. E. Ohlin, *Delinquency and Opportunity*, London: Routledge and Kegan Paul, 1961.

[90] G. B. Vold, 'Social-Cultural Conflict and Criminality' in M. E. Wolfgang (ed.), *Crime and Culture*, New York, John Wiley and Sons Inc., 1968, pp. 33-41, suggests that since customary behaviour within a minority culture group may be regarded as illegal and criminal by the dominant majority in control of the state the problem is no longer a behavioural one but of political organization. He proposes a shift of emphasis in criminology from individual human behaviour to the scientific study of political organization and the control of power in the state.

[91] F. Redl and D. Wineman, *Children Who Hate*, Glencoe, Illinois: The Free Press, 1951.

[92] G. M. Sykes and D. Matza, *American Social Review*, vol. 22, December 1957.

[93] R. K. Merton and A. S. Kitt, *The American Soldier*, in R. K. Merton and P. F. Lazarfeld (eds.), Glencoe, Illinois: The Free Press, 1950.

[94] These days it is more likely to be the elderly professor growing a beard or wearing his hair long to show that he identifies with his students.

[95] B. Bettelheim, 'Individual and Mass Behaviour in Extreme Situations' in T. M. Newcomb and E. L. Hartley (eds.), *Readings in Social Psychology*, New York: Henry Holt, 1947.

[96] R. R. Sarbin, 'Role Theory' in Gardner and Lindzey (eds.), *Handbook of Social Psychology*, Cambridge, Mass.: Addison-Wesley, 1954, vol. 1, pp. 223-58.

[97] cf. E. H. Lemert, *Social Pathology*, New York: McGraw Hill Book Co., 1951; M. B. Clinard, 'The Sociology of Delinquency and Crime' in J. B. Gittler (ed.), *Review of Sociology*, New York: John Wiley and Sons Inc.; J. Bernard, *Social Problems at Mid-Century*, New York: Dryden Press, 1957.

[98] R. K. Merton, *Social Theory and Social Structure*, Glencoe, Illinois: The Free Press, revised edition, 1957.

[99] This statement needs some modification for the conditions of today. Now the notoriety can itself be a means of enrichment. Popular public figures seem to be able to commit certain offences without losing too much prestige, sometimes their earnings improve and relatively unknown offenders have turned to publicity as a means of obtaining more favourable treatment.

[100] Sir Cyril Burt, *The Young Delinquent*, London: University of London Press, 5th edition, reprinted 1957.

[101] S. P. Breckinridge and E. Abbot, *The Delinquent Child and the Home*, New York: Russell Sage Foundation, 1912.

[102] J. H. Bagot, *Juvenile Delinquency*, London: Cape, 1941.

[103] T. P. Morris, *The Criminal Area*, London: Routledge and Kegan Paul, 1950.

[104] R. A. Cloward and L. E. Ohlin, *Delinquency and Opportunity*, London: Routledge and Kegan Paul, 1961.

[105] A. K. Cohen, *Delinquent Boys*, Glencoe, Illinois: The Free Press, 1955.

[106] W. B. Miller, op. cit., pp. 15-19.

[107] Sir Cyril Burt, op. cit.

[108] H. Blumer and P. M. Hauser, 'Movies, Delinquency and Crime', quoted by Howard Jones in *Crime and the Penal System*, London: University Tutorial Press, 1956.

[109] T. M. Newcomb, *Social Psychology*, New York: Dryden, 1950, pp. 90-6.

[110] E. Shanas and C. E. Dunning, *Recreation and Delinquency*, Chicago: Recreation Commission, 1942.

[111] The inconclusiveness of studies on the criminogenic effects of mass media has again been shown by the evidence presented to and the conclusions drawn by the US Government Commission on Crime and Violence, e.g. US Congress/ Senate, Judiciary Committee, 88th Congress, 2nd Session Hearings pursuant to S. Res. 274: Washington D.C. On the other hand, the *Final Report of the National Commission on the Causes and Prevention of Violence* published in 1969 definitely stigmatized violence on television as a 'contributing factor' (Chap. 199) to violence in the country.

[112] Perhaps it should go on to include the world and principles of the criminologist himself since it has been insufficiently appreciated that these affect the position he takes on crime and its treatment.

[113] See, for example, *Seven Tribes of Central Africa*, Elizabeth Colson and M. Gluckman (eds.), London: Oxford University Press, 1951, esp. the articles of Colson on the 'Plateau Tonga' and by Barnes on the 'Fort Jameson Ngoni'.

[114] The literature on this is both copious and varied, but there is a common theme, cf. Simon and Phoebe Ottenberg in the 'Introduction' to their *Cultures and Societies of Africa*, New York: Random House, 1960, esp. pp. 61-3.

[115] cf. W. H. Sangree, *Age, Prayer and Politics in Tiriki, Kenya*, London: Oxford University Press, 1966, especially pp. 235-6 showing the respect for and the power of elders.

[116] cf. Audrey I. Richards, 'The Bemba of N.E. Rhodesia' in *Seven Tribes of Central Africa*, op. cit.; May M. Edel, *The Chiga of W. Uganda*, New York: Oxford University Press, 1957.

[117] See Colson, op. cit., on the effects of a resettlement of the Gwembe Tonga and the fear of the reaction of the 'shades'. It should be noted, however, that this functional explanation of social solidarity in terms of human needs does rather less than justice to a complex phenomenon. There is no intention here of denying the existence of social facts apparently unrelated to basic human needs.

[118] cf. W. Goldschmidt, *Sebei Law*, Berkeley: University of California Press, 1967, pp. 243-4; M. Fortes, *The Dynamics of Clanship Among the Tallensi*, London: Oxford University Press, 1945, p. 157; V. W. Turner, *Schism and Continuity in an African Society*, Manchester: Manchester University Press, 1957, esp. pp. 169-77, where he shows how the Ndembu use of genealogical generation as a principle of local organization allows mobility whilst keeping cohesion. Gluckman in his *Custom and Conflict in Africa*, Oxford: Blackwell, 1966, shows how conflict and division can be used and balanced to 'contribute to the peace of the whole', p. 24.

[119] Gunter Wagner, 'The Abaluyia of Kavirondo (Kenya)' in Forde (ed.), *African Worlds*, London: Oxford University Press, 1963. However the concept of change is relative and in a lesser than modern sense there were both internal and external changes in tribal life which the oral historians are now uncovering.

[120] Meyer Fortes, *Oedipus and Job*, Cambridge University Press, 1959, pp. 52-4.

[121] Van Warmelo, *Venda Law*, Pretoria, 1948.

[122] J. Beattie, *Bunyoro: An African Kingdom*, New York: Holt, Rinehart and Winston, 1960.

[123] Max Gluckman, *The Judicial Process Among the Barotse of Northern Rhodesia*, Manchester University Press, 1955.

[124] C. K. Meek, *Law and Authority in a Nigerian Tribe*, Oxford University Press, 1937.

[125] Gluckman, op. cit., suggests that it is the existence of rivalries, conflicting interests and divisions which contribute to the continuation and peace of a society. A full study of the process and a consideration of Gluckman's views is not possible here.

[126] The Azande say 'Jealousy comes first and witchcraft after'. Also Gluckman says 'Witchcraft beliefs are the source of many disharmonies and quarrels . . . but witchcraft also sometimes solves quarrels which arise between men from the conflict between allegiances to different and contradictory social principles', *Custom and Conflict in Africa*, op. cit.

[127] W. H. Sangree, op. cit., p. 13. There is, of course, the 'alliance theory' of incest which maintains that incest actually supports exogamy—perhaps much as prostitution was, once at least, supposed to protect 'decent' women. In any interpretation of incest both the 'descent' theory and the 'alliance theory' have to be balanced.

[128] E. Sidney Hartland, *Primitive Law*, Methuen, 1924,p. 48. However, there appears to be a difference as the political power of a state and economic free enterprise develop. For example, it is said that in Ghana, although in the traditional system the accent was on the group as the basic unit in political organization, in marriage, succession and ownership, criminal responsibility was basically individual.

See S. K. B. Asante, 'Law and Society in Ghana' in T. W. Hutchinson, *et al.* (eds.), *Africa and Law*, Madison, Wisconsin: University of Wisconsin Press, 1968, pp. 131-2. This does not affect the basic theme here, for Asante argues that legal individualism fails to arrest the full implications of a persistent philosophical collectivism.

[129] It has been observed that the Maasai of East Africa have a cholesterol-forming diet but hardly any evidence of thrombosis or heart disease. In the absence of physiological explanation this has been attributed to their emotional tranquillity.

[130] G. H. Boehringer, in a mimeographed paper presented at the University of East Africa Social Sciences Council Conference held at Kampala, Uganda, 30 December 1968 to 3 January 1969, quotes *The Standard*, 10 June 1968, and the *Sunday News*, 3 November 1968, for the fact that a government decision was taken to resettle 2,000 families of the Wamangati tribe in ujamaa villages in order to break up the traditional pattern of Wamangati raids. He also refers to *The Standard* of 22 March 1967 quoting the responsible minister for a statement that 4,200 people had been rounded up and that the cattle thieves amongst them could be deported from their home areas and presumably settled elsewhere. (Both newspapers quoted are Dar es Salaam publications.)

[131] T. O. Beidelman, 'Kaguru Justice and the Concept of Legal Fiction', *Journal of African Law* (London), vol. 5, no. 1, pp. 5-20; also Asante, op. cit., for the view that 'This persistence of philosophical collectivism in the face of individualistic pressures in the economic and legal spheres is one of the most fascinating social developments in present-day Ghana.

[132] W. Clifford, *Juvenile Delinquency in Zambia*, op. cit., but see section on Juvenile Delinquency, below, for a fuller discussion.

[133] M. E. le Brun, *Délinquance Africaine en Milieu Urbaine*, CEPSI: No. 58, September 1962.

[134] P. Raymaekers, *L'Organisation des Zones de Squatting*, Publications de l'Université Lovanium, 1963.

[135] W. Clifford, *Juvenile Delinquency in Zambia*, op. cit.

[136] The world's urban population (i.e. in towns of 20,000 or more) is said to have increased threefold between 1920 and 1960. But whilst European towns grew by only 18% between 1950 and 1960, African towns grew by 70% (*Urbanization*, United Nations publication ST/SAO/ Ser. X/1., 1968, p. 5).

[137] *Report of Committee Appointed by the Minister of Justice and Native Affairs to Investigate the Position of Crime on the Witwatersrand and in Pretoria*, Government Printer, Pretoria, 1942. Old fashioned though they are to modern research workers, the appositeness of these remarks to the conditions in a number of the modern towns of America and Europe where cohabitation is widespread (and accepted) should not be disregarded. Here too crime rates are often high and a superficial link between the two could be made.

[138] L. J. Lebret in the foreword to *L'Organisation des Zones de Squatting*, op. cit.

[139] M. Richelle, *Aspects Psychologiques de l'Acculturation*', CEPSI, Elisabethville, 1960.

[140] *Reaching the Young Child*, UNICEF/Misc. 109, 12 January 1966, p. 138.

[141] J. Clyde Mitchell, 'The Growth of Towns' (Northern Rhodesia) in Prudence Smith (ed.), *Africa in Transition*, London: Max Reinhardt, 1958, p. 52.

[142] M. McCullock, *A Social Survey of the African Population of Livingstone*, Lusaka: Rhodes/Livingstone, Paper No. 26, Manchester University Press, 1959.

[143] A. W. Southall (ed.), *Social Change in Modern Africa*, London: Oxford University Press, 1961. See also Leslie and Swantz on Dar es Salaam.

[144] Laura Longmore, 'African Poverty and Social Unrest', *Journal of African Affairs*, 1958, 51: 291.

[145] In Zambia during the years 1958 to 1962 millions of pounds were poured into an integrated scheme for intensive rural development in the Fort Rosebury area to provide work opportunities, housing, schooling, and better local transport facilities for the people in the hope of slowing the drift of people to the Copperbelt. Its effects were not noticeable. This example may be duplicated by experience in other countries during colonial times.

[146] These psychological terms of classification (schizophrenic, paranoic, etc.) are used here in their popular connotations. It is appreciated that each one is an umbrella term for a series or range of conditions and that they could be held to be too general for practical use.

[147] It will be recalled that low intelligence was, in the earlier studies, associated with the supernumerary Y chromosome and the Klinefelter Syndrome (XXY) (see above, p. 37).

[148] C. Goring, *The English Convict*, HMSO, 1913—as quoted by E. D. Driver in his essay on Goring in *Pioneers in Criminology*, London: Stevens, 1960.

[149] H. H. Goddard, *Feeblemindedness: its Causes and Consequences*, New York: Macmillan, 1914.

[150] H. H. Goddard, *Human Efficiency and Levels of Intelligence*, Princeton, N. J.: Princeton University Press, 1922.

[151] H. H. Goddard, 'Who Is a Moron', *Scientific Monthly*, 24 pp. 41-6, 1927.

[152] But compare note 147 above.

[153] D. H. Stott, *Delinquency and Human Nature*, Carnegie United Kingdom Trust, Dumfermline, Fife, 1950, pp. 367-8.

[154] Karl M. Bowman, 'Psychiatric Aspects of the Problem', Symposium: Challenge of Sex Offenders, *Ment. Hyg.*, vol. 22, January 1938.

[155] J. Frosch and W. Brombey, 'The Sex Offender', *Amer. Journal of Orthopsychiat.*, vol. 9, 1939, pp. 761-76.

[156] E. H. Sutherland, 'Mental Deficiency and Crime', in Kimball Young (ed.), *Social Attitudes*, New York: Holt, Rinehart and Winston, 1931, ch. ix.

[157] J. Gittins, 'Approved School Boys', quoted in Howard Jones, *Crime and the Penal System*, London: University Tutorial Press, 1956.
[158] Mary Woodward, *Low Intelligence and Crime*, London Institute for the Study and Treatment of Delinquency, 1955.
[159] For a fuller discussion of the role of intelligence in crime—including a quotation from Weber to the effect that when all the handicaps are considered it is quite remarkable that the association of crime and mental backwardness is not more pronounced; see H. Mannheim, *Comparative Criminology*, London: Routledge and Kegan Paul, 1965, vol. 1, pp. 273-81.
[160] K. F. Schuessler and D. R. Cressey, 'Personality Characteristics of Criminals', *Amer. Journal of Sociology*, 55, March 1950, pp. 476-84.
[161] S. Glueck and E. Glueck, *Unravelling Juvenile Delinquency*, Commonwealth Fund, New York, 1950.
[162] E. D. Monachesi, 'Some Personality Characteristics of Delinquents and Non-Delinquents', *Journal of Criminal Law and Criminology*, 38, January-February 1948, pp. 487-500.
[163] Sir Cyril Burt, op. cit.
[164] S. Glueck and E. Glueck, op. cit.
[165] J. Bowlby, *Forty-four Juvenile Thieves: Their Characters and Home Life*. London: Ballière, Tindall and Cox, 1946.
[166] J. Bowlby, *Maternal Care and Mental Health*, WHO, Geneva, 1951.
[167] D. Burlingham and A. Freud, *Infants Without Families*, London: Allen and Unwin, 1943.
[168] R. G. Andry, *Delinquency and Parental Pathology*, London: Methuen and Co., 1960.
[169] H. J. Eysenck, *Crime and Personality*, Boston: Houghton Mifflin Co., 1964. Prof. Eysenck suggests that conscience is mainly instrumental in socialization; that conscience is the culmination of a long process of conditioning. He supports his thesis with evidence that offenders are more difficult to condition being frequently extroverted and emotionally disturbed.
[170] The term 'sociopath' is often used interchangeably with 'psychopath'. The word 'sociopath' was coined by G. E. Partridge in 1929 and the American Psychiatric Association decided in 1952 to replace 'psychopath' with 'sociopath'.
[171] R. D. Henderson, *Psychopathic States*, New York: W. W. Norton and Co., 1939. But there is a vast literature: see for example, W. McCord and J. McCord, *Psychopathy and Delinquency*, New York: Grune and Straton, 1956, and *The Psychopath: An Essay on the Criminal Mind*, New York: Van Nostrand, 1964; S. B. Maughs, *Psychopathic Personality: Review of the Literature 1947-54*, Archives of Criminal Psychodynamics, Winter 1955, pp. 291-325.
[172] Sir Norwood East, *Society and the Criminal*, London, HMSO, 1949.
[173] S. P. Butzer Spitzer and J. D. Spevacek, 'Cognitive Organizations of Sociopaths' and 'Normal Criminal Offenders', *Journal of Research in Crime and Delinquency*, vol. 3, no. 1, January 1966, pp. 57-62. For the view that sociopaths do not use their intelligence as well as others and are not as adaptable cf. M. Gurvitz, 'Intelligence Factor in Psychopathic Personality, *Journal of Clinical Psychology*, April 1947, pp. 194-6; L. J. Sherman, 'Retention in Psychopathic, Neurotic and Normal Subject', *Journal of Personality*, December 1957, pp. 721-9, who found psychopaths to have better memories than the others.
[174] op. cit., fn. 172.
[175] *Royal Commission on Mental Illness and Mental Deficiency*, London: HMSO, Cmd., 169, 1957.
[176] D. K. Henderson, 'The Psychopathic Personality', chapter in the *British Encyclopedia of Medical Practice*, 2nd edition, vol. X, London: Butterworth and Co., 1952, pp. 332-6.

[177] J. R. Cavanaugh and J. B. McGoldrick S. J., *Fundamental Psychiatry*, revised edition, Cork, Ireland: The Mercier Press, 1963, p. 497.

[178] A. M. Carr-Saunders, H. Mannheim and E. C. Rhodes, *Young Offenders*, London: Cambridge University Press, 1942.

[179] Sir Cyril Burt, *The Young Delinquent*, op. cit.

[180] M. A. Stott, *Delinquency and Human Nature*, op. cit.

[181] C. A. Bonner, 'Who and What are Sexual Psychopaths', *Focus*, July 1948, vol. 27, no. 2, pp. 103-5.

[182] W. W. J. Keiser, 'Native Juvenile Delinquency', M. Ed. thesis, op. cit.

[183] Howard Jones, *Crime and the Penal System*, London University Tutorial Press, 1956, p. 85—quoting T. Ferguson, *The Young Delinquent in his Social Setting*, 1952; Shaw and McKay, *Report on Social Factors in Juvenile Delinquency*, Nat. Commission on Law Observance and Enforcement, Report No. 13, 1932; and E. W. Hughes, *Brit. J. of Ed. Psych*, 13, 3, 1943.

[184] S. Glueck and E. Glueck, *Unravelling Juvenile Delinquency*, op. cit.

[185] For a more precise and complete record, see Kate Friedlander, *The Psycho-Analytical Approach to Juvenile Delinquency*, London: Routledge and Kegan Paul, 1947, and M. Birnbach, *Neo-Freudian Social Philosophy*, Stanford, California: 1961 (i.e. for the development of Freudian theory).

[186] Freud had monistic sexual views and conceived of woman as a defective man. See Janine Chasseguet-Smirgel, *Female Sexuality*, Ann Arbor, Michigan: University of Michigan Press, 1970, in which the image of woman born castrated, innately envious of the penis and having oedipal stage difficulties because of this, is fully discussed.

[187] A. Aichhorn, *Wayward Youth*, London: Putnam, 1936: cf. note 169 above.

[188] cf. Kate Friedlander, *The Psycho-Analytical Approach to Juvenile Delinquency*, op. cit.

[189] F. Alexander and W. Healy, *Roots of Crime*, New York: Knopf, 1935, p. 67.

[190] See the article on Dr. Thomas Szasz, 'Dr Thomas Szasz: Normality Is a Square Circle or a Four Sided Triangle', by Maggie Scarf in the *New York Times Magazine*, 3 October 1971.

[191] J. F. Ritchie, *The African as Suckling and Adult*, Rhodes/Livingstone Paper No. 9, 1943.

[192] J. C. Carothers, *The African Mind in Health and Disease*, Geneva, WHO Monograph No. 17, 1958.

[193] A. Milner and T. Asuni, 'Psychiatry and the Criminal Offender in Africa' in *African Penal Systems*, op. cit., p. 320, mention a recent survey of psychiatric facilities in Africa south of the Sahara showing only twenty-six psychiatrists, only about ten of whom were indigenous and ten of the total of twenty-six were in Nigeria. Countries like Gambia, Swaziland and Lesotho were without psychiatrists whilst Cameroun, Gabon and Congo (Brazzaville) had only one each—not indigenous. This excluded South Africa.

[194] For the cautious view that the patterns of psychiatric disorder among Africans 'are closely akin to the known patterns already familiar in the Euro-American cultures' see Milner and Asuni, op. cit. They say this despite doubts expressed by Tooth in *Studies in Mental Illness in the Gold Coast*, 41 (1950). They quote *inter alia* T. Lambo, 'Further Neuropsychiatric Observations in Nigeria', 1960 (ii) *British Medical Journal* 1966/7, for the commonness of schizophrenia and noting no predominance of any sub-variety.

[195] T. Lambo, 'Malignant Anxiety: a Syndrome Associated with Criminal Conduct in Africans', **108**, *Journal of Mental Science*, 256 (1962). Milner and Asuni suggest that it is probably only of pathoplastic significance in schizophrenia and not a disease *sui generis*.

[196] Milner and Asuni, op. cit., p. 320.

[197] cf. L. Leighton, T. Lambo, *et al.*, *Psychiatric Disorder Amongst the Yoruba*, 1963, where information regarding certain types of sociopathic behaviour was not elicited by general questioning. The norms of those formulating the questions did not correspond with the norms of those expected to answer.

[198] W. Clifford, *The Psychological Approach to Crime in Lusaka*, op. cit.

[199] See Carothers, op. cit., for the view that neurotic conditions in Africa are more likely to take culturally tolerable forms than to find their way to hospitals.

[200] Reports in the *New York Times* (Sunday), 26 December 1970, indicate great clinical interest in the possibility of brain damage being a source of aggression: but it is acknowledged that families in poor or neglected environments were more likely to be exposed to the risk of brain injury—and again the distribution of non-aggressive cases of brain damage was not sufficiently known for the necessary conclusion to be drawn.

[201] Sir Cyril Burt, *The Young Delinquent*, op. cit

[202] S. Glueck and E. Glueck, *Unravelling Juvenile Delinquency*, op. cit.

[203] G. B. Vold, *Theoretical Criminology*, New York: Oxford University Press, 1958, p. 310.

[204] E. H. Sutherland, *Principles of Criminology*, 5th edition, revised and edited by D. R. Cressey, Philadelphia: J. B. Lippincott Co., 1955.

[205] Sheldon Glueck, *British Journal of Delinquency*, VII, 2 October 1956.

[206] J. R. Cavanaugh, and J. B. McGoldrick S. J., *Fundamental Psychiatry*, op. cit.

[207] W. C. Reckless, *Criminal Behaviour*, New York: McGraw Hill Book Co., Inc., 1940, p. 2. He refers to Tadeusz E. Kuezma who in a work then recently published, *The Genetic Approach to Crime*, Poznan, 1939, discarded the use of causal relationships of factors in favour of the 'multifarious correlationships of various components'.

PART TWO

4
PREDICTION

Prediction studies merit special consideration because they have been largely instrumental in turning the attention of research workers from delinquency causation to the possibilities of delinquency control. Whilst they have yet to be developed and expertly applied in African conditions, a good deal of groundwork has been done from which basic data could be gathered for the formulation of some rudimentary tables. Meanwhile, the prediction formulae developed elsewhere remain to be tested in Africa for their application to different cultures.

The best account of the history of prediction studies is probably to be found in the first chapter of the well known work by Mannheim and Wilkins on prediction and Borstal training.[1] What follows here is merely a brief summary. Marc Ancel has suggested that Bonneville de Marsangy, who invented the criminal record (*casier judiciaire*) in the nineteenth century and who sought to systematize the records of previous convictions, was the first to show clearly that past and present conduct were indices of future conduct if properly interpreted. He believes that de Marsangy might well be regarded as the herald of the preventive treatment of crime—probably the inspirer of studies leading to prediction tables.[2]

No doubt prediction has even more venerable roots in the thinking on human behaviour and in the efforts which have been made to rationalize and improve legal administration. In its modern form, however, it aroused interest between the two world wars as a technique for deciding which offenders should be released on parole, and it burgeoned forth after the Second World War into the more ambitious sphere of forecasting the children most likely to become delinquent or determining the risk of an offender repeating his offence. In both phases pioneering work was done by Sheldon and Eleanor Glueck so that Mannheim and Wilkins divide their history into the pre-Glueck, post-Glueck and Glueck periods.

The earliest approach was probably Warner's publication in 1923 of his critique of the Board of Parole based on a sample of 680 prisoners of the Massachusetts State Reformatory of which 300 were regarded as successfully paroled, 360 as unsuccessful and the remaining eighty had not been awarded parole. He was able to demonstrate that the criteria being used by the Board (i.e. seriousness of the offence, previous record and previous record on parole (if any), conduct within the institution and whether the person to be paroled appeared to have profited, prospects of a home and work on his release, his demeanour and truthfulness before the Board) did not really indicate whether the person to be paroled would be a good risk.[3]

There was lively discussion of this study which led to considerable interest being shown in the possibility of forecasting recidivism—especially as effectiveness in this was held to be the best indicator of the value of the treatment. Warner was criticized especially for his failure to use statistics accurately.[4]

The next major contribution appears to have come from Bruce, Burgess and Harno in 1928. They extracted twenty-one factors associated with parole success or failure in 3,000 cases which they examined as part of a study they were making of the functioning of the indeterminate sentence and the Illinois parole system. They compiled a table of 'Expectancy Rates of Parole Violation and Non-Violation' weighting the significant factors equally.[5]

The Gluecks entered the field with two major series of follow-up studies. In 1930 they published their study of all the prisoners (i.e. 510) released from the Massachusetts Reformatory whose sentences expired in 1921 and 1922. Here they probed beyond the data in the usual official files, checking identities by fingerprints when necessary and interviewing a near relation in the families of about 73 per cent of their sample of persons released to ascertain precisely what kind of adjustment to society they had made. From this they selected fifty factors which seemed significant to success or failure on parole and weighted them in order of importance (using a statistical technique known as the 'mean square contingency coefficient'). From the total, six major factors were selected and developed into a prognostic table which judges might use: these were (1) seriousness of the offence, (2) arrest record for previous offences, (3) previous penal experiences, (4) work habits, (5) economic responsibility and (6) mental abnormality. For those judges faced with recidivists who had already passed through the reformatory and parole machinery, five additional parole factors were added; and the table intended for the use of parole boards had to include two additional factors covering the person's conduct during reformatory training or earlier parole.[6]

The Gluecks had the merit of keeping their interest in their samples. In *Later Criminal Careers* published in 1937 and in *Criminal Careers in Retrospect* which appeared in 1943, the Gluecks followed up their earlier groups for a total period of fifteen years following release. Despite the extension of the years and the death of some of those being monitored there seemed to be no reason to alter drastically the prime factors previously specified. However, the lapse of time emphasized some of these factors and greatly reduced the influence of others.[7]

In the areas of juvenile delinquency the Gluecks launched another predictive series. They first checked on 1,000 juvenile delinquents who had been referred to the Child Guidance Clinic of the Judge Baker Foundation in Boston extracting six factors likely to be most associated with success or failure. These were (1) the paternal discipline of the child, (2) the maternal discipline, (3) school retardation, (4) school misconduct, (5) age of the first behavioural disorder and (6) the time elapsing between delinquency and examination of the child by the clinic. The same sample of delinquents was followed in 1940 for a further ten years and this showed conduct improving by age or maturation.[8] It also disclosed five factors mainly correlated with success or failure. These were: birthplace of father, discipline by father, discipline by mother, school retardation and school misconduct. Once again prediction tables were compiled from these. To illustrate: the proportion of failures on probation in the case of boys whose paternal discipline had been good (fair, firm not lax or erratic and not over strict) was only 16.7 per cent, but boys whose fathers were extremely lax or extremely rigid or erratic had a failure rate of 62.9 per cent. It will be observed, of course, that certain factors such as parental birthplaces are mainly relevant to countries with immigrant populations. Nevertheless, it should be remembered that even within countries, migration to urban areas can create situations or problems of a similar nature.

Rounding off the juvenile delinquency series, but standing apart from it in many respects, was the Gluecks' study published in 1950 entitled *Unravelling Juvenile Delinquency*. This was a wide-ranging team study comparing a sample of 500 persistent delinquents with 500 non-delinquents, in respect of some 400 traits and factors involving body structure, health, status, neurologic and psychiatric tests, the Rorschach test, the Wechster-Bellevue intelligence test and intensive investigations of home, school and neighbourhood conditions. It was found that almost nine-tenths of the delinquents had already persistently misbehaved before their eleventh year.[9]

On the basis of the evidence collected here, the Gluecks went far beyond any previous work on forecasting the success or failure rates of treatments or predicting the results of release on parole or probation. They suggested that it would be actually feasible, by the use of their prediction devices, to discover potential delinquency in young children. They suggested three possible tables. One was based upon the five *psychiatric* traits which had been found to distinguish delinquents and non-delinquents most effectively. Delinquents were more adventurous, extroverted, suggestible, stubborn and emotionally unstable. The second table was based on the five traits of *character* structure which had been derived from the Rorschach tests: delinquents were more socially assertive, defiant, suspicious, destructive and emotionally labile. The third prediction table (known as the Social Prediction Table) was based on the five inter-personal *family* factors found to be of crucial importance in separating the delinquents from others; that is discipline of the boy by his father, supervision of the boy by his mother, affection of the father for the boy, affection of the mother, and lastly the degree of family cohesiveness. A high degree of inter-relationship between the three tables was established so that a boy shown as delinquent on one would be likely to show as delinquent on at least one of the others.

In all, the Gluecks have constructed some fifty-one tables in their forty years or so of research. Some of these deal with the prediction of juvenile and adult recidivism, male and female, some with the probable behaviour of offenders during different forms of treatment, some to identify the young offenders most likely to develop into persistent offenders, and lastly the most recent ones designed to discover delinquency-prone children before they have committed an offence.

There had been quite extensive validation of the social prediction table by 1962. In that year, Mrs Glueck referred to its application to over a thousand children in the United States and England and to 249 boys in Strasbourg, France. Retrospective applications of the table had also been made to more than 1,200 children in Japan. She said that about 90 per cent of all delinquents in these tests had been found to be characterized by the significant factors in the Social Prediction Table.[10] Significantly, a Czech team followed the Glueck scheme with studies of 500 delinquents and a control of 500 non-delinquents in 1966 and despite the differences in age groups, social formation, generational characteristics and methods of collecting data, the measure of conformity between the weighted traits in the Czech and Glueck studies was unexpectedly high.[11] Furthermore, a verification of the Gluecks' table by more sophisticated computer techniques has suggested that the predictive potential and the factors selected by the Gluecks are those arrived at by strict analytic multivariate techniques and represent findings which cannot be faulted by criticism of the Glueck methodology.[12]

Another well-known contributor to prediction studies has been Professor Vold. In 1931, he extracted forty-nine factors from the records of 542 men discharged from the Minnesota State Prison and 650 discharged from the Minnesota State Reformatory between 1922 and 1927. Again using the coefficient of mean square contingency he worked out the correlations for the combined groups. He found the highest correlation with success or failure was the earlier work record but concluded that whilst no single factor was outstanding there were few of his forty-nine factors without significance.[13] In 1936, Vold took a group of 282 Minnesota Prisoners and compared the predicted and actual outcome (correlation about 0.4) and the estimate of a parole officer and actual outcome (correlation about 0.3).[14]

Monachesi looked at prediction in relation to probation in his book of 1932.[15] Using the records of 1,515 cases of the years 1923–5 from the State Probation Office, he reduced these to fifty factors from the juvenile probationers and thirty-four factors for the adults which were related to success or failure. Like Vold, he compared the Burgess system of using all factors with the Gluecks' use of only the most significant factors and like Vold he confirmed that both gave similar results when tested against outcome. In 1945, Monachesi looked again at prediction as compared with actual results in the cases of 120 juveniles. He found fairly accurate prediction at the extremes—with the very high risk and very low risk groups—but the efficiency of the prediction device declined when used for the larger number of persons in the middle.

Still in 1931–2, there was a study of 3,000 youth parolees from the Illinois State Reformatory between 1921 and 1927. In this inquiry, Tibbitts sought to validate Burgess' technique and, with some variations, showed that it had considerable value.[16] Then in 1939, the United States Department of Justice issued what amounted to a vast validation study of the factors related to parole selection and its outcome in the cases of 100,000 offenders. This concluded that the use of prediction tables would not improve Federal parole practice.[17]

Lloyd Ohlin published in 1951 his valuable study of 1,000 cases of parolees who had completed parole, but the table he constructed from a selection of twelve of the twenty-seven factors he called an 'xperience table'. He, like Burgess, avoided weinting but used Glueck's approach of employing only highly predictive factors. He emphasized the need for field studies to supplement any classification and prediction reports and he called for regular modification of the experience table to keep it abreast of internal and external changes.[18]

There were other studies in America including Caldwell's follow-up of 1,862 probationers[19] and Reiss' attempt to predict recidivism in juvenile delinquents,[20] but the next event of major significance was the report in 1951 of the ambitious Cambridge-Somerville Youth Study which sought to compare the value of special social work services provided to 325 young people with the value of ordinary services for another 325 in a control group over a period of ten years beginning in 1935. Each boy had been given a calculated forecast of his future delinquency in 1937–8. This prognosis was based upon a careful study of the boy's physical and mental condition, school work, family and environmental situation. Prediction efficiency was judged in the cases of 100 boys of each group. The correlation between prediction and outcome was found to be 0.49 for both groups.[21]

Europe had its prediction research too, but it was largely inspired by the developments in America. Mannheim and Wilkins refer to the prediction table established by Robert Schiedt in Germany in 1935,[22] to the prognostic schedule of Erwin Frey in Switzerland (1951),[23] to the study of Erkki Saari in Finland[24] and to Mannheim's own venture into this field in his study of juvenile delinquency in Cambridge.[25] However, the most notable and technically impeccable study was that of Mannheim and Wilkins themselves—on the prediction of recidivism amongst Borstal boys. From experience based on the records of some 700 young men passing through Borstal classification centres, the authors selected ten factors for the prediction of recidivism among Borstal inmates, namely:

1. Total number of convictions,
2. Job changes during the period of licence,
3. Whether committed to approved school,
4. Longest period in any one job,
5. Average duration of jobs,
6. Number of misdemeanours in Borstal,
7. Number of convictions resulting in fines,

8. Evidence of drunkenness,
9. With whom he was living,
10. Age at first finding of guilt.

They stressed the importance of the first months after release as being crucial for success or failure. They asserted, like Ohlin, that their 'prediction tables' were systematic analyses of experience and found them valid by testing them on a complete intake of one classification centre in the last half of 1948 (that is one year later than the group from which the factors were compiled). This showed the prediction formula to be an accurate guide to future success or failure. [26] Cockett tested the Mannheim-Wilkins table on 770 discharges from Borstal in 1967 and concluded that, although less efficient in differentiating success and failure than before, it still had relevance to post-training experience.

In 1954, England studied 100 adult offenders whose probation had ended successfully between 1 January 1939 and 31 December 1944[27] in Pennsylvania, attempting to relate pre-sentence characteristics to success or failure on probation as determined by post-probation convictions. He discovered that only one-half of the failures could be predicted.[28]

This review of studies could well be extended. There has been the Glaser and Hangren investigation,[29] the United Kingdom Home Office Research Unit's ongoing programme of probation studies under Folkard,[30] Ostrihanska's prediction formula for juvenile recidivism in Poland which he found accurate on validation of 73 per cent of the cases[31] and Munkwitz's work in Western Germany.[32] Buikhuisen and Van Weringh used similar procedures on 2,166 persons convicted of drunken driving in the Netherlands in 1955 and 1956 to abstract the factors most significantly associated with recidivism in drunken driving—finding that age, need of a car for work, previous convictions for other offences like theft or violence, etc., are most crucial for prediction.[33] Prediction methods are being applied to parole and probation caseloads. For example, Nicholson reported in 1968 applying a modified Base Expectancy Scoring method to 111 male adult offenders, 71 on probation and 40 on parole. The study underlined the efficiency of the device and raised some interesting questions such as whether those who could readily be predicted as successes or failures needed supervision at all: the first group could probably get along without it and the failure group would be likely to be successful in spite of it. It seemed likely that supervision should be kept for those who score midway, that is showing that they could be either failures or successes.[34]

Finally, groups of boys have been asked to rate each other and factors have been identified which predict future indiscipline and withdrawal-assertive behaviour,[35] and decision theory and other models have been used to sophisticate this work to the prediction of behavioural intentions in choice situations.[36]

There can be no doubt, then, of the validity of prediction methods if they are carefully developed from experience of the past and present knowledge of the persons and if they take full account of the wider field-work required to fill gaps in the official files. That is to say, there can be no doubt of them doing what they are intended to do—and no more. They have a number of shortcomings, however.

It may be that the levels of accuracy now being claimed could have been claimed for far less sophisticated but so far untested methods of grading people. For example, there was an interesting analysis made in 1968 of the prognostic value of the low marks given by teachers in elementary and vocational schools in Finland which showed that 40 per cent of the group given low marks at school (for conduct and orderliness) had committed offences as against only 17 per cent of a control group.[37]

In the United Nations *International Review of Criminal Policy* in 1955,[38] the possibility of predicting juvenile delinquency was discussed. It pointed out that the fact that similar prediction tables had given similar results with different groups of juveniles living in different localities did not exclude the possibility that the results could be ascribable to factors not appearing in the table. Moreover, even if juveniles predictably became delinquent after x years, this does not validate the prediction tables. Factors other than those originally taken into account may have played a more decisive role.

More serious objection to the use of prediction tables has been taken because of their possible 'labelling' effect. Suppose a child is identified as 'delinquency prone' and treated as such—would not this classification and treatment tend to influence his development into a delinquent? This could affect the child himself if he knows he is being treated as a possible future offender; but it also affects the behaviour of those about him so that he may be subtly edged into a delinquent role. In 1970 an interesting experiment was carried out at McGill University in Canada on the difference between predicting the outcome of an event and postdicting the outcome. It was found that people predicted with more confidence of affecting the outcome if they knew the event was still to come. Being asked to say what had happened after it had happened they were much less sure.[39] This is an isolated study but it would appear to reinforce the view that labelling by prediction could greatly affect the expectations of those concerned—and these expectations if known or perceived could affect the results.

The danger of stigmatizing an individual by prediction can be better appreciated by the realization that even a single previous conviction has a very high predictive value.[40] One study of 3,500 offenders has shown that failure during a period of a suspended sentence was directly proportional to the number of previous convictions so that a valid prediction formula was constructed on the basis of this variable and the age of the offender.[41]

It should be noted, however, that whilst few advocates of prediction methods feel that the time has yet come to place tables in the hands of judges to be followed without adequate regard for the merits of the individual case or the special characteristics of the offender, they rightly defend their methods as useful on the macro-level, that is in showing what delinquency might be expected from a group. It may be that this broader level is the one at which the prediction techniques have most to offer to those concerned with crime prevention.

In Africa, it is obvious that much could be done to develop prediction tables on the material already available. If school marks for conduct have a predictive significance for delinquency this could be followed up at little cost. The files on offenders will easily provide material for a prediction device based on previous records and on age. The Glueck table could perhaps be validated or refuted for Africa with studies replicating the work already published by the Gluecks. Then, as criminology develops and local sophistication in research improves, it should be possible to study larger numbers of offenders, young and adult, in order to distill the factors most obviously associated with the success and failure of the various treatments. Whilst human nature is everywhere the same and since Africa appears to have concepts of law and delinquency (and probably psychiatric ailments) in common with so many other parts of the world (especially since the urban culture is overlaying traditional cultural differences), it is reasonably certain that prediction tables compiled elsewhere (like the Gluecks') will be validated in African countries. If this proves to be so, there should still be ample scope for more intensive work to be done to discover the factors peculiar to conditions in Africa which are also exerting recidivist pressure.

Also very important for Africa are the studies which have been made, in the Quetelet tradition, of the propensity to crime. The Council of Europe published studies on the forecasting of crime in 1969. By an agreement between the Scandinavian Research Council for Criminology and the Council of Europe a pilot study of the forecast of the volume and structure of future criminality was made. Traditional crime factors were chosen as possible predictions and population-related crime rates were used. Unfortunately, despite an approach to the problem via (1) regression analysis of population crime rates with time as an independent variable, (2) possible relationships between various crime variables and single social factors (other than population), and (3) relationships between crime variables and combined social factors, the attempt really failed to produce satisfactory prediction methods.[42] (There are other studies in this issue of the Council of Europe collected studies.) Henry suggests that such criminality varies with sex and age and as it is possible to calculate for each of these an *apparent* criminality (the proportion of men and women of each age known to have committed an offence) it ought to be possible to reach an *actual* criminality, that is equal to the proportion of men and woman who commit a crime or offence whether they are identified or not. After the ages and sexes of the future population have been predicted the trends of series of crime rates could be projected into the future.[43]

Of course, these studies ignore issues like 'dark crime' or questions of the appropriateness of the policy of law enforcement. Nevertheless, they seek to provide rough guides to future problems, and in Africa this type of macro-approach would be of especial value for planning. Most African countries are accustomed to five-year planning periods in the allocation of resources for economic and social growth. Forward estimates of the needs of the country for the prevention of crime and the treatment of offenders could be of inestimable value.

[1] H. Mannheim and L. T. Wilkins, *Prediction Methods in Relation to Borstal Training*, London, HMSO, 1955, chapter I.

[2] M. Ancel, *Social Defence*, London: Routledge and Kegan Paul, 1965, p. 39, referring to Bonneville de Marsangy's *De l'amélioration de la loi criminelle en vue d'une justice plus prompte plus efficace, plus génereuse et plus moralisante*, Part II, Paris, 1864.

[3] S. B. Warner, 'Factors determining parole from the Massachusetts Reformatory', *Journal of Criminal Law and Criminology*, **14**, 1923, pp. 172-207.

[4] H. Hart, 'Predicting Parole Success', *Journal of Criminal Law and Criminology*, **14**, 1923, pp. 405-13.

[5] A. A. Bruce, E. W. Burgess and A. J. Harno, 'The Working of the Indeterminate Sentence Law and the Parole System in Illinois', 1928, quoted in Mannheim and Wilkins, op. cit.

[6] Sheldon Glueck and Eleanor T. Glueck, *500 Criminal Careers*, New York: Alfred A. Khopf, 1930.

[7] Sheldon Glueck and Eleanor T. Glueck, *Later Criminal Careers*, New York: Commonwealth Fund, 1937; *Criminal Careers in Retrospect*, Yew York: Commonwealth Fund, 1943.

[8] Sheldon Glueck and Eleanor T. Glueck, *One Thousand Juvenile Delinquents*, Cambridge, Mass.: Harvard University Press, 1934; *Juvenile Delinquents Grown Up*, New York: The Commonwealth Fund, 1940.

[9] Sheldon Glueck and Eleanor T. Glueck, *Unravelling Juvenile Delinquency*, New York: the Commonwealth Fund, 1950. See also Eleanor Glueck, 'Predicting Juvenile Delinquency', *British Journal of Delinquency*, **2**, April 1952.

[10] See Eleanor T. Glueck, 'Workability of Predictive Techniques' in I. Drapkin (ed.), *Proceedings of 12th International Course in Criminology*, Hebrew University of Jerusalem, September 2-30, 1962.

[11] M. Veverka, 'S/a E. Glueckovych, V Nasem Kriminologiekein vyzkumu Na Brovém 1167 Praha', *Sociol Easopis*, 1969, 5/1, pp. 38-46.

[12] R. A. Labrie, 'Verification of the Glueck Prediction Table by Mathematical Statistics Following a Computerized Procedure of Discriminant Function Analysis', *Journal of Criminal Law, Criminology and Police Science*, 61/2, 1970, pp. 229-34.

[13] G. B. Vold, *Prediction Methods and Parole*, Hanover N. H., Minneapolis, Liverpool: The Sociological Press, 1931.

[14] G. B. Vold, 'Prediction Methods Applied to Problems of Classification within Institutions', *Journal of Criminal Law and Criminology*, **26**, July 1935, pp. 202-9.

[15] E. D. Monachesi, *Prediction Factors in Probation*, Hanover N. H., Minneapolis, Liverpool: The Sociological Press, 1932.

[16] C. Tibbitts, 'Success and Failure in Parole Can Be Predicted', *Journal of Criminal Law and Criminology*, **22**, May 1931.

[17] *Attorney-General's Survey of Release Procedures*, vol. IV, Parole Department of Justice, Washington, 1939.

[18] Lloyd W. Ohlin, *Selection for Parole: a Manual of Parole Prediction*, New York: Russell Sage Foundation, 1951.

[19] M. G. Caldwell, 'Preview of a New Type of Probation Study Made in Alabama', *Federal Probation*, **15**, June 1951.

[20] A. J. Reiss, 'The Accuracy, Efficiency and Validity of a Prediction Instrument', *American Journal of Sociology*, **61**, May 1951, pp. 552-61.

[21] E. Powers and Helen Witmer, *An Experiment in the Prevention of Delinquency*, New York: Colombia University Press, 1951.

[22] R. Schiedt, *Ein Beitrag zum Problem der Rückfallsprognose*, Munchen, 1936.

[23] E. Frey, 'Der Frünkriminelle Rückfallsverbrucher: Criminalité précoc et Recidivisme', *Schweizeische Criminalistische Studien*, vol. 4, Basel: Verlag für Recht und Gesellschaft, 1951.

[24] E. Saari 'Pahantapaisrus Yksilön Sopentumattomuuden Oireena, Jyväskyla' (1951).

[25] H. Mannheim, *Juvenile Delinquency in an English Middle Town*, London: Routledge and Kegan Paul, 1948.

[26] H. Mannheim and L. T. Wilkins, *Prediction Methods in Relation to Borstal Training*, op. cit.

[27] R. Cockett, 'Borstal Training: a Follow-Up Study', *British Journal of Criminology*, **7**: 2, 1970, pp. 180-83.

[28] R. W. England, Jr., 'A Study of Post-Probation Recidivism Among 500 Federal Offenders', *Federal Probation*, vol. 9, pp. 10-16 (1955).

[29] D. Glaser and R. F. Hangren, 'Predicting Adjustment of Federal Probationers', *N.P.P.A. Journal*, vol. 4, pp. 258-67 (1958).

[30] S. Folkard, K. Lyyn, M. M. Carver and E. O'Leary, *Probation Research: a Preliminary Report 1966*, HMSO, and other HMSO Reports in this series.

[31] Z. Ostrihanska, 'Prognoza recydywy u nieletrich przestepcow', *Archives of Criminology*, vol. 3, 1965.

[32] W. Munkwitz, 'Die Prognose der Frünkriminalität', *Ein Beitrag zur Ergänzung der Statistischen Prognose methoden*, 1967.

[33] W. Buikhuisen and J. Van Weringh, 'Voorspellen van recidivisme', *Ned. T. Criminal*, 1962, 10/5, pp. 223-40.

[34] R. C. Nicholson, 'Use of Prediction in Caseload Management', *Federal Probation*, 1968, 32/4, 54-8.

[35] H. B. Gibson and R. Hanson, 'Peer Ratings as Predictors of School Behaviour and Delinquency', *British Journal Soc. Clin. Psychology*, 1969, 8/4, 313-22.

[36] I. Ajzen and M. Fishbein, 'The Prediction of Behavioural Intentions in a Choice Situation', *Journal Exp. Psychology*, 1969, 5/4.

[37] I. Järvenpää, 'The Prognostic Value of Low Marks for Conduct and Orderliness in Elementary Schools and Vocational Schools', *Monthly Statistical Review*, Bureau of Statistics of the City of Helsinki, 1968, **19:** 12, pp. 491-526.

[38] No. 7/8, January-July 1955.

[39] M. Rothbart and M. Snyder, 'Confidence in the Prediction and Postdiction of an Uncertain Outcome', *Canadian Journal of Behavioural Science*, 2/1, 1970, pp. 38-43.

[40] S. Shoham, *Crime and Social Deviation*, Chicago, Henry Renery Co., 1966, p. 12.

[41] M. Sandberg and S. Shoham, 'Suspended Sentences of Imprisonment in Israel', report submitted to Israel Society of Criminology, January 1964: quoted by Shoham, op. cit.

[42] J. Jepson and L. Pak, 'Forecasting the Volume and Structure of Future Criminality', *Collected Studies in Criminological Research*, vol. IV, Strasbourg, Council of Europe, 1969, pp. 25-209.

[43] M. L. Henry, 'Forecasting Research in the Social Sciences with Special Reference to Demography', *Collected Studies in Criminological Research*, vol. IV, Strasbourg, Council of Europe, 1969, pp. 9-22.

5
SPECIAL PROBLEMS

The discussion of special problems which follows is included partly because these are issues of particular importance in Africa, partly because they are subjects on which a certain amount of data is available and partly because they illustrate some of the approaches which the criminologist needs to consider in his development of criminology in Africa.

HOMICIDE

The term homicide covers both intentional and unintentional killing, brutal murders, judicial executions, 'ritual' murders and death on the roads, political assassination and infanticide. Suicide is also a form of homicide although it is usually dealt with separately. Killing engenders the greatest insecurity in a society and stirs the deepest fears. The presence of cold calculation, brutality, wantonness or irrationality repels and horrifies; the drama and the mystery so frequently investing murder not only stirs the public imagination but gives continuing life to a whole industry of magazines, books, films and plays. There was more than a grain of truth in Juvenal's observation that 'even those who do not wish to kill anyone would like to be able to'.

Bohannan introduces his own and his contributors' essays on African homicide with the words: 'The main question is this: do Africans kill themselves and one another for the same reasons and in the same situations as Europeans and Americans?'[1] In trying to answer this he presents 755 cases of killing in seven different African tribes, yet he felt that he and his colleagues had 'barely scratched the surface'. The criminological significance of this work is primarily to be found in the structural analysis which Bohannan applies. Having reviewed the Western literature on homicide and suicide he uses Durkheim's classifications of suicide in terms of social solidarity, or its absence in all homicide, and finds that it throws light on data which he and his collaborators have collected. He concluded on the limited evidence before him that there was amongst the tribes little or no egoistic homicide (or suicide in Durkheim's terms) and only a moderate amount of anomie homicide and suicide. Moreover, the Western impact had been uneven in its local effect on homicide and suicide.[2] He did not deal with 'ritual' murder and could give little account in his kind of work of the urban situation.

In recent years in the West, criminologists have been looking beyond the offender and trying to study crime in situational terms. Because so many murders are committed within families, between friends or neighbours, a whole science of victimology has grown up, drawing attention to the way a murder may be provoked or induced by the victim himself or herself—or at least by the contribution which the victim makes to the production of the situation which leads to the murder.[3] The other fact that so many murderers are otherwise law abiding and frequently do not commit any other offence in their life span has also led to their becoming the subject of special investigation,[4] and indeed when the matter of criminology is broken down in this way into sociological situations rather than legal definitions, it is often true that the most serious or prevalent crimes have their own typologies.[5]

However, the most serious modern problem of homicide in the form of murder is that of the wild, sadistic, cruel murder sometimes of complete strangers—senseless killings like the sadistic slaying of a girl of ten and a boy of twelve in the 'Moors Murders' in England in 1966, or the murder of Sharon Tate and her entire house party in California in 1969. Observation of the offenders in cases like these casts doubts on Dostoevsky's contention that murderers ultimately repent.[6] One is reminded here of the explanation of an extra Y chromosome or the studies of psychopaths, but one is also faced with the issue of whether the kind of society which we have produces these types, or at any rate leaves them without the guidance and control necessary for adaptation.

In the context of such speculation, it is interesting to observe that neither in Bohannan's account, nor in the writer's experience is there much evidence of 'pathological' killers of this type in Africa—yet. Of course there are cruel murders and killings with great violence: there are 'senseless' killings too in the occasional case of someone 'running amok'—these happen in Europe and America, when (from mental illness or sheer pressure of the social situation) a person 'cracks'. But the 'affectionless', completely self-centred type of killing, regarded as pathological elsewhere, has little or no recorded history in Africa. It may be that the studies have been too few and too sketchy—this cannot be denied. But it should not be dismissed too readily that the structure of society, the kinds of social controls, the patterns of relationships, are really responsible for the absence of this type of killer. Either he has not developed at all—or he has no scope to act so anti-socially. It is probably not merely the scale or cohesion of society which is operative here. There may be more subtle factors at work and the West might profit from further studies of this situation.

In a book published in 1963, Wyden suggested that the hiring of persons to commit murders is a practice probably more widespread than generally thought, that it is reasonably easy to escape detection for this kind of offence and that we all have the 'make-up' of hired killers.[7] He pointed out that the hirer, the hired and their victim are rarely the only people who know about the murder: there are many who know what is being planned and who take no action to prevent it. Although Wyden was not conducting a scientific study he felt able from his examples to suggest that psychopaths appear most frequently in the psychiatric examinations of hired killers and that a hired killer does not like working alone—preferring the moral support of an assistant or an accomplice.

The hiring of a killer seems to be rare in Africa. It is not a factor in Bohannan's study and it hardly ever occurred in the writer's experience in Central, East and West Africa.[8] This is due, no doubt, to the smallness of the communities and to the difficulty of keeping such an arrangement secret. However, something like hired killing is present on a very wide scale, for in many parts of Africa aggrieved persons will frequently seek spells or potions from witch doctors, which might be intended to cause sickness or the death of another. When a death or a sickness occurs there are frequent visits by relatives to diviners to discover who is bewitching them—and frequently the belief that a person is responsible for the bad luck is a motive for killing.[9]

Most of the recorded murders in Africa appear to be derived from the pattern of relationships—the killing of close relatives, wives or associates. Van Henting called homicide a dyadic social relationship between the perpetrator and the victim, but Bohannan extends this (for Africa at least) to the more immediate community. He argues that the offender-victim relationship is interconnected with all the other social relationships and that these make their remote or more immediate contribution to the situation from which the crime arises. No one with a knowledge of tribal Africa would underestimate the interleaving and interdependency of the different parts of the social web of relationships, roles and responsibilities. And, as shown above, these relationships frequently extend above and beyond the existing tribal group so that in Bohannan's tables of cases there were twenty-nine cases where murder or a killing had been committed out of fear of witchcraft or sorcery or as a retaliation for supposed bewitchment. The administration report from Kolambo in Barotseland in 1957 states: 'Witchcraft investigations which took place in the last quarter of 1956 were largely concerned with the "Kaliloze" gunmen' who had been killing old women thought to be witches.[10]

Bohannan found few cases of premeditated killing or murder in the legal sense amongst his homicides; for example only four cases out of the ninety-nine homicides amongst the Gisu and only four out of the fourteen cases amongst the Luyia. It is also likely, for the reasons already given, that murder would not go undetected in rural areas. On the other hand, in such simple conditions it is always possible that a person may die from apparently natural causes so that without post-mortems and immediate medical investigations the prospect of making a murder look like natural death should not be overlooked.

The writer produced figures for Northern Rhodesia (now Zambia) from the early 1930s to 1958 and was dealing mainly with areas actually policed, that is the urban or near urban districts. On an admittedly rough and ready comparison with some of the figures for England and Wales, he suggested that the Northern Rhodesia figures for murder and manslaughter for certain of the years he covered could be proportionately higher than the figures for England and Wales. In 1951 for example, he calculated that whilst England and Wales recorded one convicted murderer for every 2.25 million people, Northern Rhodesia recorded five per million.[11]

These are probes—Bohannan in one kind of area, the writer in another. A great deal more data gathering is required before conclusions are drawn as to the high or low rates of murder and manslaughter in Africa. In particular it should be noted that the economic motive will begin to play its part more noticeably in the towns where there is more to steal—and in urban areas the pattern of social relationships will be different. The economic roles may be separated from the social roles, the nuclear family will tend to supersede the family of wider lineage and clan relationships. Some links will have been broken but new ones will have formed and the influence of different types of reference and peer groups can certainly be expected. The effects on murder patterns would be interesting to trace.

Murders following upon drinking sessions were recorded by both the writer and Bohannan. 'Not only is . . . drunkenness itself a frequent cause of violence,' said one magistrate in Northern Rhodesia, 'but in addition the unlighted streets of the locations make the drink-bemused African an easy prey to criminals.'[12] Beer drinking is of course traditional in Africa: beer brewing is connected with tribal ceremonial and drunkenness after feasting is recorded from the earliest accounts of tribal life. The point is that beer drinking, like nearly everything else, was a part of the total community life; it established new relationships during betrothal and marriage, it was part of reconciliation feasts after quarrels and disputes had been settled and it had a customary rather than an intrinsic value.

In the towns, drinking has its Western connotation of diversion and entertainment. Certainly, it still has social significance and value, but far different from the tribal system. This may play its part in throwing the newcomer to the town off his social balance; but it has to be remembered that alcohol nearly everywhere else in the world has had an association with criminal conduct, and drunken brawls have, ubiquitously, led to assaults and often to killing.

Ritual murder has received very little attention in the literature so far. Bohannan has no cases for consideration and the expression 'ritual murder' seems to cover a variety of situations. Perhaps the best known case is the outbreak of such murders in Basutoland in the 1950s. These were committed by sub-groups within the tribes and appear to have been directed against political figures. It has been suggested that they were instigated by the colonial power's misunderstanding of the role of the chief in local societies and their attempt to provide him with a more authoritative position than he was entitled to—thus provoking a form of rebellion within the tribes by the influential groups who felt their rights and power affected. Naturally a great many people would know of the offence but were too afraid to give evidence.

The following passage appeared in the 1932 Report on African Affairs in Northern Rhodesia:

> Three charges of 'chinkula' murder were brought against individuals who, in the belief that 'unnatural' children would bring disaster upon the community destroyed infants because they cut their upper incisors before the lower ones.[13]

In an early report on the Nandi it was said that if a Nandi killed a member of his own clan he would be regarded as being unclean for the rest of his life—unless 'he can succeed in killing two other Nandi of a different clan and can pay the fine [compensation?] himself'.[14] Presumably, these latter types of killings might qualify to be called ritual.

These brief notes suggest that ritual murder could be a fascinating subject for study by criminologists of all disciplines. Practically nothing is known about its significance for Africa generally, its incidence, its survival in urban settings or the possibility of its translation into a modern form with psycho-analytical 'meanings'.

INCEST

If there is a natural law then incest is an example of a natural crime. Margaret Mead has shown that the incest rule forbidding sex relationships between son and mother, father and daughter, brother and sister is a constancy in all known cultures.[15] In Africa, the relationships may be wider since matrilineal, patrilineal and bilateral lines of descent and family relationships make far-extended families sometimes with intricate cross-cousin linkages and restrictions. Many of these may be lost as families drift into towns and the knowledge of one's exact position in the lineage structure begins to be dissipated due to family fragmentation. It is a fair assumption, however, that these inter-family taboos on sex may be amongst the last to fade; and therefore incest as a crime will tend to be rather more widely construed than in the West. It will be more widely construed but the relationships considered incestuous will differ when one moves beyond the three mentioned by Margaret Mead. Audrey Richards says of the Bemba 'marriage within the matrilineal clan is not permitted, although people themselves express this taboo in terms of incest rules.'[16] The Lozi do not allow a man to marry a woman with whom he can trace genealogical relationship in any way. Such a marriage might occur but it is cursed and divorce is not allowed.[17]

Hughes has shown that the UK Sexual Offences Act of 1956 (s.10) makes no mention of any restriction on sex relationships between uncles and nieces, grandson and grandmother, step-father and step-daughter: but he shows too that in the United States these are included as incestuous relationships, and in almost half the States concerned first cousin relationships are forbidden.

It is practically impossible to give any realistic account of the incidence of incest, first because it is a close family affair and it is known that far more cases occur than are ever reported, secondly because even when known the evidence may be difficult to collect and thirdly, because the element of consent and its treatment in the law often means that incest and rape overlap and some of the cases of rape may be cases of incest.[18] Whilst all this is probably equally true of the conditions in African towns, it is highly probable that the close community living, the fear of supernatural reaction on the community and the revulsion felt towards forbidden inter-clan or lineage connection would tend to bring to public notice most of the cases which occur in tribal or country areas. Not only would the participants find it difficult to maintain secrecy, the community vigilance against the spiritual danger would be likely to bring to notice any example of this type of offence.

If this be true, then incest may be an offence of only very rare occurrence in rural Africa—and not only because it remains unreported or undetected. In Bohannan's book on homicide and suicide it arises only once,[19] and although it is discussed very fully in the literature on tribes, the cases quoted are few and far between. Vansina reported that 'very few cases of incest are actually known' amongst the Kuba[20] and he describes a case in 1953 where a man who had committed involuntary incest hanged himself in classical style to escape public scorn as soon as he discovered it.[21] Amongst the Ngoni, however, where a proposed marriage appears to conflict with the rules of incest because of some distant relationship between the couple, it is likely to be conveniently forgotten, and when marriage against such rules by older people happens to have the effect of rendering their children's marriages 'incestuous' (for example by a man marrying his daughter-in-law's mother or his son-in-law's mother) the court might oblige the husband to give up his wife so as to preserve intact the earlier marriage of his or her child.[22] But usually amongst the Ngoni 'incestuous liaisons between people whose parents are still alive are hampered from becoming proper marriages by the refusal of the woman's parents to accept any marriage payment from the man.'

In the study of crime in Northern Rhodesia of the years between 1932 and 1959 it is significant that incest is hardly mentioned and it certainly does not show up on the police reports or the reports of the administrators which were used to compile the study.[23] This does not mean that incest did not occur at all but that if it did occur it was dealt with (a) within the tribe—probably by dissolving the liaison, by compensation, or (where this was not effectively prevented by the penal law) by the more severe punishments of customary law in cases of incest or (b) by administrative rather than legal action in those areas regularly policed and served by magistrates' courts.

Every possible theory has been put forward and disputed and the peculiar significance which it [the origin of the incest taboo] has assumed for psycho-analysts has added to the heat of the discussion.[24] Why people act with revulsion towards incest was explained by Westermarck as due to a natural aversion to sexual relations between near kin between whom there is usually 'a remarkable absence of erotic feelings'.[25] White, on the other hand, thinks that this instinctive revulsion is contradicted by the severe laws which societies enact to prevent incest. These would not be necessary if it held no general attraction. White and others believe incest to be repulsive because of its socially harmful effects—its confusion of family roles as father or brother becomes a husband or lover or a mother or sister becomes a wife or mistress. This creates stress and tension, threatening the family unit on which society depends. And, as we have seen, in simple conditions of natural dangers outside the group, this could mean a threat to individual and collective survival. White's particular argument is that exogamous marriage strengthens the family, extends its interest and security via wider social relationships, and promotes economic development.[26]

The Freudians have a more dramatic, race-development, approach to incest in terms of the Oedipus complex and its effect upon a child's wish to possess the opposite parent and crush competition. It is a deep-rooted immemorial aversion based upon a real desire, and it affects not only the treatment of incest but a large number of other social relationships. This gives the incest taboo a much wider significance than it would have in respect of incest alone: it is found underlying not only such things as homosexual behaviour and fetishism, but also difficulties in marriage and social adjustment.

Both theoretically and practically there would be value in collecting more apposite data. Africa presents societies at all levels of growth and at practically all degrees of complexity, so that there is still a rich treasure awaiting the criminologists who can organize a sufficiently intensive and extensive study of incest. As this book goes to press there is a report of one Caribbean country making incest an offence for the first time in its legal history—and this in 1973.

SEXUAL OFFENCES GENERALLY

The types of sexual behaviour likely to be prohibited by the law will depend upon the culture and local standards. This is illustrated by the way laws have been altered in Western countries recently with regard to adultery, homosexuality, obscenity and prostitution. As values have changed so the law has been adjusted. Africa has had its way of dealing with sexual deviation (adultery, incest or 'unnatural offences') by customary law, usually by means of compensation, but the different values introduced by Muslim and Christian missions as well as the standards of imported penal laws have greatly affected the picture. The penal law may have prohibited indecent exposure on the Western Coast, for example, where women are frequently naked to the waist, or in areas where tribesmen did not cover their private parts. Here the penal law was not usually enforced rigorously but if such persons came to town they would need to conform to local standards by covering themselves. Sex play before marriage may have been tolerated in the tribe but Christian missions prohibited such conduct amongst converts. Polygamy sometimes became bigamy according to the place and the law applied. There is therefore a great deal still to be written in Africa about the conflict of laws and the different standards and conceptions of sexual deviance. Here it is possible to deal only with the penal law offences and sex offenders as these appear before the courts.

Sex offenders have for long been the special province of the psychologists, psychiatrists and psycho-analysts. Straightforward punishments, and straightforward explanations of sexual promiscuity did not seem to suffice with so many of these persons coming before the courts for attacks on children, indecent exposure or sexual deviations like transvestism, voyeurism, fetishism. Only the medical—especially the psycho-analytical—practitioner laid claim to a more scientific approach to these difficult and sometimes bizarre individuals. Failure to control instinctual drives, repression or inhibitions leading to irrational (or rational) explosions in the form of anti-social sex behaviour, and of course a wide range of emotional conflicts or mental illnesses, could all be adduced to explain, if not always to correct, their behaviour.

It is said that the first paper on the sexual offender to appear in the United States was Karpman's study of a case of obscene letter-writing in 1923.[27] This was a time when psychology was just beginning to be used in criminology. A year later, Sir Norwood East, a distinguished prison medical specialist, published his study of exhibitionism in England[28] dividing these offenders into two groups—the psychopathic and the depraved—but allowing that some exhibitionists will be both psychopathic and depraved. Sir Norwood, whilst having no doubt that there were genuine medical cases amongst those who were prosecuted for sex offences, very firmly rejected the idea of classifying all such offenders as medical cases. So in his work on exhibitionism he believed that prison could still be a deterrent.

Later writers have disagreed. For instance, May Romm in 1942, found in her cases elements of narcissism, castration fears, fear of homosexuality and masochism. She questioned the treatment usually administered to exhibitionists arguing that a patient would invariably expose himself not only sexually to other people but socially to the risk of arrest to gratify his need for punishment and to avoid bringing the underlying factors into consciousness.[29] In direct opposition, Taylor denied the existence of psycho-neurosis in cases of exhibitionism; but his cases were not psycho-analytical studies.[30]

There has been no suggestion in anything written on Africa so far that indecent exposure of the kind known in the West is either experienced or prosecuted. It appears to be hardly known and it could well be that the satisfaction which such exposure seems to afford the offender depends on the general attitudes to sex and its practice. Africa may not know it because it has a tolerant tradition which robs such an act (exposure) of its vicarious value. If this is so then it will be interesting to see the effect of greater permissiveness on the incidence of this offence on both sides of the Atlantic.

The work on homosexuality is voluminous. Wolbarst thought homosexuality congenital.[31] Henry and Galbraith thought it to be 'phylogenetic and embryologic' finding that homosexuality indicated a 'constitutional deviation'.[32] Loeser dealt with homosexuals in military service and divided them into four groups; endocrine or constitutional, psychological (Oedipus complex), regressive (compulsive-obsessional neurotics) and psychopathic. He believed that only the third group (the compulsive-obsessed neurotics) would benefit from psychotherapy and that these are not true homosexuals.[33] To leap to 1968, Ovesey argued that in true male homosexuality the prime motive is sexual satisfaction and the person does not feel anxious about it. However, this motive is not isolated: it is a deviant need to which a person has been brought by fear of the heterosexual function originating in early parental intimidation. The inhibition may not start in the sexual sphere but fears tend to spread and the homosexual love subject is chosen because it seems safer.[34] There is also a possibility that genetics may be more influential in the production of the homosexual than has previously been supposed. If this kind of conduct is well known in Africa it is certainly not as a criminal offence. Few cases come before the courts and whilst anthropological literature contains very occasional references to tolerated homosexual practices, it only really comes to light where men are crowded into dormitories as in some of the prisons.[35]

One investigation of offenders subject to what the authors define as 'heterosexual pedophilia' (that is the expressed desire for immature sexual gratification with a prepubertal female child) leads the researchers to divide these offenders into three groups—the adolescent, middle-aged and the senescent, each group with its own characteristics;[36] and a distinct victimology has developed for sex offences.[37]

Of course, a vast number of sex offenders may be ordinary people who have done publicly and anti-socially or illegally what a great many ordinary people are doing less conspicuously. Sir Norwood East had the merit of balance when he argued that not all sex offenders are deviates.

Above all, the question of what 'deviate' really means and whether the law should not be changed to permit a good deal of previously forbidden behaviour is certainly topical.[38] Britain has legalized homosexuality in private and in the United States of America there are clubs and associations for homosexuals and lesbians openly operating as such. Even where the law is still strict, its enforcement is greatly tempered with leniency and understanding. It is widely understood that laws against sex practices which are as old as man himself create unnecessary problems for the administration of law. Benjamin and Masters have argued that in the United States a local attempt to combat prostitution 'creates problems of law enforcement with which no police force in a large city is able to cope, without committing more and worse offences than those it has been detailed to suppress'.[39]

Among psychiatrists many sexual and other offences are held to be due to compulsive behaviour. It is interesting, with conditions in Africa in view, to note that Cressey has criticized this resort to 'compulsion' as being a loose classification of behaviour not properly understood. He has suggested a re-examination of 'compulsive crimes' in terms of a social psychological framework of motivation, identification and role playing.

One of the aspects of racial discrimination, whenever it occurs, is the fear of attacks by the members of the 'out group' on the women of the 'in group'. At least this has been a feature of the racial fears and reactions of whites in the United States and Africa. Thus, the death penalty was available as a punishment for rape in Kenya from 1927 to 1955 due to six cases of assault and attempted rape by Africans upon European women and girls in 1927.[40] Rape is always visited with severe sanctions in the imported penal systems and in South Africa its treatment according to race is discriminatory.[41]

One of the contributions of the study of crime in Northern Rhodesia, to which reference has so frequently been made, was that it showed the possibility of cross-racial sex offences to be remote in the case of rape but much less remote when it came to the lesser sexual misdemeanours.

The number of cases of rape was small and showed something of a variation over the years. In 1932, a high of twenty-seven cases had been reported and the offenders convicted. In 1954, there had been thirty-two convictions, but only eleven the following year and only nine in 1956: in 1957, this had risen to nineteen cases and in 1958, the last year of the survey, only twelve convictions had been registered. Between 1953 and 1958—the years for which information was available—there had been no rape of a European woman by an African reported and only one case of an African woman being raped by a European. There had been three cases of attempted rape during the years 1953-8 which were inter-racial: in 1958, an African was convicted of attempting to rape a European woman; in 1955 a 'coloured' (i.e. mixed blood) person had been found guilty of attempting to rape an African woman; and in 1953 a European had been convicted for the same kind of offence.

Convictions for indecent assaults on females between 1932 and 1958 remained fairly constant in absolute numbers and, since the population had grown, they actually decreased in significance. There were thirty-eight such offences in 1932, forty-two in 1951, and thirty-three in 1958, and the years in between showed a hovering about these figures.

As far as is known at the time of writing there have been no similar studies of rape rates and patterns of sex crimes in other African countries. Riley showed no cases of rape in his study of files at the Training Centre and Remand Home in Addis Ababa, and a report of crime in Ghana gave a low incidence of murder and rape despite a rise in population between 1959 and 1964.[42] Nor have there been any studies of sexual offenders. Obviously, this is a field of great value for exploration not only because of the significance of comparison with other countries but also because of the different tribal approaches to the control of sexual behaviour and the overlay of an urban culture. It is likely that the over-all picture in the towns will not be very different from that to be observed in towns all over the world; but the superficial view needs more careful sifting and analysis for those elements specific to the African scene and of greater value in seeking an understanding of local problems.

Amongst the 'unnatural' crimes, sodomy, buggery and bestiality are terms hardly even encountered in the accounts of crime in Africa which have been published, and they only very rarely arise in anthropological writings. Of course, buggery is generally covered by what has been said already on homosexuality although unnatural connection between man and woman is also comprised by this term. It is certain that whatever the real incidence of unnatural crimes in Africa only very few actually find their way to the courts. Beidelman has given one good reason for this—and incidentally one of the rare references to bestiality in the literature.[43]

Prostitution is not usually a criminal offence except in the cases of public soliciting. However, the growth of towns in Africa has increased the profits to be made from prostitution as well as increased the number of young girls who are either separated from their families, divorced, widowed or the victims of a legally and socially confused and unstable pattern of family life. This is too complicated a subject for discussion here in any depth,[44] but (a) the long history of labour migration taking young and often married men from their villages to towns, (b) the 'work camp' character of many of the early industrial developments, (c) the inadequate housing or unsuitable conditions for families in urban areas, (d) the difficulties of travel reducing the number of home visits a migrant labourer might pay to his family back home, (e) the economic role of the woman in the cultivation of fields (and sometimes the possession of family property) which often kept the married women in the villages when their husbands left for town, (f) the consequent breakdown of the levirate which gave a home and family to widows and the collapse of other systems of tribal security for the unattached woman—all these and other things have contributed in Africa to a general condition of matrimonial instability and uncertainty.

This has sometimes encouraged infidelity in women left for very long periods in the village (sometimes without an income except what they might grow for subsistence) and it has very obviously created a market for prostitution in the urban areas.

In a rural area survey in 1934, Lucy Mair examined some fifty-eight households and found nineteen men and seven women living alone—and a 'broken home' history in 50 per cent of these households[45]—and concluded that whilst it might not be possible to establish conclusively that marital infidelity and divorce were increasing, it was clear that sanctions which used to operate to discourage divorce and infidelity were no longer operative. Premarital conception was increasing for example and was no longer severely punished.[46] Lyndon Harries also mentioned a report from Angola to the effect that extramarital pregnancy was becoming more marked with the disappearance of the older fear of a girl's spirit wreaking vengeance on a man who 'wronged' her by making her pregnant.[47]

The position in towns has also been studied. Mitchell, comparing the proportion of town marriages dissolved, found little difference between urban centres on the Copperbelt of Zambia and the surrounding rural areas,[48] but when the *duration* of marriage was taken into account the urban instability was more marked and that this was not only due to tribally mixed marriages.[49] Mitchell was addressing the 1961 Annual Conference of the Northern Rhodesia Council of Social Service which concluded, amongst other things, that although there was a general instability of marriage and the divorce rate was high on the Copperbelt, there were special characteristics of a matrilineal society which aggravated the position, that is (a) the breakdown of a marriage in the early stages was apparently not viewed in matrilineal societies as a cause for any great concern, and (b) the children belong to the wife's kin and not to the husband's—an arrangement which allows the maintenance of the children in a divorce case to be treated very lightly.

An *ad hoc* study of the situation on the Copperbelt, made for the same Conference, reported that there seemed to be little professional prostitution in the strict sense of the word. Even the 'bad' women pretended to love a man for his generosity, his social abilities, his looks or his clothes: such a woman would flatter the man into inviting her to have intercourse rather than offering it to him. But, it was added, 'the amateur knows quite well how to provoke the man if she is after his money'. On the evidence available, it was suggested that most of the cases usually described as prostitution are probably a transference to the towns of the relatively free sex play in certain tribal conditions. The Kasai women were apparently being specially watched by the police because they belonged to one of the few polyandrous tribes in Africa,[50] but there seemed little evidence that Kasai women were more promiscuous than others.

Dr Lehmann, who was working in a copper mining township, described the periodical police raids rounding up women who were in the mine housing area without permits. They were fined about ten shillings, which 'is not really prohibitive', and the practice of returning such single girls or women to their rural areas had been abandoned as unrealistic: they either never got there or were very soon back in town. She concluded that some husbands regard their wives' adulteries as a source of income. 'How far they encourage them is difficult to find out. Others are extremely jealous and inflict cruel punishments which are quite legal if they have paid the *mpango* [bride price]'. Dr Lehmann goes on to quote a case which Epstein reports where a clash arose between Luvale law and modern urban ethics. Here a man who had given a husband money and blankets for the right of sexual access to his wife complained when he found that another person had the same kind of agreement with the husband. This was no offence according to Luvale custom but the urban native court decided it was a bad contract and fined both husband and wife.[51]

However, it seems that the practice of sending marriageable girls back to the villages and a certain tolerance of juvenile indulgence also contribute to the situation. Mitchell found a definite inequality of numbers of young people of puberty on the Copperbelt,[52] and Lehmann reports that mothers preferred 'to send their marriageable daughters back to the villages. But the boys who would like to marry them are in the towns and therefore many girls run away and try to find a husband—or at least a man to live with—on the mines . . . it is the first step towards becoming a professional prostitute'.[53]

Discussing this problem, Dr Lehmann makes the telling point that these are girls who form a new group and a new problem. 'Less than fifty years ago no healthy girl was left unmarried when she had passed puberty'.[54]

Information about prostitution in other parts of Africa has been difficult to come by. However, in the writer's knowledge of Africa, there has always been a brisk trade in prostitution around the beer halls of Southern Africa's cities and townships and along the suburban roads at night where girls are picked up by passing motorists. A similar trade flourishes in the streets of Kinshasa and Nairobi and is not difficult to find around the hotels of Togo, Ghana and Dahomey.

Whilst there is no data to prove or disprove it yet, it appears that this trade has 'visibly' increased with the growth of the towns.

In Ethiopia, it seems that although some sexual licence—often due to early marriage and frequent divorce—was known, it was the Italian occupation which really introduced, in its full form, the practice of paid sexual promiscuity. This flourished so much that by 1962 a survey of drinking houses in Addis Ababa (population 500,000) showed 6,000 licensed drinking places with more than 9,000 girls employed—most of them in part-time prostitution.[55]

Prostitution is frequently fed by the practice of a family benefiting, in some way, from sending its young girls out for service. Forde writing about the Yako says: 'It is likely that the general practice of polygynous marriage has been made possible only through the purchase of foreign children, mainly from Ibo country west of the Cross River who are known as *Yafoli* and adopted into the household and kin.'[56]

This kind of informal 'adoption' is well known far beyond the shores of Africa and occurred in the Mediterranean until very recently. Nor was it always a purchase of girls for marriage in Africa: the writer's own experience of the West Coast confirms the practice of the well settled urban families bringing in girls from the villages (with their parents' consent, of course—and usually after a payment and/or an understanding about future benefits) in order to do the housework or, more particularly to look after the children. (These girls were appropriately known as 'boyesses'.) When this arrangement broke down or the girl reaching puberty became a possible rival attraction to the husband or older sons, she might be sent away. Without the fare to go home, she might be easily seduced and recruited for prostitution: even if she had the fare she might be unwilling to leave the town, and in the search for somewhere to live fall in with the 'wrong company'.

In the Sudan, there was the practice, a few years ago, of bringing in girls from Ethiopia to work in the brothels. It was said that these girls from outside who had not undergone a clitorectomy were preferred by the clients as being more responsive.[57]

Studies of prostitution have been fewer than the ubiquity of the profession might suggest. Henriques had published a very readable survey of prostitution in history and in the contemporary world, criticizing the hypocrisy of trying to 'curb' the profession.[58] Lombroso argued that prostitution is often a woman's substitute for delinquency, and this theme has been taken up by many criminologists seeking to explain the low rate of female crime as compared with male delinquency. If it is a substitute then perhaps the male clients are also substituting for a good deal of male delinquency.

Glover, in a psycho-analytical study of prostitution, says that many female psychopaths are prostitutes and even 'normal' prostitutes have psychopathic traits when closely examined. It has not yet been established that prostitution is female delinquency in essence, however, and African studies from very different social groupings could make a significant contribution to world understanding of it. After all, the pattern of prostitution may have special features on a continent about which it has been said that: 'Almost universally a marriage according to native law is potentially polygamous', and that the monogamy existing is of necessity rather than choice:[59] on a continent where customary, Christian, Muslim and ordinary legal marriage give rise to incredible complications: on a continent of tribes within which prostitution in the commercial sense has little or no significance because although the sexual relationship is a private affair it is hedged about with such beliefs about danger and uncleanliness that there are great pressures to formalize any sexual liaison and to render the relationship socially innocuous. The relationship between prostitution and delinquency may be very different on a continent where so many of the prostitution-producing patterns in other parts of the world are reversed.

Although nothing has been written and studies have yet to be made, the writer can say from his experience of several different parts of the continent that there are many sexual offences well known in the West but not evident in Africa. Psychopathic sex crimes are quite unknown in the forms they frequently take on both sides of the Atlantic. Voyeurism and transvestism also are virtually unknown. Although ordinary curiosity may occasionally lead to a charge which might be considered voyeurism, the persistent offender with an obvious addiction to this type of offence may not yet have emerged. Only one case of transvestism[60] and none of fetishism have been reported—probably because it is more natural for Africans to act out any such urges in a group rather than live a double life. Similarly, sexual attacks on children are not usually experienced and it could well be that the aberrations from which these derive only arise at a later stage of urban culture when several generations of faulty child development have combined to produce perversions of this type.

PROPERTY OFFENCES

Excluding traffic offences, it is usually the crimes committed against property or for economic gain which absorb most of the police time and attention in any country. This means theft as interpreted to include such aggravating elements as robbery, housebreaking, burglary or extortion: and it includes such related offences as forgery and the uttering of forged notes or coins, fraud, embezzlement or conversion, false pretences and forms of cheating such as giving short weight. In a different category, but still incorporated as property offences, are such crimes as malicious damage, vandalism, arson and the destruction of crops.

The significance of property offences would be difficult to overemphasize. They accounted for 87 per cent of all crime reported by the United States Federal Bureau of Investigation in 1965 and this proportion was maintained in 1966 and 1967.[61] In England and Wales, larcenious crime amounts to some 80 per cent of the total, and on a recent visit to Kuwait the writer was given figures showing a predominance of property offences in the towns. In Israel, more than 40 per cent of all offenders between 1960 and 1965 were offenders against property,[62] and it seems that in Ghana property offences are at least 37 per cent of the crime reported.[63] When combined with assault, property offences amounted to two-thirds of all offences in Tanganyika in 1962,[64] and in 1952 crimes relating to property already constituted 36.7 per cent of all serious crime in South Africa.[65] The list could easily be extended from Africa or elsewhere: for economic crimes multiply for fairly obvious reasons as populations increase and urbanization spreads. The shift from personal to property crimes with industrialization or urbanization is very marked. Thus: 'The study of different types of crime shows an important shift over the years (1932–58) from offences against the person to economic offences such as stealing, breaking and entering, etc.'[66]

While the figures given in *African Penal Systems* are not always comparable, it is interesting to note the striking differences between those offered for Lesotho, Botswana and Swaziland (countries with relatively modest degrees of urbanization) and the figures given for Central, East and West Africa (areas with some of Africa's largest cities). Apart from stock theft, which in Basutoland, constituted the most common single offence, the predominance in the less urbanized countries is of offences against person.

However, there appears to be a further stage in the urbanization process beyond which violence begins to return and to reassert itself. Between 1964 and 1969, the use of firearms in the commission of murder in the United States had risen by 71 per cent and armed robbery had increased by 117 per cent. In the first six months of 1969 armed robbery accounted for 40 per cent of the 13 per cent increase in crimes of violence.[67] In Africa too there has been an emergence of violence in the larger cities in recent years. There were eighteen robberies per million of Northern Rhosesia's population in 1956 which seemed at that time surprisingly near the European proportions.[68] Boehringer refers to the rising figures for robberies in East Africa—or at least to the growing concern about this type of offence.[69] But, when violence returns to the cities in this way in the later stages of urban growth, it is apparently a different kind of impersonal aggression which does not greatly affect the steady trend to more economic crime. It differs greatly from the personal crimes arising out of close personal relationships which characterize pre-urban societies. For the new violence in cities is usually related to theft or gambling or to organized crime for economic advantage. Apart from armed robbery or robbery with violence, the use of force to establish crime syndicates or aggressiveness in gang activities are generally the increased manifestations of violence—and their economic motivation is clear.

The shift to economic crimes with urbanization is understandable. For property crimes to develop, first there has to be something worth stealing, and secondly, there needs to be a fair prospect of avoiding detection or evading arrest. Theft was rarely a problem in tribal Africa simply because, *within* a tribe, these two conditions did not very often occur. As between tribes, the situation may have been rather different (as we shall see), but the crimes dealt with by the rural customary courts were personal offences more than anything else. By contrast, theft assumed large proportions in the *urban* customary courts.[70]

Zarr, writing of Liberia, offers an African application of Merton's aspiration/illegitimate means theory. He points out that the urban newcomer is exposed for the first time to an attractive array of commercial establishments often with the goods laid out before him. He is under considerable pressure to acquire what he needs in circumstances where legitimate means are limited. Zarr suggests, furthermore, that the communal concepts of a tribal society by which a needy person may help himself to the property of others who have more without occasioning any great social disapproval, could well contribute to theft being, to an urban newcomer, much less of an offence—or, at any rate, much less reprehensible.[71]

Actually the process of disorientation and the difficulties of adjustment for a newcomer to an African city are probably much more complicated. It is not only the temptation, the expectation of communal tolerance because of necessity, or even the likelihood of avoiding notice which need to be taken into account. There is much more that is usually taken for granted by settled town dwellers which would be likely to confuse a newcomer and cause stress. The problem of learning to earn money and to budget the spending of money over fixed periods is quite complex to someone who has been more accustomed to sowing and reaping by season, rising and retiring with the sun, to organizing his life without a clock and to simply collecting or making the things he needs. There is also the significance of what Veblen called 'conspicuous spending' in the towns: for the first time status and prestige seem to depend on possessions—not so much of land, relatives or cattle, but of movable and often perishable property.

But, of course, it remains to be demonstrated that the problem of theft in African towns is particularly ascribable to newcomers. It is just as likely that the majority of these property offenders are persons who were born in urban areas or who have not only found their way around the towns, but have been there long enough to learn how to steal efficiently.

As *between* tribes in the rural areas, the fact that the concept of theft is frequently limited to the community or tribal society has given a certain amount of trouble. Jacqueline Costa confirms that to the people of certain pastoral tribes in French-speaking Africa, stock theft is less a wrongful act than an exploit bringing prestige to the perpetrator. 'The word "chorset" meaning theft, does not, of course, apply to the taking of cattle from foreign enemies.'[72] This makes it a real problem for the country in which such tribes live. Thus in Malagasy and Niger, stock theft has been visited with severe penalties for a number of years, whilst Guinea uses its socialist philosophy to make all stock a part of the public property in an effort to extend the feeling of community obligation and so eliminate animal theft.[73] Boehringer refers to cattle theft as one of the most difficult crime problems facing East African countries. He says that all have special police units for stock theft and all provide deterrent penalties. Kenya provides a fourteen year maximum sentence and twenty-four strokes. In Tanzania, it was an offence under the Minimum Sentence Act of 1963.[74]

Otherwise, it appears that theft was a comparatively rare phenomenon in indigenous society. Seidman says that among the Konkomba of northern Ghana no one would steal sacred objects such as bows and arrows and that clothing is practically held in common.[75] Vansina provides a list of the cases heard by a *Chefferie* court from May 1952 to May 1953 which shows only 21 cases of theft in the year as against 246 other cases classed as criminal—including 74 assaults.[76]

But theft was known, deplored and discouraged even within a tribal society, rare though its occurrence might be. There is a Nandi proverb that a 'born thief' will respect nothing, not even hospitality (he will steal even from his host), and Lindblow observed that 'even a cursory glance at what has been written about the judicial system of the Bantu people is sufficient to show that well nigh everywhere the punishment for theft is surprisingly severe'.[77] Hollis found theft amongst the Nandi to be regarded as a mean and contemptible crime to be severely dealt with: a first offender would be beaten and fined four times the value of what he had stolen; a second offender would be tortured by having a thong or bow-string tied round his head and twisted to an extent which branded him for life, his houses and granaries would be burned, his crops destroyed and his cattle confiscated.[78] Forde, on the Southern Ibo, says that in the past the punishment for theft depended on circumstances. Petty theft by women or unimportant persons might be punished by shaming on the first occasion, the offender being tied up in public to be ridiculed and degraded. Persons guilty of persistent theft were liable to lose the protection of their close kin who connived at their abduction by the victim's lineage for the offender to be sold into slavery.[79]

In the course of the study of juvenile delinquency in Zambia in 1964, tribal elders were closely questioned about the different types of wrongdoing and one gave the following interesting account of theft as it developed in this part of Africa:

> Theft has been regarded from the earliest times as a serious offence although there was very little to steal then as compared with today. It consisted mostly of food, groundnuts, maize, cassava, sugar cane or sweet potatoes. These might be stolen from the fields, gardens or granaries. Meat, fish, fowls, etc., might be stolen from houses. Usually a child's theft would be from his home where he might begin by helping himself to the relish in the pot without his mother's consent. If such misbehaviour is not checked at this stage it could get worse and extend beyond the family. With the coming of the Europeans, children were able to steal

other things which were easily carried unseen such as money, soap, sugar, clothes and blankets.[80]

It seems, therefore, that as village people have acquired more goods, and more valuable goods, of their own the temptations and opportunities to steal have increased. Moreover, the increasing problem of theft even in many of the rural areas of Africa today no doubt reflects the contact, especially via migrant labour, with urban standards, values and ways of life—with personal ownership and possession gradually reducing the significance of sharing and communal ownership within the tribe.

From the criminological point of view property offences offer a vast field of study. Apart from the background to the increases in economic crime treated here, there is the typology of criminal behaviour. 'Theft' is an umbrella term for a wide range of different types of conduct. Stock theft has been discussed, but stealing from the person—usually pocket-picking—is prevalent and there are ingenious strategems waiting to be analysed.[81] Stealing by servant is another category of crime which would repay careful study in the light of the long tradition of males in domestic service in Africa and the changes between colonial times and independence. A study (such as Cressey's)[82] of persons convicted of violations of trust would be valuable, particularly as Africa has widespread experience of informal combinations of wage-earners pooling their wages. A group of four may agree to pool their earnings each week so that once a month one of the four takes all. A full discussion of this practice is not possible here but in the writer's experience not a single case of default ever came before the customary courts, which dealt with a great many complaints of far less consequence. How does this kind of trustworthiness compare with the many offences in which a breach of trust is alleged? Corruption is another aspect of trust which would be an interesting study.

Similarly it would not be difficult to provide very valuable criminological data by replicating in Africa Wattenberg and Balistrieri's investigation of automobile theft.[83] In this study 230 auto thieves were compared with 2,774 other offenders and were found to be different in that they had a higher than average family income, only 1 per cent working, being mainly white, and coming from more ethnically homogeneous populations. Moreover, they usually operated in gangs. It should be noted, however, that this study suffered to some extent from its over-dependence upon police data: it would be more interesting to develop a team study of selected offenders of this kind with psychiatric or social workers joining with sociologists to obtain the information required.

Although it has not been mentioned elsewhere, the writer discovered a surprising amount of forgery and uttering in the collection of data from Northern Rhodesia. This was surprising because forgery is a relatively sophisticated offence which one would not expect to find in any large measure in the conditions of developing Africa. It is again a form of property crime which would be worth following up. Lemert found that 'naïve check forgery' which constituted 75 per cent of all forgeries in the United States did not follow the ideas of crime being derived from cultural conflict, delinquency areas, emotional disturbances or differential association.[84]

The different forms of robbery, burglary or house-breaking offer fascinating areas for closer study in the special conditions of Africa. Is it true, for example, that some of the armed bandits in Kenya are remnants of the Mau Mau who have never been able to settle down to conventional life? Is there any significant difference between the patterns of these crimes in East and West Africa, and do they take special forms in countries like Ethiopia or Somalia with significant cultural differences? We cannot know until writers in these countries begin to describe and define their groups.

Shoplifting, fraud and stealing from places of work have all been the subject of studies elsewhere and they need more attention in African conditions. Of course, one can expect similarities in the results of such studies due to the overlay of urbanism; but there are likely to be significant differences which might be valuable locally in finding solutions. In the Zambia study there were details of two interesting cases of false pretences. In Lundazi in 1956, the District Commissioner reported that a police station labourer had gone through the township posing as a detective equipped with photographs of wanted men and a set of handcuffs. In this role he was able to successfully steal two bicycles and escape to Nyasaland (now Malawi). It seems that a real detective who followed him into the township was immediately arrested by the chief headman and had difficulty in establishing his identity. The second case was from Mankoya in Barotseland. Here the offender would arrive at a village on a gaily decorated bicycle, blow a whistle and shout in English 'Fall in' (he was an old soldier). His fame having spread, the villagers would line up, whereupon he would invite them to shake a small bottle of what appeared to be water. If the water foamed or 'boiled' the person shaking it was accused of witchcraft or of having charms. If it did not boil the person was free of any taint of witchcraft. The 'diviner' then collected for his services. But in fact there were two bottles, one of water and one of ear-drop fluid which the old soldier distinguished by a notch on the cork.

Finally, the other types of property crimes should not be neglected. Arson has a particularly interesting place in African development and no doubt has special local features which distinguish it from the Western pattern of fires frequently started by people with an abnormal proclivity for burning or by those who wish to cover crimes or make profitable insurance claims. In tribal Africa, where huts are thatched, arson has frequently been the manifestation of revenge,[85] and it has sometimes been used as a political weapon in the towns. The burning of huts by night was especially feared in the villages for obvious reasons and was frequently associated with witchcraft.[86] Failure to report such an occurrence immediately might lead to suspicion of complicity. Sometimes burning was a means of execution, that is setting fire to the offender but whilst he was inside;[87] and several tribes feel it essential to burn the hut of a person who has committed suicide (as well as the tree he used) so as to cleanse the community.[88] However, Orchardson reported a strangely tolerant attitude rowards burning amongst the Kipsigis. After a burning no one was blamed severely in case it should happen to someone else: although compensation was payable it was not regarded as a punishment or fine. This was apparently due to the tribal memory of a disastrous bush fire during the migration of the Kipsigis.[89]

THE USE OF DRUGS

The world revolution in the use of drugs—especially synthetically produced drugs—has been gathering momentum for some years. An average of 7,500 new addicts were enumerated in the United States each year from 1953 to 1967.[90] Arrests for Narcotic Drug Law violations were four times as great in 1968 as in 1960 and the arrests in 1968 were 64 per cent more than in 1967.[91] Since then, the situation has deteriorated considerably on both sides of the Atlantic.

There has been a 2,000 per cent rise in confiscations of pills smuggled over the Mexico/USA border at all control points: in 1965, 65,000 'units' were seized; in 1968 it was 5,500,000 'units' mostly manufactured in the United States but sold without prescription in Mexico and reimported.[92] A television account of drug addition in New York in 1969 said that in this city alone, 120 persons die of drugs every month and 50 per cent of these are teenagers. In April 1969, it could be said that the chances were even that a crime would be committed by an addict looking for a 'fix', and the commanding officer of a police precinct in Harlem said that 60 to 80 per cent of his crime could be attributed to addicts who now out-numbered the police four to one. Even the number of children born in addiction (to addicted mothers) was increasing.[93]

Whilst the position is not quite so bad in other parts of the world, the shift to drugs is very obvious. The United Kingdom recently legalized the sale of drugs on prescription for addicts so as to obviate the need to commit other crimes to get funds for drugs and to cut out the black market. In fact, the use of drugs in the United Kingdom continued to grow, but there is reason to believe that it may have peaked and now be more amenable to control. Iran, which in the 1950s prohibited the growth of the opium poppy, has recently reintroduced the cultivation in limited areas and under careful control —on the grounds that this is necessary because of the growth in illicit traffic.[94] The trade in drugs has grown substantially in Israel, and in Brazil the federal censorship department has announced that it will ban references to drugs in newspapers, magazines, books and on the air.[95]

Ramsay Clark does not think that the hard drugs like opium are the problem for the United States. He points out that in 1900 there were an estimated quarter of a million to one million addicts as compared with only about seventy thousand today, but the use of methedrine (speed) pep pills, amphetamines, barbiturates, LSD and other chemical synthetics is spreading very fast.[96] Marijuana is so widely used that there are comparisons being made with the use of alcohol, and campaigns are waged for its legalization. The difficulty is that the use of the psychotropic drugs often leads to the use of harder and more dangerous drugs.

At a 1971 Assembly of Interpol it seemed that most countries were involved in the drug traffic as consumers, processors or growers. Efforts are being made to control growth by subsidization of substitute crops and hard sentences for 'pushers' are matched by rehabilitation programmes. At the same time the climate of toleration of the use of softer drugs is growing in some places.

Hemp or marijuana is historically a euphoriant which has been used by people throughout the ages. About the year 2737 B.C. the

Chinese Emperor Shen Nung wrote a book about drugs and medicines in which he outlines the uses and effects of marijuana.[97] Linnaeus gave the hemp plant its name of *Cannabis sativa.* Its name hashish derived from Hashzshin, leader of the assassins—the Muslim group of fanatics who used the hemp to prepare themselves for the killing of Christian intruders.

Africa has known the use of *dagga, bhang, rongory, takrouri, yamba, chanvre, oui, muti wa mwana,* or marijuana for many years. Africa's use of drugs is almost entirely restricted to hemp and its derivatives. It grows freely and is in fairly general use although prohibited by the laws of most countries.[98] However, this wide use does not mean that it is widely abused. This depends on the area and on the country.

One of the few studies of drug use in Africa was reported by Haworth at a meeting of the Zambia Council of Social Service in 1965.[99] He selected a group of fifty men, six of whom had been born in towns and thirty-six in the rural areas—the rest did not know where they were born. He found that the average age of learning about *dagga* smoking was just under sixteen years. The informants told him that the effects of *dagga* smoking wear off within two to three hours and many used it more than once a day, morning being the most common time. They were evenly divided between those who took it alone and in company, but three times as many took the *dagga* with beer as those who took it on its own. Many mentioned the extra strength it conferred besides its ability to take away shyness. Half the total sample said that they could work better after taking *dagga*; but seven said they could not work as well after as before. Five were gradually stopped from working because of *dagga,* three lost their jobs, seven were arrested by the police and eighteen were involved in some kind of trouble with relatives. Seven of the *dagga* smokers held that it improved health but twenty-five thought that it caused ill health and another ten believed that it did not affect health at all.

A number of the informants said that tribal chiefs and the police officially condemn *dagga* but used it themselves. Thirty of the total of fifty held that women should not use *dagga,* six said they should and five held that it did not matter. Surprisingly, forty-two of the total sample were against *dagga* being sold openly like tobacco or beer.[100]

There is surprisingly little written on the use of drugs in a tribal setting. Junod describes the renewal of drugs used by the medicine man amongst the Thongas referring to the villagers being assembled and inhaling the smoke through reeds:[101] but these are apparently drugs used as medicines rather than as stimulants or 'escape' devices. Most of the comments on the use of food or drink for diversion are confined to beer or alcoholic beverages. Thus we read that for the Lovedu drunkenness is no disgrace and perhaps exhilarating;[102] that the Buganda people were in the habit of gathering at night at the home of someone who happens to have beer to offer,[103] and that the Twa enjoyed eating meat and drinking 'much beer' when and where they could get it.[104]

Beer brewing is widely spread and, as we have seen, has a ceremonial significance in tribal settings, being linked to all kinds of celebrations and rituals. This has carried over to the towns where, however, it is now largely commercialized.

Hemp smoking of one kind or another has usually gone on alongside the beer drinking, though it would be going much too far to suggest that it was a regular practice for any large number of people. All that is known is that it is fairly general and not usually so repudiated by society as in some other regions of the world. In the prisons repeatedly visited by the writer in Central Africa, hemp smoking was a regular diversion and prisoners seemed to have little difficulty obtaining supplies. Tanner describing conditions in one East African prison gives figures showing that nearly 10 per cent of those inside were there for the manufacture and possession of drugs.[105]

A newspaper article of 1968 draws attention to *bhang* as a growing menace in Kenya. This claimed that police maintained that there were more *bhang* growers, dealers and smokers today than there ever were—and blamed the unemployment in the cities for much of this. It pointed out that the hemp grew wild all over Africa: in Kenya its original home was said to be Nyanza Province and Western Province around Kakamega, but its growth had now spread all over the country. Growers smuggled it into towns on buses, trains, in taxis, or hidden in baskets of maize or banana leaves—even in bicycle tyres. The article alleged that users took the drug in 'hubbly-bubbly' water pipes, in cake mixed with herbs and spices or, most popularly, in ready rolled cigarettes at anything from sixpence to one shilling a time. Although the penalties for possession of *bhang* in Kenya could be severe (up to ten years in prison and/or a shs. 20,000 fine) the number of prosecutions had risen from 2,124 cases in 1960 to 4,324 in 1966. In 1960, 1,362 lbs of the weed were seized in raids by the police: in 1966 it was 3,500 lbs.[106]

It is inevitable that the spread of interest in the new synthetic drugs will reach Africa via the urban culture and the use of *dagga* may become more widespread. For the moment, however, Africa has only a relatively mild problem of drug abuse and its interest should be in keeping it that way. With this in mind, it might not be too soon for there to be some searching inquiries made into the types of drugs locally used, the characteristics of the users and the best procedures for their containment and control.

GRAFT, CORRUPTION, WHITE COLLAR CRIME AND THE COSTS TO THE ECONOMY

Crime is a wider phenomenon than is presupposed by the sensational murders, burglaries, robberies or widespread stealing familiar in any of the larger urban settings. There is a great deal of crime which escapes attention because it is slick, sophisticated and often beyond the scope of ordinary police systems to deal with.

Sutherland coined the phrase 'white collar' crime for the respectable individuals (or corporations) who contravene tax or labour regulations, charge more than they should for their products or behave in a fashion which is just as criminal in its way as the depredation of the less fortunate individuals who do not enjoy legal advice and safeguards and are more visibly 'criminal'. The scope for this type of crime in Africa may be restricted as yet but it is undoubtedly growing and if breaches of currency regulations or the evasion of Africanization rules be taken into account it is likely that the numbers of crimes in this category would increase. So far there have been no studies of this type of offending in Africa; but undoubtedly there is ample material in government offices to provide data for such an investigation. Even very broad accounts at this stage would pave the way for more detailed studies later. Where large businesses have been recently nationalized it might be possible to uncover evidence of past conduct which could be classified as 'white collar' crime. On the other hand, care should be taken to curb any over-eagerness to find scapegoats. Actions would always have to be judged against the background of the prevailing standards or norms of behaviour in the society. In this respect the Western concept of 'corruption' could be wrongly applied to the gift exchanges and some of the normal practices of a traditional African consumptionist economy. It is clear that not all 'tipping' or 'gift-giving' is evidence of venality.

A brave start on a most delicate study has been made by Simpkins and Wraith.[107] Corruption and graft is as well known in Africa as it is in so many other areas of the world.[108] No country or region has the monopoly of this type of crime and it is usually the most difficult to uncover since those involved are so frequently the ones wielding the power to investigate or to hamper investigation. On the other hand, Africa is not wanting in the number of upright and incorruptible citizens who, given the opportunity, will act promptly against venality in public places. This antagonism to questionable practices is sometimes behind the changes of government or of government ministers or officials who have been discovered in their corruption. Moreover, Africa probably has a great deal more to lose by graft and corruption than the more highly industrialized countries, if only because its resources are still so limited: it usually has to build up confidence in its serious efforts to develop in order to attract foreign capital and technical aid and it is still in need of a firmer economic and social infrastructure on which to build its own future growth.

A great deal more information is required as to the real extent of graft and corruption; and criminologists in Africa could possibly distill a good deal of this from the regular work of the courts—even if this means by-passing the really big rackets. Sometimes, the real problem of graft is the dispersion over thousands of individuals rather than its sensational concentration in the hands of a few.[109] And even where there is official protection, many smaller cases will come before the courts. Of course it should not be overlooked that the courts themselves may have questionable procedures. A fascinating aspect of this whole problem lies in anthropology and in the correct interpretation of the older African attitude to money. No attempt has yet been made to separate acceptable levels of giving from bribes or to draw lines for the tolerable limits of nepotism.

Wraith and Simpkins used an administrative rather than a criminological technique in their analysis so that their data leaves much to be desired. Nevertheless, they broke the ground, and criminologists should not be slow to follow through. The larger scale corruption in the higher realms of government should probably, by definition, not be dealt with by criminologists alone. It needs the government itself to spring-clean its own house from time to time and occasionally to hold the kind of public hearings which, apart from informing the public, enable the social scientists to obtain the material they need for deeper studies and for the devising of better programmes for the prevention of these offences.

The extent to which a criminologist can be useful in this field will therefore be determined by the honesty and frankness with which the authorities face up to their difficulties. Naturally, there will always be those with a vested interest in inhibiting inquiries, but as government business becomes more and more subject to public scrutiny the criminologist finds increasing opportunities for pursuing his studies. However, a degree of ingenuity is implied and the student of crime in this field may find himself obliged to become something of an expert in business and administrative methods if he is to distinguish the abnormal from the normal—or to understand how far the normal departs from the declared policy or from the publicly understood standards. It is always conceivable that there could be situations in which corruption might be the norm and then it would be a question of asking what corruption really meant in this society and whether it could be regarded as a form of crime.

All these are bigger problems that cannot be fully explored in a book of this kind. The quotations from speeches or writings which would have readily confirmed the prevalence of corruption and financial mismanagement in certain African countries have deliberately been omitted from this discussion so as to avoid any unfair stigmatization of a nation which might result. But such evidence of an allusive nature is available backed by dismissals from office or prosecutions for abuse of office. And the purpose of this brief comment is to incite more research in the direction indicated by such data as is available. Each country well knows, though it may not always be able to tell, the extent to which corruption represents a problem for its administration and its services. It could well be the case that the countries which are the most open about such difficulties and which publicize most of their activities are the ones with the least to hide. It would be unjust therefore to select certain countries for reference simply because the facts are more readily available there.

Corruption thrives on secrecy and collusion. The criminologist can only get into this area when the facts are known to the authorities if perhaps not always yet known to the public. But if authorities are really concerned about such problems they will doubtless come to depend upon carefully devised criminological studies to demonstrate the extent of corruption. After all, it may be possible to indicate the range of corrupt activities from interviews with all concerned in a way which protects identities and avoids stigmatization. Criminology itself has not become greatly involved in this kind of work.

Only one other matter can be dealt with here, namely, the costs to the economy of (a) crime generally, (b) corruption and (c) white collar crime. The basic concepts are not sufficiently clear and delimited for such costs to be estimated without some very questionable assumptions being made. Nevertheless there have been some useful studies in this area in other countries and it would be interesting to see similar attempts being made in Africa.[110] One thing is clear at the outset: contrary to common belief, graft and corruption do not *necessarily* retard development. They may serve to concentrate wealth which can then be invested in development but to do this the citizens or taxpayers have to be cheated or otherwise separated from their goods. It has been suggested above that corruption is bad for developing countries, but this is not because of the simple transfer of wealth, which can be good as well as bad if total economic investment is the only consideration; it is because corruption can lead to a loss of the confidence on which a country depends for its effort by the working public, by outside investors and by those responsible for its administration.

Therefore, into this concept of the costs of crime intrude social costs as well as economic costs and a range of less tangible effects which need to be taken into account since they affect the human behaviour of which crime is an integral part. In Africa, as yet, practically nothing is known of the costs and effects of crime on the national efforts being made to develop the countries. This could possibly be a very rewarding type of investigation—not only for the understanding of crime but for the benefit of national growth.

JUVENILE DELINQUENCY

Juvenile delinquency is perhaps as significant in Africa as in any other part of the world—although in absolute terms it is still very far from the volume of juvenile crime familiar in the more highly industrialized countries. It is significant, however, because just as children's problems in the nineteenth century triggered a chain reaction of social improvements, so, in Africa, it was often the complications of handling effectively the young persons coming before the courts in the urban areas which led to the appointment of probation officers, the setting up of special institutions and the gradual development of a range of social services.[111]

Perhaps for similar reasons juvenile delinquency has been one of the earliest phenomena to attract criminological attention. As the various references in this book will have shown, there have been several studies of juvenile delinquency in Africa. Paul Raymaekers carried out a descriptive study of the pre-delinquent and delinquency situation amongst juveniles in Leopoldville (Kinshasa) in 1960/61.[112] Some years before this, figures for juvenile crime had been given by the Annual Reports of the Department of Social Welfare in Zambia[113] and by other Annual Reports in other colonial territories,[114] and in 1964, the writer was commissioned by the United Nations to do a study of juvenile delinquency in Zambia as part of a series of five world studies of the phenomenon.[115] This included not only a study of the concept of delinquency but a control group study.

The same subject had been covered more superficially in a broader study of the development of crime in Zambia between 1932 and 1958.[116] Weinberg provided a comparative analysis of delinquent and non-delinquent groups in Ghana in 1964.[117] Riley produced a study of juvenile crime in Ethiopia and Ross and Yeweinsshet Beshah-Woured have also made investigations of juvenile delinquency in Ethiopia which appear to be unpublished.[118] Perhaps this list could be extended: a paper on social stigma as a factor in juvenile recidivism in Nigeria prepared by Lambo and Clairemonte has been recently published[119] and there may be other studies in preparation.

Most of these studies tend to confirm what is known about juvenile delinquency in other countries. The disruption of the family, unemployment, lack of education—or truancy—emotional instability and residence in delinquency areas all appear to apply. But these are first studies and the apparent similarities may overlay some very important differences.

It should go without saying that the whole idea of juvenile delinquency in Africa should be approached with great caution. It is not at all clear, for example, what Raymaekers really means by pre-delinquency and delinquency or how he would distinguish them: if the latter refers to young persons convicted by the courts then he may not have been aware of the official numbers which are really very small. In the national statistics issued by the *Service de l'Enfance Délinquante* of the Ministry of Justice for the years 1965-67[120] the details appearing in the table on page 151 were given.

It is true that these figures referred only to cases reaching the service via the *Etablissement de Garde et d'Education* and not via the parquets. It is true too that the service was dealing mainly with the larger towns.

Nature d'infraction (Type of offence)	1965	1966	1967	Total	Total 1960/67
Attaques contre les personnes (Attacks against persons)	13	18	18	49	102
Viols (Thefts)	156	197	258	611	1,041
Actes de vandalism et de destruction de biens (Acts of vandalism and destruction of property)	—	—	—	—	17
Débordements sexuels (Sexual offences)	31	28	25	84	142
Usage de stupéfiants ou d'excitants (Drug taking)	6	1	3	10	25
Vagabondages itinerants (Vagrants)	15	40	38	93	131
Totals	221	284	342	847	1,458

Nevertheless, the picture, even with totals doubled or trebled, would be far from the situation described by Raymaekers. But it all depends upon what one means by delinquency. There are many parts of the world, and many parts of Africa where the 93 cases of 'vagabondages itinerants' would not have been classified as delinquent—they would have been classified as children or young people in need of care and protection: and the age of criminal responsibility enters into this. In Zaïre, minors under eighteen years of age were not criminally liable at this time.[121]

Raymaekers was dealing with a broader concept of juvenile misconduct which might lie just outside of the realm of legal action or might encompass a great deal of unreported or unprosecuted crime. The same report of the *Service de l'Enfance Délinquante* seems to support him when, in its comments on the above figures, it explains that:

> In general these young people have been in the habit of living for several years from pillage [*rapine*] stealing and rape [*viols*] so that they do not see why they should not continue. Moreover an extraordinary dissolution of morals, divorces, taking of girls, rape and abortion are in full operation; music, bars, innumerable for example in Kinshasa and the large cities. This extravagant way of life prevents the young people appreciating their misfortune.

Zaïre is a very special country with a special history, however, and during its years of disruption and disorder a great many young people both suffered and had to learn how to fend for themselves in the turmoil—even if this meant committing a crime. Even so the grave pictures painted by Raymaekers and the above comments are hardly substantiated by a total of eighty-four 'débordements sexuels'[122] in the three years shown. And the 611 thefts[123] could probably have been exceeded in countries which had had no such disorders. Neighbouring Zambia for example recorded 1,799 juvenile offenders in 1965, 1,902 in 1966 and 1,748 in 1967.[124] Any one of these years shows a greater number of juvenile offenders in Zambia than the total of 1,458 offenders recorded in Zaïre for the whole period 1960-67.

Obviously, something is wrong with the comparison and we are at once on guard against any facile statements about juvenile crime which mean different things in different countries because of the different laws and in connection with which the areas actually policed have a great effect upon the figures. Pierre Zumbach investigating juvenile delinquency in Cameroun reported in 1962 that the problem is practically non-existent in the villages and small towns but predicted a considerable increase in the towns and cities like Douala and Yaounde in the next fifteen years.[125] Again, the problem might have been one of areas policed, the extent to which the laws are enforced and the legal and social conceptions of juvenile crime.

Ethiopia reported a fast increase in juvenile crime in the cities of Addis Ababa, Asmara and Dire Dawa but admissions to the Training Centre and Remand House at Addis Ababa showed a decrease from 312 in 1958–59 to 95 in 1961–62 followed by a sharp rise to 229 in 1962–63.[126] In Sierra Leone the number of juveniles brought before the juvenile courts increased from 512 in 1959 to 1,686 in 1963 and admissions to approved schools from 76 in 1962 to 132 in 1963. Tanganyika was said in 1964 to have had a constant upward trend in juveniles found guilty over a period of eight years.[127] In January 1969 the re-educational school at Kamiha in Togo had only thirty boys between thirteen and twenty years of age of which nineteen had been committed by the courts and eleven had been placed in the institution by the Ministry of Social Affairs as being in need of care and protection.

Only one or two deeper studies have been done. As part of the study of crime in Northern Rhodesia, juvenile crime in the country was traced over a period of nearly twenty years. From 229 offenders in 1939, the figures rose to 1,167 in 1958, but the great increase came between 1948 (303 offenders) and 1957 (974 offenders) and, over all, the most persistent rise was in the twelve to sixteen year age group.

There were also a couple of recession years in juvenile crime when the numbers fell, for example in 1953 by 30 per cent from the previous year and in 1956 by 10 per cent (from 1955 figures), but they always rose again to new heights. To decide whether the phenomenon being examined was really juvenile crime and not just youthful waywardness the types of offences were examined. It was found that theft and offences of 'breaking and entering' predominated and that most of the actions for which juveniles had been brought before the courts were actions for which they would have been undoubtedly prosecuted had they been adults.[128]

The Trend's Study of Juvenile Crime in Zambia commissioned by the United Nations in 1964, allowed a more comprehensive and intensive study of the problem to be made. First the concept of juvenile delinquency was examined for its significance in an African setting. A study was made of the concepts of youthful waywardness and youthful misbehaviour in tribal conditions and in the attitudes of newcomers to the towns—without using the term 'delinquency' at all. It was found that traditional and indigenous notions of youthful misbehaviour of a serious nature were in close accord with those of juvenile delinquency as defined in the penal codes.[129]

The close study of juveniles from 1939 was carried over to 1962 in which year 1,888 offenders were found guilty and the trends were compared to changes in police strength over the years to see if there were any indications that the increases in juvenile crime were no more than increases in police activity. The evidence was too ambiguous to show any clear relationship: but its ambiguity if anything strengthened the notion of juvenile crime as a growing social problem.

Thirdly, a tracing of juvenile crime in three towns, Lusaka, Kitwe and Livingstone, revealed that there seemed to be a correlation between the growth of crime and the *rate* of growth of cities. Finally, the study was completed by an in-depth investigation of a group of juvenile delinquents at the approved school and a control group of non-delinquent school boys. This indicated *inter alia* that tribes and tribal differences had little effect, having been the same for both delinquents and non-delinquents. There were no marked differences between delinquents and non-delinquents in their attitudes to crime generally, to the police or the courts. The greatest differences between delinquents and non-delinquents emerged from their home backgrounds: three times as many parents of delinquents as parents of non-delinquents were divorced and twice as many non-delinquents as delinquents were living with both parents. About 75 per cent of delinquents were out of touch with their parents as compared with 25 per cent of non-delinquents. And twice as many non-delinquents as delinquents had good relationships with their parents. Although delinquents were lower in education than their counterparts it seemed that (compared with figures for the total population) they had been amongst those favoured by educational opportunities.[130]

Another control group study was being carried out at about the same time in Ghana confirming these Zambian conclusions. This verified that delinquents experienced more stress in the family situation than did non-delinquents. Delinquents more frequently than non-delinquents (i) resided with guardians farther removed than their parents and close kin, (ii) were shifted to other families, (iii) were shifted for unfavourable reasons, (iv) experienced the first family shift before the age of five, (v) were truants from the family and (vi) were affected by the broken home. Secondly, delinquents were found to be more alienated from school values and practices than were non-delinquents. Thirdly, this study appeared to substantiate the view that delinquent conduct is learned behaviour; that is those who become delinquent were exposed and susceptible to the influence of delinquent associates.[131]

The most recent study of stigma and factor in juvenile recidivism takes the line that with value orientation held constant 'little or no stigma attaches to a young person's learning his trade at an approved school rather than a trade centre' and raises the interesting point that the lack of stigma contributes to the low rate of recidivism; that is the person released from the approved school is not seriously hampered by the fact that he received his training there. However, the value orientation taken was that of all the children (at the two approved schools in the Western State of Nigeria) whose value system was 'predominantly traditionalistic'.[132]

No assertion was made about the children of the modern 'élite', which probably means that the study was of children not yet fully exposed to the influence of modernization (urbanization?), i.e. to the disruption of families and values noted above in the areas from which most delinquents came. If this is so, then it is further confirmation of the idea of growing delinquency in its full sense being a function of the urban culture with all its implications.

It will be clear that the studies of juvenile crime in Africa are becoming more and more sophisticated. They are the most numerous of the serious studies done and they may be said to be amongst the best in criminology so far. Since this is where crime really begins it is to be hoped that the work will extend widely. What is important now, in this period of transition, is to trace the process of transformation from traditional to urban values and to discover the extent to which the kaleidoscopic urban over-culture may be concealing some of the stabilizing influences which mean so much in this search for effective prevention.

[1] Paul Bohannan (ed.), *African Homicide and Suicide*, Princeton, New York: Princeton University Press, 1960.

[2] ibid., p. 266.

[3] See M. E. Wolfgang, *Patterns in Criminal Homicide*, Philadelphia, 1958, also von Hentig, *The Criminal and His Victim*, New Haven, 1948.

[4] See J. M. Stanton, 'Murderer on Parole', *Crime and Delinquency*, vol. 15, no. 1, January 1969, showing that murderers are generally a good risk for early release from prison.

[5] See H. Mannheim, *Comparative Criminology*, London: Routledge and Kegan Paul, 1965, p. 170, for a general discussion of the typological classification of offences.

[6] Pamela H. Johnson, *On Iniquity: Some Personal Reflections Arising out of the Moors Murder Trial*, New York: Scribner's, 1967. See also review of this by Mannheim in *Crime and Delinquency*, vol. 15, no. 1, 1969.

[7] P. Wyden, *The Hired Killer*, New York: William Morrow Co., 1963.

[8] Although he does recall a case in Malawi where in the customary courts a man who had assumed the guise of a crocodile and killed for a number of people actually sued for his payment! Note too the role of secret societies on the West Coast: these could be used to get rid of 'enemies'.

[9] Bohannan, op. cit.

[10] W. Clifford, *Crime in Northern Rhodesia*, op. cit.

[11] ibid., p. 46.

[12] ibid., p. 121. Also for the view that 'the law-abiding African detests the beer hall and anyone who is involved in the policy of compelling him and his wife to patronize it and to give up private brewing for profit'.

[13] For an account of this belief among the Bemba see Audrey Richards, op. cit.

[14] A. C. Hollis, *The Nandi: Their Language and Folklore*, Oxford University Press, 1909, pp. 73 ff.

[15] Margaret Mead, 'Some Anthropological Considerations Concerning Natural Law', *Natural L. F.*, **6**, 51 (1961) quoted by Graham Hughes in 'The Crime of Incest', *J. of Crim. Law, Criminology and Police Science*, vol. 55, no. 3, September 1964, pp. 322-31.

[16] Audrey I. Richards, *The Bemba of N.E. Rhodesia*, op. cit., p. 181.

[17] M. Gluckman, 'The Lozi of Barotseland' in *Seven Tribes of British Central Africa*, op. cit.

[18] cf. G. Hughes, op cit., p. 323.

[19] Bohannan, op. cit., p. 176.

[20] J. Vansina, 'A Traditional Legal System: The Kuba' in Hilda Kuper and L. Kuper (eds.), *African Law Adaptation and Development*, Berkeley: University of California Press, 1965, p. 116.

[21] cf. B. Malinowski, in Molene *et al.* (eds.), *Crime and Custom in Savage Society*, London: Kegan Paul, 1926, pp. 77-79, describes the young Tobriand Island incestuous lover who jumped to his death from the top of a palm tree when he was publicly denounced.

[22] J. A. Barnes, *The Fort Jameson Ngoni*, op. cit., p. 226.

[23] W. Clifford, *Crime in Northern Rhodesia*, op. cit. Also a later study of 'Female Crime in Lusaka' uncovered no instances of prosecution for incest amongst the sixty-two women offenders.

[24] H. Mannheim, *Criminal Justice and Social Reconstruction*, London: Routledge and Kegan Paul, 1946.

[25] Westermarck, *History of Human Marriage*, 5th ed., 1921, p. 192, quoted in Weinberg, *Incest Behaviour* (1955), p. 237.

[26] White, 'Definition and Prohibition of Incest', *American Anthropologist*, vol. 5, p. 416 (1948) quoted by Graham Hughes, op. cit., see also Morris, 'Sex Taboos, Sex Offenders and the Law', *Amer. J. of Orthopsychiatry*, vol. 9, p. 554 (1939) quoted by Hughes, op. cit.

[27] B. A. Karpman, 'The Sexual Offender (A Case of Obscene Letter Writing)', *Psycho-analytical Review*, vol. 10, July 1923, pp. 1-46.

[28] Sir Norwood W. East, 'Observations on Exhibitionism', *Lancet* II, August 1924.

[29] May E. Romm, 'Compulsion Factors in Exhibitionism', *Journal of Criminal Psychopathology*, vol. 3, April 1942, pp. 585-96.

[30] F. H. Taylor, 'Observations on Some Cases of Exhibitionism', *Journal of Mental Disorders*, vol. 93, July 1947, pp. 631-8.

[31] A .L. Wolbarst, 'Sexual Perversions: Their Medical and Social Implications', *Med. J. Rec.*, vol. 134, July 1931, pp. 5-9 and 62-5.

[32] G. W. Henry and H. M. Galbraith, 'Constitutional Factors in Homosexuality', *American Journal of Psychiatry*, vol. 90, May 1934, pp. 1249-70.

[33] L. H. Loeser, 'The Sexual Psychopath in the Military Service', *American Journal of Psychiatry*, vol. 102, July 1945, pp. 92-101.

[34] L. Ovesey, 'Homosexuality in Men', *Manitoba Medical Review*, vol. 48, no. 3, 1968.

[35] See R. E. S. Tanner, 'East African Experience of Imprisonment' in *African Penal Systems*, op. cit., pp. 301-2.

[36] A. K. Gigeroof, J. W. Mohr and R. E. Turner, 'Sex Offenders on Probation: Heterosexual Pedophiles', *Federal Probation*, vol. 32, no. 4, 1962.

[37] cf. S. Sutherland and D. J. Scherl, 'Patterns of Response Among Victims of Rape', *American Journal of Orthopsychiatry*, vol. 40, no. 3, 1970, pp. 503-11.

[38] See N. Morris and G. Hawkins, *The Honest Politicians Guide to Crime Control*, op. cit.

[39] H. Benjamin and R. E. Masters, *Prostitution and Morality*, New York: Julian Press, 1964. There is a long history of police involvement in the vice they seek to control, especially documented in the US but also found in other parts of the world. Prostitutes and pimps are often police informers or in other ways buy their measure of official toleration of their activities.

[40] Foran, 'The Kenya Police 1887-1960' (1962), quoted by J. S. Read in *African Penal Systems*, op. cit.

[41] See details given by D. Welsh in 'Capital Punishment in South Africa' in *African Penal Systems*, op. cit.

[42] R. B. Seidman and J. D. Abaka Eyison in *African Penal Systems*, op. cit.

[43] T. O. Beidelman, 'Kaguru Justice and the Concept of Legal Fiction', *Journal of African Law* (London), vol. 5, no. 1, pp. 5-20.

[44] For a full treatment of the question of family change as it presented itself in the 1950s see A. Phillips (ed.), *Survey of African Marriage and Family*

Life, London: Oxford University Press, 1954 and A. R. Radcliffe Brown and D. Forde (eds.), *African Systems of Kinship and Marriage*, London: Oxford University Press, 1950.

[45] L. P. Mair, 'African Marriage and Social Change' in *Survey of African Marriage and Family Life*, op. cit., p. 71.

[46] L. P. Mair, op. cit., pp. 153-4; she adds however that the Hausa were probably an exception.

[47] M. A. Lyndon Harries, 'Christian Marriage in African Society' in *Survey of African Marriage and Family Life*, quoting a letter from a Pastor Joao, Capuca, Chilesso, Andula, Angola.

[48] J. C. Mitchell, 'Aspects of African Marriage on the Copperbelt of Northern Rhodesia', *Rhodes-Livingstone Journal*, XXII, pp. 1-30.

[49] J. C. Mitchell, 'Measures for Marriage Stability' (Working Paper for the Northern Rhodesia Council of Social Service Conference on Marriage and the Family, Lusaka, 15-17 September 1961).

[50] D. Lehmann, 'Marriage, Divorce and Prostitution of African Women in a Changing Society' (paper prepared for Northern Rhodesia Council of Social Service 1956: given at NRCSS Conference on Marriage and the Family at Lusaka 1961), *NRCSS Report of Annual Conference*, Lusaka: Government Printer, 1961.

[51] No reference is given by Dr Lehmann but a bibliography to the Report includes A. L. Epstein, 'Urban Native Courts on the Northern Rhodesia Copperbelt', *J. African Administration*, 1951, pp. 117-24; *The Administration of Justice and the Urban African*, 1953 Colonial Research Series; *Judicial Techniques and the Judicial Process*, Lusaka, Rhodes/Livingstone paper, no. 23, 1953; 'Divorce Law and the Stability of Marriage Among the Lunda of Kazembe', *Human Problems in British Central Africa:* 'The Role of African Courts in Urban Communities of the Northern Rhodesia Copperbelt', *Human Problems in British Central Africa*, vol. 13 (1953), pp. 1-17.

[52] J. C. Mitchell, *African Urbanization in Ndola and Luanshya*, Lusaka, Rhodes/Livingstone Communication, no. 6, 1954.

[53] D. Lehmann, op. cit.

[54] ibid.

[55] H. Mayed, 'Prostitution and Venereal Disease in Addis Ababa', August 1962, quoted by J. Riley in his *Report* of December 1964 to the Ministry of Native Community Development.

[56] D. Forde, 'Double Descent Among the Yako' in A. R. Radcliffe Brown and D. Forde (eds.), *African Systems of Kinship and Marriage*, op. cit.

[57] Information given to the writer by a local psychiatrist. It should be noted that the hospitality of wife-lending is also known in Africa and the long separations of young married people lend their own influence to the development of prostitution.

[58] F. Henriques, *Prostitution and Society*, 2 vols., London: Macgibbon and Kee, 1963.

[59] A. Phillips, *Survey of African Marriage and Family Life*, London: Oxford University Press, 1954.

[60] In Kampala, Uganda, in early 1971; reported in the *Uganda Argus*. Though the exact reference was not available I was informed that the African accused was made to divest himself of the woman's *busuti* he was wearing and to appear in court in a shirt and trousers.

[61] See *Report of U.S. Presidential Commission on Law Enforcement*, op. cit., and comments by E. M. Schur, *Our Criminal Society*, New Jersey: Prentice Hall Inc., 1969, p. 26.

[62] U. O. Schmelz, 'Differentials in Criminality Rates between various Groups in Israel's Population' in I. Drapkin (ed.), *Studies in Criminology*, vol. XXI,

Jerusalem: Hebrew University, Magnes Press, 1969, p. 277.

[63] Figures given by Siedman and Abaka Eyison on 'Ghana' in *African Penal Systems*, op. cit., p. 63.

[64] ibid., Read's article on Kenya, Tanzania and Uganda, p. 99. See also L. A. Fallers, *Law Without Precedent*, Chicago: University of Chicago Press, 1969, p. 87, where he lists cases heard during 1950 by a sub-county court. Here, too, theft is outstanding.

[65] *Official Yearbook*, no. 27, 1952-53, pp. 446-7, quoted by Freed, *Crime in South Africa*, op. cit.

[66] W. Clifford, *Crime in Northern Rhodesia*, op. cit.

[67] Figures issued by Federal Bureau of Investigation, Department of Justice in *Uniform Crime Reports*, Washington, D.C., 23 September 1969, and quoted by *New York Times Encyclopedic Almanac*, 1970, p. 230.

[68] W. Clifford, *Crime in Northern Rhodesia*, op. cit., p. 51.

[69] G. H. Boehringer, *Developments in Criminology in Tanzania*, op. cit., referring to figures for Uganda and to newspaper editorials in the *East African Standard*, June 1968 and *Sunday Nation* of 8 September 1968.

[70] W. Clifford, *Criminal Cases in Urban Native Courts*, Lusaka: Government Printer.

[71] G. H. Zarr, 'Liberia' in *African Penal Systems*, op. cit., p. 194. See also R. B. Seidman, 'The Ghana Prison System' in *African Penal Systems* for the view that among the Fante it was not theft for a starving man to take food. He quotes Sarbah (Fante National Constitution 30 (1906)) for the opinion that the 'sensibility of many persons to the criminality of theft is not so great'.

[72] I. Q. Orchardson, in A. T. Matson (ed.), *The Kipsigis*, Nairobi: East African Literature Bureau, Eagle Press, Nairobi 1961, p. 114. It should be noted that this kind of limited obligation is a function of nationhood. During the two World Wars the stealing of enemy property carried no moral stigma amongst Western nations and was frequently rewarded. Orchardson also points out that whilst the Kipsigis would take the cattle of others they regarded theft amongst Kipsigis as *sogoranet* or unnatural.

[73] Jacqueline Costa, 'Penal Policy and Under-Development in French Africa' in *African Penal Systems*, op. cit., p. 372-3.

[74] G. H. Boehringer, op. cit., footnotes 16-18. These include quotations from newspapers referring to the resettlement of tribes: in one case eleven Samburu tribesmen were killed and more than £20,000 worth of stock were stolen in a raid in Eastern Kenya. About 4,000 head of cattle were stolen by about 60 Gabbra tribesmen.

[75] R. B. Seidman, 'The Ghana Prison System' in *African Penal Systems*, p. 432.

[76] J. Vansina, 'A Traditional Legal System: the Kuba' in Hilda and Leo Kuper (eds.), *African Law, Adaptation and Development*, op. cit., p. 108.

[77] G. Lindblow, 'The Akamba in British East Africa', *Archives d'études orientales*, J. A. Lundell, Uppsala, 1920, 2nd. ed.

[78] A. C. Hollis, *The Nandi: Their Language and Folklore*, London: Oxford University Press, 1909.

[79] D. Forde, 'Justice and Judgment Among the Southern Ibo under Colonial Rule' in *African Law, Adaptation and Development*, op. cit., p. 91. It should be observed, of course, that all such penalties are now superseded by statutory penal code sanctions.

[80] W. Clifford, *Juvenile Delinquency in Zambia*, United Nations Trends Study, SOA/SD/CS.3, p. 7.

[81] See details of offences committed given by the offender in W. Clifford, *Profiles in Crime*, op. cit.

[82] D. R. Cressey, *Other People's Money*, Glencoe, Illinois: The Free Press, 1953.

[83] W. W. Wattenberg and J. Balistrieri, 'Automobile Theft', *American Journal of Sociology*, vol. 57, 1951/2, pp. 575-9.

[84] E. M. Lemert, 'An Isolation Closure Theory of Naive Check Forgery', *Journal of Criminal Law, Criminology and Police Science*, vol. 44, 1954, pp. 296-307.

[85] See for example, Bohannan (ed.), *African Homicide and Suicide*, op. cit., and especially p. 33 where a man set fire to a hut in anger; pp. 164-6 for an orgy of killing and arson in revenge.

[86] I. A. Fallers and M. C. Fallers, writing of the Basoga in *African Homicide and Suicide* say that sorcery (*bulogo*), poison (*butwa*) and arson (*kwokya*) are regarded as similar forms of deliberate killing because all are secret and usually perpetrated at night.

[87] Two women were reported burned alive at Port Herald near the Shire River in Malawi by the local people who alleged that they had created a crocodile which killed a young girl. The police were investigating the murder (*The Sunday Mail* (Central African Newspaper) of 11 February 1962 quoting the London *Sunday Telegraph*).

[88] Bohannan (ed.), *African Homicide and Suicide*, pp. 70 and 143.

[89] Orchardson, op. cit., p. 114.

[90] US Department of Justice, Bureau of Narcotics and Dangerous Drugs.

[91] US Department of Justice, Federal Bureau of Investigation, *Uniform Crime Reports*.

[92] CBS Television News, 8 August 1969.

[93] CBS Television, '60 Minutes', Tuesday, 1 April 1969. On 14 January 1970 a TV feature on the 42nd Precinct of the New York Police Department reported one-third of all arrests there were addicts: also one-third of all burglaries were committed by addicts.

[94] See lecture by Dr A. M. Khalifa to *Fourth United Nations Congress on the Prevention of Crime and the Treatment of Offenders*, 1970, op. cit.

[95] *New York Times*, Sunday, 10 January 1971, said that at least a thousand words were on the censorship list, including 'trip'.

[96] R. Clark, *Crime in America*, New York: Simon Schuster, 1970.

[97] N. Taylor, '*The Pleasant Assassin: the Story of Marijuana*', in P. Solomon (ed.), *The Marijuana Papers*, New York: New American Library, 1968, p. 35.

[98] See Jacqueline Costa, 'Penal Policy in French Africa' in *African Penal Systems*, op. cit.

[99] A. Haworth, 'Psychiatric Aspects of Juvenile Delinquency' in *Annual Report of Zambia Council of Social Service*, Lusaka: Government Printer, 1965.

[100] ibid.

[101] H. A. Junod, *The Life of a South African Tribe*, New York: University Book Inc., 1962, p. 454.

[102] D. Forde, *African Worlds*, op. cit., p. 78, but drunkenness is bad if it leads to neglect of duties or to dissension.

[103] L. P. Mair, *An African People in the Twentieth Century*, New York: Russell and Russell Inc., first published 1934, reissued 1965.

[104] J. J. Marquet, *The Premise of Inequality in Rwanda*, London: Oxford University Press, 1961, p. 18.

[105] R. E. S. Tanner, 'The East African Experience of Imprisonment' in *African Penal Systems*, op. cit., fn. 2, p. 315.

[106] *Sunday Nation*, 21 July 1968: article by Vivienne Barton. This article also described *miraa*, another drug in common use which is not prohibited by law, but for which growers and dealers have to be licensed. *Miraa* was said to be a 'stringy green stalk' produced mainly in the Meru district around Mount Kenya, and it was chewed for its juice which had an intoxicating effect. It was used mainly by the Coast Arabs and Somalis.

[107] E. Simpkins and R. Wraith, *Corruption in Developing Countries*, New York: W. W. Norton and Co., Inc., 1963.

[108] See 'Social Defence Policies in Relation to Development Planning' (Secretariat working paper for the Fourth United Nations Congress on the Prevention of Crime and the Treatment of Offenders, Kyoto, Japan, 1970), para. 87 for the view that mismanagement and incompetence in administration, can also be criminogenic.

[109] See the illustrations from licensing, contracting, renting market stalls, taking fees for otherwise free hospital services, the abuse of veterinary facilities and the venality of local government generally, in Simpkins and Wraith, op. cit. The nomenclature of graft was reviewed at a meeting of Asian experts held in Tokyo recently. In some parts of Asia it is referred to as 'tea money', 'coffee money', or 'whisky money', e.g. in Afghanistan *choi kuli* (tea money) is a euphanism for a small bribe.

[110] See J. P. Martin, 'The Cost of Crime: Some Research Problems', *International Review of Criminal Policy*, no. 23, UN publication, sales no. 65, IV, 4. Also S. Gary, 'Crime and Punishment: An Economic Approach', *Journal of Political Economy*, 1968, **76**, March-April, pp. 169-217. See, too, B. M. Fleisher, *The Economics of Delinquency*, Chicago: Quadrangle Books, 1966.

[111] Most welfare services of any type in Africa (apart from tribal institutions) began with religious missions, but government involvement in colonial times may be traced to the need to provide staff to deal with urban problems—especially those of young people.

[112] See *International Review of Criminal Policy*, no. 20, and Raymaekers, op. cit.

[113] See for example, *Annual Reports for 1958/1959*, Lusaka: Government Printer, 1959-60.

[114] For example Tanganyika's Annual Reports for the Judiciary.

[115] United Nations, SOA/SD/CA.s, 30 April 1967.

[116] W. Clifford, *Crime in Northern Rhodesia*, op. cit.

[117] See S. K. Weinberg, 'Juvenile Delinquency in Ghana: a Comparative Analysis of Delinquents and Non-Delinquents', *Journal of Criminal Law, Criminology and Police Science*, 55, p. 471 (1964).

[118] See note 36 to S. Lowenstein's article on Ethiopia in *African Penal Systems*, op. cit.

[119] T. A. Lambo and P. Clairmonte, fn. 132, p. 161 below.

[120] Given at the United Nations Consultative Group for the Prevention of Crime and the Treatment of Offenders in Geneva, August 1962.

[121] See articles on Zaïre (then Congo, Leopoldville) in *African Penal Systems*, op. cit.

[122] Still only 142 when traced back to 1960 (see above).

[123] Still only 1,041 when traced back to 1960 (see above).

[124] Figures given to the United Nations Consultative Group, Geneva, op. cit.

[125] *International Review of Criminal Policy*, no. 20, 1962, p. 45.

[126] See working paper 'Rapid Social Change and Juvenile Delinquency in Africa', produced for United Nations Expert Group Meeting in Social Defence, Monrovia, 12-21 August 1964, E/CN.4/SODE/4.

[127] ibid.

[128] W. Clifford, *Crime in Northern Rhodesia*, op. cit., pp. 63-71.

[129] But cf. T. A. Lambo, 'Social and Health Problems of Adolescence in Traditional Cultures of Africa', paper submitted to WHO Expert Committee on Health Problems of Adolescence, *WHO Report*, September 1965, no. 308, p. 6, in which he concludes that 'Juvenile delinquency was not properly conceptualized as a syndrome, social or biological'. This was taken to mean that 'the age of criminal responsibility was much higher than that stipulated in the formal criminal laws of the countries of Africa'. However, some of the francophone countries have raised the age of criminal responsibility to eighteen and it is arguable that in traditional societies full responsibility as adults begins with initiation—and this usually occurs at puberty, i.e. before the age of legal liability in many countries.

[130] W. Clifford, *Juvenile Delinquency in Zambia*, op. cit.

[131] S. K. Weinberg, 'Juvenile Delinquency in Ghana', op. cit.

[132] T. A. Lambo and P. Clairmonte, 'Attribution of Stigma as a Factor in Juvenile Recidivism in Nigeria: a Preliminary Enquiry', MS privately communicated to the author.

6
PREVENTION AND TREATMENT

GENERAL

It is conceptually impossible to separate the prevention and treatment of crime. Measures taken to deal with criminals or to help an offender to avoid future trouble with the law are obviously as much preventative measures as they are forms of treatment. A good police force, successful in detecting crime and arresting offenders, is a preventative of future crime. Thus all forms of treatment are preventative. The converse, however (that all forms of prevention are forms of treatment), may not be true. For instance, the redistribution of income or an extension of the educational system with a view to reducing poverty and ignorance and ultimately reducing crime, are obviously preventative measures; but one would have to strain such a concept to regard it as a form of penal treatment. So too, investments in better child care may be preventative but they become effective as a treatment only when, in fact, a delinquent act has been committed and improved child care measures are applied to the particular child. In the distinction we make here the term 'prevention' will be taken to include mostly the measures necessary to prevent delinquency whether or not they have a treatment aspect. The term 'treatment' will relate to action after a crime has been committed.

PREVENTION

In Africa it might be possible to classify a wide range of health, educational and welfare policies, indeed a great deal of the investment on general or national development, as being crime preventative. There can be no doubt that they are—in so far as they reduce the pressures of ignorance, poverty or maladjustment which make for delinquent conduct. There is, however, something just a little spurious about citing measures which are preventative of a wide range of other things because they cannot help having an effect on crime. It is like claiming foul weather as a preventative of street demonstrations, or good health as a preventative of accidents. Furthermore, the link between crime and these other general measures is not as direct as has been supposed. As they prevent crime deriving from poverty they may encourage it from boredom, as they avoid crime from ignorance they may engender a more ingenious and sophisticated type of crime. It is significant that crime rates usually rise with development.

It would be much easier to discuss the prevention of crime if the great deal of research which has been done so far had produced more precise information as to causes. It is only known that crime is associated with social changes like industrialization and urbanization, with social conditions such as a high degree of social mobility, poverty, ignorance, emotional disturbance and mental disability, and with faulty child care.

Even these need qualification as we have already seen. Thus crime is associated with poverty, but greater affluence in recent years has brought more crime so that one must necessarily modify this by saying with Edison, that 'poverty consists in feeling poor'.[1] Therefore, it is less abject poverty which invokes delinquent behaviour than (presumably) the inequalities which exist within a society. A conspicuous maldistribution of incomes is likely to arouse need anxieties, greed and acquisitive tendencies all of which have their criminal aspects. Similarly, mental disability is related to crime only in so far as social conditions increase the pressure on the mentally disabled. Thus, one could as readily argue that the real factor at work is the growth process of society which increases the stresses and strains and forces people towards those short cuts which are criminal.

So too, with child care: whilst there is sufficient evidence to believe that psychopathic and maladjustive behaviour results from child neglect or faulty handling, we still do not know exactly what kind of process is involved. The trend is towards a great deal more permissiveness in child upbringing, but the advice of experts tends to be conflicting, sometimes even contradictory, as to the best way of handling particular situations. There was a period when punishment of any kind served little or no purpose since it satisfied guilt feelings or inhibited natural behaviour. According to one extreme view the authoritarianism in a home unfitted children for the democratic principles of life outside. This was followed by a period when punishment with love had a place, but only if it were consistent and so logical: healthy inhibitions were not to be despised. There are now experiments with autistic children which may show punishment to be an effective communication with and support for children otherwise unreachable. There was a time when rewards and minor deprivations (for example of spending-money or small pleasures) were good substitutes for corporal chastisement. Later such sanctions were to be regarded as more cruel than a sharp slap given in love and as rapidly forgotten. Even now it is not always easy to get agreement on the 'best' course of action with children in a given situation. We are still only guessing at the effects in later life of certain kinds of treatment of children.

In this situation of incomplete knowledge of the causes of crime, then, it is clear that countries may readily assume that measures taken to improve child care, to even the distribution of income, to eradicate feelings of inequality and poverty, to relieve the mental strain of modern living, will all serve to reduce crime—at least that amount of crime with which these factors are associated. The fact that we do not know more should not hamper the use of what we do know—even if we know it only in general.

(a) Prevention in the Early Stages of Childhood

Prevention, then, must begin at the earlier stages in terms of child care. The flow of delinquents from deprived, maladjusted children is too well documented to require emphasis here. To begin to prevent crime, any country needs to look first and very carefully at the condition of its children.

In this respect, Africa begins with a great advantage over many other parts of the world. In Africa it is generally true that children are well cared for, that children are desired, and that children enjoy a secure feeling of 'belonging' from their earliest years. Taking Africa as a whole, the 'unwanted' child, likely to grow up with all kinds of resentments and anti-social tendencies, is very much the exception.

In the tribe, children confer prestige, ensure greater productivity and reciprocal care for their parents and grandparents in old age. Illegitimacy is rarely a problem except in so far as it leads to disputes as to which family should have the child. And a child in a rural area is rarely without care if the parents die or prove unable to look after it; the extended family system provides many relatives only too ready to take the child in and, as a member of the clan, the child would be well protected and provided for.

The one possible exception to this has been the infant whose mother dies in childbirth. Here the absence of a wet nurse at the appropriate place and time could mean death from starvation. There are no synthetic or processed baby foods easily available where tribal conditions prevail and a child unable to take solid food is sometimes in danger of death.

For many years now, religious missions and voluntary bodies in Africa have offered services for motherless children of this type and there has, typically, been no difficulty in restoring these children to their families when they were able to eat solid foods. Indeed, in the Kivu area of Zaïre evidence has been found of herbal treatments which produce lactation even in girls before menstruation or in women after the menopause. Corroborative reports have been received from Zambia, Malawi and Tanzania. The *Institut pour le Recherche Economique et Social* at Bukavu, and later the Belgian authorities, instigated research some years ago on the fifty herbs known to be associated with the 'medicine', but so far the exact formula has proved elusive.[2] Obviously this tribal device to produce lactation further testifies to the desire to provide for motherless infants and to preserve life. It is another illustration of the value placed on children in the traditional conditions of Africa.

Of course, Africa is still affected with malnutrition on a wide scale and too many children are badly fed and suffering from the general poverty in rural areas as well as in the crowded urban settlements. These are general problems of economic underdevelopment, lack of knowledge as to diets, budgeting and hygiene. The children suffer with the rest of the population—but not more so because they are children. Usually every effort will be made to feed, rear and protect them, partly because of a genuine love of children but also partly because of the prestige and status, the clan benefits, and economic advantages of children. An additional child may be an extra mouth to feed but it is also a vindication of manhood or womanhood, an extra assurance of their clan's future, a rise in tribal status for the parents and an addition to the family labour force. A child from many points of view is an asset. His acceptance, care and recognition within the tribe protects him from many of the doubts, insecurities and emotional conflicts imposed on children in towns. Even in the African towns the emotional 'belonging' of children is markedly stronger than that experienced by children in the more developed parts of the world. There is a carry-over of tribal attitudes towards children into the urban areas which is often the despair of family planners. Though children are beginning now to be neglected, even abandoned, by feckless parents in urban areas, or especially by prostitutes who find them a hindrance to business, the tradition of wanting, loving and caring for children is still very strong in Africa.

This is a situation which has been changing rapidly in the past few years. The disintegration of close child care of this kind by a whole tribe is part of the process of modernization and certainly not to be deplored. But from the delinquency point of view it is significant that the prospects of children getting into trouble have increased as they have become separated from relatives and more of an economic liability than an asset.

As schools have been established throughout the rural as well as in the urban areas the need for a child to be educated has been widely accepted. This meant, at first, a great family sacrifice of children to schools when they might have been working, if only herding the cattle or helping their parents in the fields, and it was resisted by many. Some of the early missionaries had to go out into the bush to persuade children to come to school and had to argue with parents to allow them to do so. Not infrequently, it seems that they had to spend time bringing children back into the schools when they ran away.[3] This did not last long, however, for the significance of schooling was quickly appreciated and soon the schools found that they were having to turn away applicants. For many years there have not been—and still are not today—enough schools for those wanting them.

With so few Africans educated it was these who moved into good positions and who had many more opportunities when independence came. The disproportionate rewards of education increased the demand for more schools: the sacrifices were now perceived as being only short term with a great many advantages in the long run. There is still a great need for more and better schools in Africa, but the danger ahead is that the economy cannot expand fast enough to provide all these educated young people with the kinds of jobs for which they feel qualified. In most countries there is a growing number of unemployed young people with primary or secondary education. From the point of view of delinquency this is a great risk. This, however, introduces a rather different aspect of the problem to which we will return below.

In a very real sense then, the question of caring for children will depend very largely upon the ability of the economy to provide adequate incomes, nutrition, good education and better opportunities for everyone. The timing is also important however. Job opportunities will need to expand to keep pace with improved education. In urban conditions and modern Africa the traditional picture has been the most changed. The large towns recreate in Africa many of the problems of housing, sanitation, family disintegration and mental strain typical of towns everywhere. Whilst children are still wanted, the facilities for caring for them adequately have dwindled. The extended family cannot easily be transferred from a rural to an urban area. First of all there may not be jobs for everyone; but in any case there will not be housing, and even if there is housing it will not be the housing for all relatives in the same street or neighbourhood. Thus, the extended family is scattered either to different towns or by the dispersion within a town itself. Nor is the marriage (now unsupported by relatives on both sides) always so secure. Divorce mounts and casual liaisons increase. And clearly, a very large part of the security traditionally a birthright of a child in Africa is shattered in this domestic, economic and social transformation.[4]

Secondly, the family income is strictly curtailed. Whilst in a rural area an extra child may mean additional production (an additional income to offset the extra person to feed), in an urban area extra children are an additional burden on a wage which does not stretch proportionately to the size of the family and a liability as the same wage must now begin to cover costs of education. More than this, the housing will generally be inadequate and additional children will increase the problem of over-crowding and sanitation.

Whilst, as we have seen, illicit sexual relations are not unknown in rural areas they are the exception rather than the rule and their consequences are taken care of by the traditional system: an illegitimate child has no difficulty in finding a home or someone to care for it. Indeed, as already shown, the argument which generally comes before the customary courts or the tribal elders is an argument as to who should have the right to do this. There is no feeling of liability. In towns, prostitution and casual marriages are widespread and a great many more children are spawned than can be cared for. Moreover, those who have borne the children may have personal, family or professional interests in disposing of them quickly. Thus, in many parts of Africa there are orphanages or children's homes, official and private: religious missions and volunteer societies are very often active in this kind of work. This has not prevented many children being on the streets, without family care and living by their wits. There is usually not enough money to provide for them all.

From a preventative point of view, therefore, it is necessary to ensure in any country that each child has a right to a minimum of subsistence and care. It is obviously impossible for every country in Africa at this time of limited resources to guarantee all the health and educational services which may be necessary for all children everywhere. It is essential, however, if there be a genuine interest in preventing crime, that every child should have someone to look after it, sufficient food to live and basic instruction for life. When these are lacking, crime can be expected whether or not these be the mediate or immediate causes. As a preventative of crime, any government must look closely at its provisions for child care.

Generally speaking, the towns have grown so large and the problem of young people without care is now so great that it is no longer possible to leave this entirely to benevolent or voluntary organizations. It may well be better for a government to employ religious bodies or others able to obtain the appropriate staff or to train people for the work. If the government relies on such voluntary aid it must assure the standards and adequacies of the services by grants-in-aid or supplementary assistance. Where this is not possible on a large scale, local services have to be provided either by the government or local authorities, and if the latter then it will usually be necessary for the central government to have a small inspectorate to make sure that the care being given in voluntary or local authority institutions is adequate to the need.

The mention of institutions raises an interesting possibility that the problems of child care in Africa—at least in so far as they relate to neglected or deprived children—might possibly be dealt with without the number or size of institutions which have been necessary in the developed countries. The love of children, the large size of most families, and the general tradition of helping each other could mean that African countries may develop the kind of foster-care services which could reduce if not eliminate the need for institutions—and could especially dispense with the large Dickensian orphanages which one occasionally finds. It is apposite, however, that the developed countries have found difficulties with the foster-care system, especially where this has meant children being moved too rapidly from one foster home to another. Many authorities in developed countries have had to return to institutional care on a big (if now more enlightened) scale. In all this, Africa has an opportunity to experiment for the best system to meet its own requirements.

Child care does not end, however, with care of neglected or deprived children. There are many delinquent children who have not really been deprived unless one likes to argue that by definition delinquency means deprivation of some sort. In delinquency the evidence is that a great deal of the harm in the up-bringing of a child may be perpetrated by good, loving parents who cannot agree. In the first place there is the concept of the 'broken home'. Clearly many children suffer because homes break up as a result of unfaithfulness, quarrelsomeness, interference by relatives, etc. Even where there is no physical separation, the emotional effects of disunity, inconsistency and bitterness in a home can be devastating and might predispose a child to behavioural disorders amounting to delinquency. Therefore, preventative measures for crime would not overlook measures to preserve marriages and to avoid widespread separation, disharmony and divorce. This, with the problem of prostitution, is really a question of national morality which will be differently interpreted in each country. The important thing to note, however, is that the fragmentation of homes and extra-marital relations on any wide scale will inevitably increase the problems of child care and ultimately serve to recruit delinquents.

Apart from promiscuity and a general slackening of the traditional moral system there is the problem of ignorance about child care. A great many parents just do not know how to look after their children, and as we have seen, the old rural traditions are no longer effective in the towns. If the social controls were there, and if children could be helped to mature and assume adult responsibilities with their peers, then the whole process would be simplified. In town, however, the social controls are no longer effective, the relatives to enforce them are scattered, and the increased mobility and opportunity for young people means that there is no longer an acceptance of the old patterns of life. Indeed, the problem is complicated by the fact that improved education provides children with a greater knowledge of modern life, its demands and requirements, than their parents could ever give them. In towns it is often the children who are the guides and leaders for the family rather than parents leading the children. Young people have a greater economic independence and their behaviour is not as circumscribed as in a tribal area.

Programmes which seek to strengthen the role of the parent, which seek to provide information on child care and which help families to interpret for themselves some of the things going on about them, are all crime preventative (in so far as our present knowledge enables us to say this). They will bring more knowledge and understanding to bear on the problems of town living as these arise. In this connection, home visiting services manned by experienced social workers can be extremely valuable as can services which make use of the natural meeting places, for instance the markets, baby clinics, labour exchanges and local government offices for disseminating information to parents. Courses in child care, budgeting, home economics, nutrition for women and courses to help workmen adapt to town living are all to the good.

If the research which has been done on crime so far means anything at all, it signifies that strong family life carries less risk of crime and particularly less risk of delinquent children. 'Strong family life' may need more careful definition, but although scientific confirmation may still be awaited, one can argue on the evidence available that there is less crime, and more especially, less juvenile crime amongst (a) rural and traditional societies, (b) amongst Jews, Chinese, Japanese and others with a strong family tradition in American towns, and (c) amongst Americans in Cyprus or Indians in Zambia—still societies with a strong pattern of family life. Thus it is reasonable to conclude that measures taken to keep family life strong will prevent crime.

However, urbanization and industrialization are making inroads on family life and the disintegrating effect is much greater and more widespread than the efforts now being made to help families stay together and to bring up their children effectively. It should be noted that some of the societies with little crime mentioned above have found ways of keeping the benefits of family life in an urban and industrial society. They, too, are feeling the centrifugal pull of modern town and industrial life but they have slowed the pace—often by creating barriers between their systems of living and those of the rest of the population.

Africa needs urbanization and industrialization. It also badly needs the stability and the roots in the past of strong family life. Its future may well be decided on the way in which it solves this dilemma. It could well learn from the examples quoted from other parts of the world, but its genius for modernizing without losing the best of its own traditions will remain its own.

(b) Prevention in Schools

This section must inevitably overlap with the last. There is some difference, however, in that the emphasis on preventative measures for younger children must be on the family, on care and nourishment, on guidance and control by the family, whereas the emphasis on preventative work amongst older children is not only on the family and the school authorities but on peer groups which are now beginning to exercise much more influence. There is a need to keep up a reputation with others in one's clique, gang or class, and to develop the respect of one's fellows. Even the approval of home and school authorities cannot compensate for the loss of face amongst one's peers.

Schooling itself is a preventative of crime if properly used. This is especially the case in Africa where the magic of schooling to promote, to endow status, to win recognition and ensure success is still deeply felt. Getting into school is like getting onto the moving staircase to better things. It is a corollary, of course, that failing to get onto that staircase has its own frustrating and bitter consequences which could predispose some of the weaker souls to seek out illegal backdoors to success and eminence. Therefore, in a general sense, the wider education is spread in Africa, the less likelihood there is of delinquency. This has been borne out by the few studies which have been done and which show most juvenile delinquents to be out of school and/or unemployed.[5]

There is a very important proviso, however, namely that the education provided must be relevant to the circumstances. It must not serve, as it has so far done and continues to do in many parts of Africa, to build an army of unemployed because young people have been educated to a higher standard than the available work requires. From now until the end of the century it is undeniable that a vast majority of young people will have no means of earning a living other than from the land: yet, year after year, people flow out of the schools in rural areas and make for the towns to find jobs equivalent to their new educational standing—or to find means of continuing schooling itself. They have little chance of doing either and they leave behind them a source of income just waiting to be developed in most areas.

This is, of course, a very difficult subject. One cannot determine easily how much education the state should regard as basic and take responsibility for. It is a standard which rises with national income as far as one is able to judge. And there are some who say that it is better to educate far beyond economic need as it will plant a seed of dynamism in the economy—more educated young people will *force* answers to the economic and social problems. On this argument, it doesn't matter that labourers have degrees or dustmen are philosophers of high qualification: it all adds to the healthy thrust for change and improvement. This is all right providing those who advance such views are prepared for the kind of change that might well occur and accept the kinds of solutions that might be forced by education for its own sake and regardless of local circumstances.

At the extreme, such an argument could lead to a frustrated, partially educated youth inciting revolution and eventually seizing power—then imposing on the nation a more ruthless and practical solution within which people might be forced to develop the land, and education might become the reward for good party service.

If this seems too high a price to pay then there is a need to restructure many of the present educational systems derived from earlier colonial eras to meet the needs of modern Africa. Thus, crime prevention by way of schooling does not just mean extending opportunities for education but extending opportunities for education relevant to the conditions of the country and appropriate to the young person's prospects of earning a decent income. The extension of schooling and its relevance for the environment are not the only measures likely to prevent crime at this stage of a young person's career. There is also the quality of education and the provisions that can be made to provide for an awakening desire for participation, and for those who fall behind in the race for success via the classroom.

It would be difficult to go at all deeply into the quality of education in Africa without this becoming a treatise on education itself. It is obvious, however, even to the casual observer, that over the past two decades, education in Africa has developed much more in terms of quantity than in terms of quality. Not only is it impossible in such a short space of time for the secondary and higher levels to be advanced without robbing the primary schools of some of their best teachers—it is evident that the primary schools have also been robbed of teachers to serve as politicians, diplomats abroad, administrators and members of parliament. This drain from the school system was unavoidable as political independence created the need for ever greater numbers of educated young people to fill the highest offices. But if the quality of primary education is impaired, the quality of other forms of education is also affected since each level begins with children inadequately prepared. This aspect of education needs careful study and attention if education is to mean what the term implies and if it is to be a means of preventing delinquency as well as of developing and training the mind and personality, so valuable in promoting achievement and success.

Any educational system has to be geared to the needs of all those it reaches and not just the majority. The greater number of those passing through the schools are moving into a political atmosphere in which they will need to know about the country and its domestic and foreign affairs, before they leave school. This becomes necessary if only because the majority of the total populations in Africa are below twenty-five years of age and therefore they become activists and beneficiaries of political systems even before leaving school. Any political party can make use of this to indoctrinate young people and already it is interesting to see the extent to which school children are brought into the streets for processions and celebrations. A scrupulously correct educational system might eschew politics altogether, leaving young people to learn for themselves. The sensible middle course would seem to be to accept the inevitable and to use the school period to encourage young people to participate in the control and conduct of their own affairs, giving them as much background information about political issues as they need. In most of Africa thus far, this aspect of youthful participation in political affairs has not yet been grasped and more effort is needed to make a distinct community of the school—a place where young people can be trained for life.

Such a preparation for life would mean the school having its own clubs, groups for public action and other youth organizations as well as its regular curriculum. Indeed, the curriculum could well be modified by the needs and developments of the community groups. These would, in Africa at least, help to solve the problem of differences of standards between school authorities and peer groups. In Europe or America there is often the need to provide something extra for young people's groups outside the schools. In Africa, the traditions of communal life are still deep rooted; the gregariousness and capacity for acting in concert could help schools to become something unique in the preparation of young people for later life. They would be educational but something very much more—apprenticeship institutions for all kinds of later activities. The trend in education in Africa might well be, therefore, towards the comprehensive type of school (schools taking boys and girls and providing for academic, technical and commercial education within the same group of buildings) and this would make the youth community a more realistic concept. This may seem a long way from crime prevention, but such youth communities could be helped to deal with delinquency in their midst—measures which are likely to be much more effective than anything the state could devise. Needless to say, this implies extending some form of education to the young people who at present do not get to any type of school at all.

Finally, there is a need for special facilities and services for those who do not keep up with the rest. The backward or wayward child needs special attention and teachers need to be trained to deal with him—which brings us back, of course, to the quality of education and the quality of teachers.

There will be few children who will drop out of school because they do not like it. In Africa there is such pressure on children from the tremendous drive of young people for education that not to like school is to declare oneself odd in the extreme, and few children will do this. Where truancy occurs, it is of a different type to that found in Europe or America. It does occur, however, when there are long walks to and from school and many diversions, when a child cannot find his school fees or afford the accepted uniform: and in all such cases it will be easier to avoid school if the child is not getting on so well educationally and is perhaps being mocked about this by his fellows in class. There are also those children who may be slightly ill, suffering from undernourishment or emotionally or mentally handicapped. There are few services to accommodate such children in Africa who do not fall into the normal stream, and there are so many others queuing for the places at school that it may seem better to replace those likely to demand extra attention. In this way, many delinquent careers are shaped unwittingly. Special counsellors or experienced social workers may be required on the school staffs, but if the community school idea is to find favour then such counsellors will be needed anyway. Above all, it needs a close association of parents with teachers and special courses in teacher training to enable a teacher to identify such problems as they arise.

(c) Prevention out of School

In many of the countries of Africa there are as many children and young people out of school as there are in the schools. What can be done for the large numbers who cannot be reached by the school system? Essentially there are three main lines of approach—the family, the youth organization and the police.

Families could do a great deal more to guide and help their young people who cannot get into a school and who cannot find work. If these children are too young for independent work then they can often be used effectively by the mother in her agricultural chores or used by the father either in his work or in his obligations around the house. This should in no way hamper the continuation of schooling at home, and the government (local or central) could make books available and develop widespread correspondence courses for children unable to complete ordinary schooling. Of course, one of the problems about a child becoming useful at home is that after a year or two at school he has no wish to be used in this way and in many parts of Africa a boy would scorn helping his mother in the fields—considering this to be 'women's work'. Even so, it is possible that a grouping of families to decide what to do about their unoccupied children could produce ideas: it could lead to a number of developmental self-help projects in which young people could take the lead. The main thing is for the families to become involved in dealing with the problem. At the same time the families could be encouraged to become involved by special government schemes to retrieve the situation—from grants for self-help services to informal types of teaching for such youngsters. The object should be to fill their time profitably and wholesomely (without exploiting them as child labour) until such time as the expanding economy can absorb them in work or find the money for more schools.

Some countries have already realized that the problem is beyond the reach of the ordinary leisure-time youth organization, and many African countries have full-time youth services absorbing thousands of young people in disciplined and uniformed corps or brigades, offering a half day's education or technical training for half a day's work on selected development projects such as road building, forest clearance, land conservation and agricultural production. Normally a young person volunteers for two years of such service, but in some countries he may be conscripted. These youth corps are about the most direct and effective means yet devised of dealing with the out-of-school or unemployed, although they are costly and, despite their size, accommodate but a fraction of the number needing this kind of help.

There is still, therefore, a major role for the conventional youth organizations to fill. They have usually accepted that the youth unemployment situation is beyond them. It is an economic issue for the country, not simply a youth problem. On the other hand, for many years they have sought to offer service beyond their customary concern with sports and pastimes. Nearly all such organizations have a motto of service to the community and many of them have related this to modern developmental issues by organizing week-end and holiday work or self-help projects of one kind or another to absorb and challenge their members and to help neighbourhoods and rural communities to improve their conditions of life. Some of the youth organizations have set up special centres, open during the working day, to provide out-of-school and unemployed young people with a place to gather, with sports and games, with informal educational classes and sometimes (by means of generous outside grants) technical training.

There is a need for greater ingenuity in using existing youth organizations to mitigate the situation of the young person who finds himself without schooling or employment. Youth leaders can bring school and parents into close touch or devise informal ways of educating children by the use of the youth club facilities. Youth clubs are often represented on national youth councils and could combine to provide facilities which they might not be able to offer separately. If rural development is the keynote of national development, as it so often is, then young farmers' clubs could be set up to provide full-time activities for the out-of-school youth—a very informal kind of practical education in agriculture. The opportunities abound but a great deal of ingenuity is required to make the best use of available youth services.

The third main way of reaching the out-of-school young person is via the police. Many of these aimless youngsters are on the streets and therefore frequently under the eyes of police officers. Instead of waiting for them to commit offences, it should be possible for police forces to develop special youth branches to follow up and guide such young people; to take them back home if they seem to be in moral danger, or in need of care; to refer them to other social services if their families are not available or do not seem sufficiently interested. Such services already exist in developed countries and one or two countries in Africa have experimented with them (e.g. Zaïre), but rarely on this kind of preventative scale. In America and England the police run their own sports clubs for young people, and as policemen are on shift work, these clubs operate throughout the day and night—thus being available to young people with nothing better to do. There is much to be done in Africa in this way; although the moves already made in this direction are encouraging, much more could be done.

(d) Prevention by Reducing Unemployment

It must be admitted at once that this section has no panacea to offer for the paralysis and disorder of urban unemployment which spreads over the length and breadth of modern Africa. Figures are rarely available: few studies have been made to demonstrate the size of the unemployment problem, but its magnitude and gravity make it the continent's most serious social, economic and political issue.

The two aspects of the problem which concern us most are that the unemployment in modern Africa is primarily urban and predominantly youthful. It is easy to observe that urban unemployment is by no means the only form of labour waste: under-employment in the rural areas is widespread and there is a degree of mobility and instability which detracts from the value and potential of any labour force. Nevertheless, it is, without doubt, the growing concentration of frustrated workless people in the towns which poses the immediate problem—or threat! Moreover, this large scale dislocation of needs and resources bears most grievously upon the young. For by far the greater number of the urban unemployed are school leavers with expectations beyond anything that the economies are, as yet, capable of satisfying. Indeed, on the most hopeful of projections, it is quite apparent that for the rest of this century jobs will not be available of a level to meet the growing expectations of the educated and partially educated body of young people thronging the towns.

There are many reasons given for this structural unemployment. Obviously there is usually some work for all these young people on the land, but so often at unacceptable subsistence or near-subsistence levels—and without the stimulation of urban living. Therefore they stay in towns, each one hoping to become lucky in the employment lottery for the few available places in offices, commerce, schools or the non-manual sections of industry or the public utilities. The educational system, too, has usually aroused expectations beyond reality. Moreover, status attaches to the role of a 'student' waiting for further schooling which is lost once a menial form of employment has been accepted and this keeps many from being employed even when some type of manual work is available.

But the facts are ominous. Even if all the young people returned to the land they would not be able to achieve much more than subsistence levels in those areas where agricultural exploitation of the land involves mechanization and therefore less need for agricultural labour. Secondly, even if the economies industrialized swiftly they would usually have to introduce automation, thus requiring less labour, in order to be competitive on world markets. These two considerations alone hold out little prospect of future openings for any larger labour force either in industry or agriculture in most of the countries of Africa south of the Sahara. These are generalizations, of course, and it would be unwise to regard them as applicable always—but they are not an unfair assessment of the dilemma facing most countries.

Nor can governments hope to escape their quandary by deficit budgeting for development—such as helped Europe and America climb from the trough of depression before the Second World War. For, in those cases, the countries had to stimulate and sustain aggregate demand so as to bring into effective operation the existing industrial plant. To do the same thing, or to attempt to do it, in conditions of economic underdevelopment would be to cripple the economy and to risk runaway inflation, for in such conditions the necessary plant does not exist yet and the means of satisfying any stimulated demand remains to be created. Moreover, unless rigid controls were established, the spending pattern of recipients of government money would be likely to augment the demand for imported goods, aggravating the unfavourable terms of trade, debasing local money values and further increasing inflation. It has to be acknowledged that the kind of structural unemployment which accompanies the growth of towns, industrialization and extended education in the developing areas of the world, is something quite new—a problem for which even the best economists have not yet devised an answer.

From a criminal standpoint the influence of all this is significant, whether or not it be held that unemployment causes crime. The range of frustration, the aimlessness of wandering the streets, the opportunities for urbane deviation or living by one's wits: it would be surprising indeed if these were not intimately connected with the breeding of crime in the towns. It would follow, therefore, that measures to reduce unemployment are part of any country's action to prevent crime. What those measures should be are difficult to speculate on at this particular stage. Clearly, all economic development is, by definition, a diminution of unemployment. But even the most generous investment and the most effective technical improvements take time: it is estimated that Japan remained a primary producer for over thirty years after the absorption of technical aid for industrialization.

Whilst, therefore, unemployment in African countries might be reduced in time by the steps taken to develop the economies generally, it seems certain that this will take more time than these countries can afford. It appears unlikely that they will be allowed to sacrifice a generation—perhaps two generations—before making a substantial impression on the growing army of discontented workless in Africa. General measures to take effect in the long term will not be enough—something will have to be done in the shorter run. The question is still, what?

For some time economists and social scientists with an interest in this problem have been drawing attention to the need to consider much more seriously the possibilities of labour-intensive as against capital-intensive investment. However inefficient this might be in the usual way, there are public works programmes in the forests, mountains or savannah of Africa which might employ manual skills as effectively as machines which need fuel, spares and maintenance (all of which become increasingly difficult to supply as one moves further into the interior), and are not nearly as mobile as human labour where roads and clearings are not there to allow manoeuvrability. It is possible, too, that, to some extent, developing countries might be able to exploit their labour surpluses, either to develop their hinterlands and infrastructure by using full-time labour corps (giving clothing, food, pocket money and technical training in return for work), or by preferring industries which need more labour than machinery.

There are also, as we have already seen, a number of relatively cheap ways of occupying, profitably—and even creatively—the thousands of unemployed youth flocking to or roaming the streets of the emergent towns. All kinds and types of voluntary youth organizations can be grant-aided to undertake schemes for unemployed youth—the founding of co-operative settlements for self-help production, the running of special shelters or hobby or vocational training projects, the development of sports interests and the associating of these young people with a variety of community improvement programmes. Ingenuity will be required, but there is really little excuse for a country doing nothing much for its idle young, leaving them to their own devices until the weaker or more aggressive amongst them are tempted, challenged or forced to act illegally for want of something better to do. Sheer desperation may yet force some countries to become what Churchill once called the 'reserve employer of labour'. There are political as well as social (if not always economic) reasons why they should. Meanwhile, it will remain difficult to discern the more fundamental factors in criminal behaviour in Africa as long as this army of unemployed is growing and its expectations rising beyond all practical possibilities.

(e) Postscript for Adults

Almost the whole discussion so far has been about the prevention of crime amongst young people. The reasons for this focus on youth derive, of course, from future thinking about countries with 60 per cent or more of their populations under twenty-one. Youth is the logical group on which to concentrate preventative attention. It must not be assumed from this, however, that most crimes in Africa south of the Sahara are committed by juveniles or that juveniles form the majority of the continent's offenders. The very opposite is true.

In 1967, the Ghana Police Report showed 46,566 adults as convicted of the different penal offences—but only 336 juveniles. In Togo, in January 1969, there were 328 persons held in the central prison at Lomé: but only eight were minors awaiting trial and the country's only approved school had no more than thirty boys in care—not all of whom had been committed by the courts. Similarly, between 1955 and 1963 in Zambia, with total convictions between 53,300 and 61,163 annually, juvenile convictions rose from under 327 to 2,766—and fell to less than 2,000 three years later.[6]

Certainly, in most African countries juvenile crime showed a significant and, usually, a progressive increase over the years; but so did the total crime rate, and even with crimes most frequently committed by juveniles their share of the total only rarely exceeded 50 per cent, the rest being adults. Thus, although in certain types of crimes in some of the countries there have been quite alarming increases in juvenile offences (for example thefts by juveniles on the Copperbelt in Zambia increased by 60 per cent between 1960 and 1966, and breaking and entering by juveniles went up by 60 per cent in the same years),[7] adults are still responsible for most of the crimes.

However, two facts have to be borne in mind. First, the age division is difficult to draw precisely in Africa without uniform systems for birth registrations. Age for official purposes may often depend upon a good memory or will be assessed by appearance. Secondly, it is equally true that aged criminals are probably rarer in Africa than they are in any other part of the world. It is not usual for criminals over forty to predominate in any area and in Africa their share of the total is very small indeed. Therefore, the majority of delinquents in any country, African or not, are 'young', even if not too young. Moreover, considering the large number who, though now adults, really began their delinquent careers as juveniles, there is ample justification for the concentration on preventative measures for the young.

Nevertheless, no preventative programme can be entirely juvenile or youthful in objective. There must be a need to direct adequate attention to the discouragement of crime amongst older people or promote better standards of conduct amongst adults. If, in turn, this preventative work amongst adults is regarded as a means of reaching *their* children too (if only by example), then it might be rightly considered as being doubly preventative.

Interestingly enough, although the emphasis changes, the preventative measures for adults are remarkably similar to those for juveniles. For instance, early character training and the development of a balanced personality have their obvious relevance for adults via their relevance for younger offenders. So, too, for adults as well as juveniles, education as a means of avoiding crime must rank very high. Whether it be formal education (for instance regular systematic classwork, intensive courses to reach basic levels or to improve qualifications for school drop-outs, or for adults denied schooling in their younger years or for those wishing to add to their attainments), or informal education (for example general knowledge about nutrition, home-making, the use of technical equipment), or vocational training or instruction in public affairs to improve democratic processes, the educational approach is still an important feature of a crime prevention programme for people of nearly all ages. Indeed it has been argued in some states that the entire reformative system for potential and actual delinquents is no more than a form of re-education in the art of living.

By the same token, all the social supports for the family which are so significant in short-circuiting juvenile delinquency, have an aspect of obvious value in inhibiting adult crime of a certain type. Basic relief or social security schemes which protect adults and their families from the sudden interruption of earnings by sickness, disability, unemployment or family crises should also merit a rating as crime preventative in so far as they reduce the amount of crime which could be attributed to insecurity or the need to procure sustenance for dependants. In the same way, better housing, leisure facilities and the development of positive sub-cultures (that is not completely antithetical to the society in which they subsist) are important.

This is the place, too, to consider briefly the need for the maintenance in a society of certain levels of conduct by the cultivation of value standards. This aspect of crime control and prevention should not be excluded simply because it carries moral or even ideological overtones. It is clearly very much more difficult for adults to avoid stealing from work when everyone about them is doing so—and when they are viewed as being abnormal if they don't. It is more difficult to be honest when handling other people's money if there is a tradition, perhaps even an expectancy, of self-interest and dishonesty. In business or professions there is a similar need to foster standards which reinforce whatever may be the legal minima of service to the public. It can be argued that if the practice of dishonesty or other anti-social behaviour becomes widespread, then it is more normal than abnormal, and the law should be adjusted accordingly. Whilst this is true, it is also important to recognize that every law—even the most widely accepted—needs the support of non-legal standards or norms.

Nor should it be overlooked that one does not have to contribute to the idea of absolute rationality in human behaviour to recognize that there are ways of making crimes more difficult to commit or more risky to attempt. A campaign to ensure that motorists lock their cars or install anti-theft devices can make it more difficult to steal a vehicle or borrow one for a joyride. Street lighting in many parts of Africa might be more effective than extra police patrols in reducing robberies, whilst more stringent audit procedures might be more useful than laws in discouraging financial mismanagement and fraud.

The pattern of crime amongst adults, and the types of criminals, are so varied that apart from the broad, population-wide, measures, such as those described above, there are a large number of specific preventative services which arise here as they do in connection with other age groups. Thus, a certain number of offences proceed from mental illness, mental defect or physical abnormalities and most of these call for adequate medical and health provisions for these special cases before there is conflict with the law. Again, a number of adult offenders are in trouble because of the abuse of drugs, alcohol or motor vehicles and such abuse may be prevented as much by licensing, the building of adequate roads and communications and a rational policy on the import, sale and distribution of alcohol or drugs, as by any vigorous police action or penal security.

Finally, in this brief commentary on the prevention of adult crime, consideration must be given to an approach which is less of a prevention than a permission. For some years now there has been pressure in the developed areas of the world for a series of legal reforms which amount to a reduction of a number of actions listed as criminal. This decriminalization of the law has been most notable in the repeal of laws against suicide or attempted suicide, abortion, vagrancy and homosexuality between consenting adults. Naturally, this reduces 'crime' though it does not seek to inhibit the behaviour previously considered as crime.

In Africa, there is also a need to do something for the occasional older person who commits offences, not as part of a continuing pattern of habitual criminality running throughout his life, but as a desperate response to the growing inhospitality of the world about him. To some extent this factor was dealt with above in the general observations on the significance of social security preventatives. But the aged in Africa are a rather special case since many of them belong to the first generation of men who have lived most of their working lives away from their tribes. Traditionally, they should be able to return to their native villages and be assured of care and consideration from the extended family. To earn this kind of protection and maintenance, however, they should have been sharing their earnings over the years with their relatives. Where they have not or could not do this they are not likely to be very welcome as they become dependants. In any case a large number would find it difficult to discover their children or close relatives at the villages since these areas have often been depleted of young people. The older people remaining in the village might not be able to look after yet another of their age group even if they wanted to do so. In addition, the mobility of people within and between towns means that many older people unable to work are often without homes or food and, partly to obtain sustenance, partly to maintain a social status and partly to keep an interest in the world about them, or simply to attract attention, they may be induced to steal, become vagrants, or otherwise act anti-socially or conspicuously break the law.

Throughout Africa, the measures to provide for aged persons in this predicament are only just being taken. Public assistance is more relevant to their predicament as a rule than the limited schemes of social security which might protect the next generation of the aged but are not designed to cover those who have not paid into the schemes over many years. Moreover, special homes and health care are needed—and these are expensive and difficult to provide in areas of under-development. The problem is not yet serious enough to attract public attention but a problem it is; and until solved by long-term social security provisions and short-term allowances and/or institutions for these older people who need them, it will continue to supply society with a small number—but a number difficult to handle—of 'golden age' offenders.

TREATMENT OR RE-INTEGRATION

The fundamental issues underlying the treatment of offenders have not been resolved in any society yet; and the theoretical arguments about deterrence, retribution, reform and efficiency are likely to continue. Justice, effectiveness and humanitarianism are not always combined harmoniously in a given case. Recently, it has been argued by some that treatment is a myth, and that, in any case, society has no right to treat offenders.

In modern times the question of whether to visit crime with vengeance is excluded as a serious possibility—yet when public indignation is roused by outrageous crimes or when insecure political régimes deal ruthlessly with any opposition, it is sometimes difficult to believe that modern man has really outgrown his elementary passion for revenge. Reform is the popular and unchallengeable ideal but it may mean measures which do not even require the formal court appearance and which might be hampered by a committal to prison, whatever the seriousness of the crime committed. As for retribution—punishment to fit the crime—this seems likely to be reinstated if the arguments for treatment—making the sentence fit the offender—are rejected.

All this leads to issues far deeper than can be dealt with here, but in approaching the question of the treatment of offenders it must be acknowledged that much of the difficulty about evolving effective systems anywhere in the world stems from the uncertainty persisting as to the fundamental objectives of the system, that is, deterrence, retribution or reformation. It will be clear for instance, that most traffic or licence or registration offences are dealt with by fines fixed in consideration of the gravity of the charge (retribution) and where the numbers of such cases are large there is little scope for the individualization of treatment (reform). Similarly, as penalties are made more severe in circumstances where it is hoped to discourage certain crimes, the influence of deterrence as an aim of punishment is very clear. Finally, as we have seen, reformative measures, taking into account the situation of the offender and the best hope of improving his conduct for the future, might lead to offenders receiving benefits, in, say, jumping the line of people waiting for employment or in receiving, as prisoners, special forms of training; and this still cannot go too far without a reaction from those who think it unfair to the people who might not have committed crime. In other words, running throughout the treatment systems in nearly every country there is a certain vacillation about the general and specific objectives of penal sanctions—an uncertainty which has its effect upon the actual work.

Historically, the treatment of crime has shifted from death, exile, mutilation or compensation to imprisonment, the suspended sentence, probation, fines and formal admonitions. Some arrangements like 'binding over' to keep the peace or obtaining a surety for future good conduct have ancient roots, and communal penalties (that is punishing a community or kin group from which the offender comes), whilst reaching far back in the human chronicles of the treatment of crime, are not infrequently evoked to meet modern crisis situations, for example terrorist and anti-terrorist campaigns, or where local communities are believed to be shielding outlaws.

Africa has inherited its approach to the treatment of crime from its colonial era. Some prisons now standing were erected in the nineteenth century and the legal systems followed the colonizers as surely as Roman law went with the Legions. Similarly, treatment systems were European in origin and made few concessions to tribal traditions. Customary law was often retained but in the civil more than in the criminal sphere. Here justice often demanded a uniformity of treatment which could not always be guaranteed by local and often varied customs. Moreover, there were practices, such as the killing of witches, which could not be tolerated as a standard for the country as a whole or which were irreconcilable with the ethical and legal standards the colonizers were bringing with them.

Nevertheless, the importation of foreign treatment measures for offenders was often blind to the better and more effective arrangements locally available. Most conspicuously, the immemorial tradition in Africa of seeking to settle a dispute by the offender compensating adequately those he had offended was almost totally neglected in penal matters in favour of modern statutes decreeing fines or imprisonment (benefiting the state but not necessarily the offended). This is not surprising. It even took reformers in the European countries themselves until the 1960s to obtain action to compensate adequately the victims of crimes. Looking back now it can be appreciated that in some respects the customary way in Africa of handling an offence by compensation was in advance of the imported European practice based mainly upon the dignity of the state. Since, however, such compensation in Africa could even apply to murder, it is not difficult to appreciate the early problems of reconciling law and custom.

Independent Africa has had to accept and modify these existing legal and penal systems: but independent Africa has yet to begin devising in earnest an indigenous policy for the treatment of offenders and there is as yet no real evidence of a 'new look' at African penal systems in the light of local conditions, traditions and possibilities.

There are ways in which both law and penal systems could become instruments for the simultaneous development of the country and the better reform of criminals. Instead of being negatively designed to deter from anti-social conduct, legal and penal systems could be devised to promote the kind of behaviour most desired—an important consideration for any country seeking to develop socially and economically. This has been done by countries determined to outlaw racial and religious discrimination, to enforce soil conservation, to encourage self-help or to control migration. At least it has been done so far as the enactment of appropriate laws were concerned—but the sanctions to enforce these laws have been as ever, admonitions, fines, corporal punishment, probation and, in the last resort, imprisonment. Little thought has been given yet to devising penal sanctions to support the aims for which the laws were enacted.

It is in the light of some new approaches to the treatment of offenders in Africa that these various sanctions will be reviewed and examined here. There is a need for the new African nations to find their way back to first principles if they are to devise a penal system both appropriate and constructive in the context of their development needs.

(a) The Legal System

It may seem odd to begin a discussion of the different forms of treatment by a review of the legal system: but criminal law is, after all, the formal cause of crime,[8] and there are many examples in Africa of laws which have multiplied the number of offenders passing through the legal system. Of nine hundred cases dealt with by local courts in Zambia in 1960 only 22 per cent were criminal in the sense of being offences against persons or property: the rest were made up of infringements of all kinds of residence, forestry or other regulations.[9] In Southern Rhodesia, even in the 1950s, the Police Reports found it necessary to make a distinction between 'serious' crime and the rest. Since then technological change, increasing traffic and social mobility everywhere in Africa, has increased the number of minor or technical offences bringing people before the courts and as the range of behaviour covered by legal regulation increases so do the numbers of people passing through the penal system and its institutions—people who have no need of special treatment or else who have a need of more specialized treatment than the penal system can provide.

Decriminalization, that is the removal of the crime label from certain types of behaviour no longer regarded as reprehensible or anti-social, has been dealt with above in connection with crime prevention but its relevance to treatment will need no underlining. Most countries need a regular review of their legal systems to repeal outmoded laws and reduce inconsistencies, in order to prevent the abuse and wastage of their treatment facilities and reformative institutions. These are often filled by people who do not need them.

Another significant link which needs to be forged in an effective treatment system is that between legal provisions and penal facilities. Too often in the past there has been a readiness to enact laws without adequate attention being paid to the capacity of the penal system to deal with the consequences. This is often why prisons become overcrowded, probation caseloads become too large for adequate supervision and guidance; and frequently the reason why the classification of cases for more individual treatment becomes difficult, sometimes impossible. Penal policy and the budget appropriations for penal treatment have to be brought into line. It was not so necessary when large numbers of offences were capital and the offender could be efficiently, inhumanely, disposed of. This situation no longer applies and a reformative system of treatment implies budgeting obligations.

Finally, the question of discretion within the legal and penal systems is important. Where systems are too rigid, the administration of law and the dispensing of justice becomes crude and often inappropriate. Judges are hampered in determining sentences according to the needs of the cases; and committals for offences to certain institutions might become unavoidable as well as irrevocable or beyond adjustment later—even after the objectives of the committal in a given case have been fully achieved. This is, however, a more difficult question than can be examined here since it raises issues of uniformity of treatment and who to really trust in the administration of justice.

The point is, however, that a penal system may be as good—or otherwise—as its legal system will allow it to be and laws and sanctions have to be taken together to obtain a reasonable perspective.

(b) Prisons

Generally speaking, prisons in Africa south of the Sahara tend to be of four main types: (1) old fashioned high security buildings modelled on old European counterparts—but usually with communal rather than individual cells; (2) *ad hoc* collections of huts, chalets or tents, some of the more permanent of which often preceded formal prison buildings and occasionally bid fair to outlive them; (3) camp-type groupings of permanent or temporary buildings set up more recently to provide accommodation and work facilities outside the older and less satisfactory structures; and (4) new farm prisons—usually open and often experimental.

Prisons for offenders are not an entirely Western importation to Africa. Anthropologists and early administrators have described prisons and the practice of incarcerating offenders amongst some of the larger and more politically organized tribes—especially in West Africa. But obviously, to develop in any way prisons needed tribes of both a certain size and of a settled way of life.

Prisons—or the keeping of offenders in forms of custody as a punishment—are hardly relevant to the simplest tribes, for the nearer one is to survival conditions the less time there is to devote to the care and supervision of offenders: they are either correctable (and their offences redeemable by some form of compensation) or they are incorrigible and therefore fit only for exile or the death penalty. To put it another way, if they are regarded as incorrigible or have committed offences not redeemable by compensation then they are dangerous to the survival of others and for this reason more than anything else they have to be removed permanently from society. If the wrong committed is dischargeable by compensation or if the offender can be reinstated, then, even if it be murder, he will not be permanently affected by his crime. In this case attention is concentrated upon providing the victim or his relatives with satisfaction for the wrong committed against them and upon restoring peaceful relations. Once this is done—the debt discharged and the balance of harmony restored—the offender is reabsorbed by society.

Thus, at the simplest levels of existence, any idea of holding the offender as a punishment—depriving him of liberty—does not apply.

It is where there has been conquest by a more powerful people, or where one tribe has gradually extended its domination over a number of smaller peoples, that a more formal system of authority begins to prevail and regular systems of law enforcement and sanctions for non-compliance are introduced. Where offences can now extend to acts or omissions regarded as being against a superior or outside rule (perhaps as well as being contrary to local customary or internal precepts), then the older recourse to compensation and peacemaking may not always be sufficient to satisfy the superior power—and exile or death might be regarded as too extreme. It is in such circumstances that 'prison-type' institutions have been found. However, it should be added that the instances of the use of imprisonment before the arrival of colonial peoples in Africa are few and relatively insignificant for our purposes.

More central to this discussion is the fact that the prisons in Africa, indeed many of the actual buildings still in use, were erected by colonial powers and used to bolster their authority as they imposed their rule throughout vast territories. They reflect the colonial era just as much as law, language, civil service and many of the school systems still do. The Ussher Fort Prison at Accra belongs to the eighteenth century though it has been improved. The Lomé Central Prison was built by the Germans. The Livingstone Prison in Zambia, the Bukavu Prison in Zaïre and the Njabule (Central Buganda) Prison in Uganda are of the same period—although the last named was established, not by the colonial government as such, but by the native Government of Buganda in 1894,[10] doubtless with European advice.

It has not been difficult for experts from developed countries to come to Africa and to find fault with the prisons which have been erected. Even by some of the now outmoded standards, they have not always been impressive. Usually, groups of prisoners are accommodated together and often locked in at night. Not infrequently, there may be no more than two blankets to sleep in—on the concrete or stone floor. Toilet facilities tend to be inadequate and sometimes rather primitive. Security lighting may be of low standard, clothing simplified and prison educational facilities poor. Classification is in very broad categories and prison staff may be untrained or only very partially prepared for their task. However, the conditions frequently complained of in Africa can still be found in the developed countries since many of the problems arise from overcrowding, structural problems or shortage of staff. In August 1969, the Manhattan Detention

Centre, New York, built to accommodate 945 men had over 1,950 inmates![11]

There are the modern prisons of Africa, of course, like the large maximum security prison at Njili in Kinshasa built just before independence, the giant rural farms of Uganda, the army camp-like structure of one-storey buildings at Broken Hill erected in the 1950s or the four modern prisons at Gaberone, Francistown, Lobztsi and Ghanzi. Moreover, Africa has a variety of work-camp expedients which had to be devised by district officers to deal with minor offenders in areas far removed from the more formal processes of law.

Yet, old or new, modified or adapted, it is generally true, in Africa south of the Sahara, that the prison system and the penal thinking behind it usually reflects that of the erstwhile metropolitan powers. There is, as yet, too little evidence of serious attempts to rethink the significance of prisons in the light of African conditions.[12]

Certainly, there were provisions for extra-mural labour in Tanganyika (as early as 1933), Kenya, Lesotho and Botswana and the practice, in one form or another, can be found in other African states. There are examples, too, of rural work centres for prisoners and different forms of detention camps, but these approaches also related to the pre-independence periods in most of the countries concerned and for want of resources have not usually been pursued with vigour by the authorities.

The prison in Africa remains central and crucial to the concept of the treatment of criminals and the frequent recourse to prison sentencing for first offenders, in most of the countries with which we are concerned, attests to its 'popularity' with the courts.[13] Interestingly enough, it is usually those who are concerned with the administration of the prison systems in these countries who complain most of the flow of first offenders or unsuitable offenders which they are expected to receive, and who constantly advocate methods for keeping people (especially women, young people, and possibly the aged or mentally sick) out of prison—or releasing them on a form of parole as soon as possible. Correspondingly, we might note that in England the Prison Administration had reduced 'hard labour' to a superfluous technicality long before the courts stopped using it and it was repealed by law.

Recourse to imprisonment in Africa is not, however, so much a desire to punish an offender by segregation as it is a reflection of the failure so far to devise suitable alternatives. The use of corporal punishment has been declining and though it has more recently been fostered by the Minimum Sentences Act of Tanganyika[14] it seems unlikely to survive for very much longer. In most areas of Africa it is already very largely restricted in application to juvenile offenders. Any vast extension of probation, supervised work, or parole depends upon the covering of great distances by larger numbers of staff than the relative importance of crime might justify. Fines, of course, are often regarded as insufficient to register public dissatisfaction, or they are self-defeating when the offender is not earning—and they are not nearly as popular with those offended as the straightforward payment of compensation.

While there is undoubted scope for experimentation in adapting the penal systems of Africa to something more locally appropriate and less dependent upon prisons, the poverty of most countries south of the Sahara makes it difficult to envisage alternatives on a genuinely country-wide basis. With national incomes so very low the first moves (in the larger countries, at any rate) may have to be limited and localized. Thus, the fact that extra-mural labour schemes have not always extended into rural areas has not been due to the unwillingness to use this in preference to prison but to the absence of an administrative structure to supervise and guide it. Having public work departments, or having district officers who can find gardening work or forest clearing, is not enough.

There is a need to devise ways of using penal labour which would otherwise be wasted in imprisonment in the systematic development of the country. This means not the *ad hoc* or haphazard use of people offered for a short time by a court which does not want to send them to prison, but a scheme which absorbs each one automatically and gives him a place and a creative role in the building of his own nation. Such projects are not always easy to work out for entire territories but the usefulness of working out a variety of small local schemes should not be under-estimated.

There is an interesting aspect of this which might have inhibited experimentation with extra-mural labour schemes so far. The International Labour Organization and many of its member states have signed conventions against the use of forced labour. Obviously, forced labour is reprehensible to the concept of democracy, but there is a vast difference between this and the *bona fide* provision of extra-mural labour as a substitute for imprisonment. The first is a device to invade liberty; the second a way to preserve it as long as possible even when it has been forfeited or jeopardized by a breach of the penal law.

In the development of modern Africa, it is skilled labour which is needed most. Where this is available from people who would otherwise be imprisoned it should be used. Furthermore, it might sometimes be possible to break down the separate processes in skilled work in such a way that they can be taught quickly and effectively to men sentenced to extra-mural labour.

Extra-mural labour is not the only way of avoiding the over use of imprisonment, however. It should not be difficult, even with the present limited resources, to make greater use of fines, compensations, probation, detention centres or attendance centres and parole in preference to incarceration. This will be argued in the consideration below of each of the measures. Here the problem is how to deal with those who are likely to find their way to prison even though these other penalties are in full use.

Perhaps reality demands that every country should have at least one maximum security institution for the apparently irredeemable recidivists or the specially dangerous offenders. In Africa, however, the nature of crime and the possibilities within the countries make it possible that, given the resources for the staff and facilities, it might be possible to develop prison systems composed of smaller, more scattered, carefully classified, mobile camps adapted to the development needs of the nation, as well as being more appropriate to the individual needs of those taking this kind of retraining for a return to the community.[15] Road maintenance companies, road building units, fishing camps, harvesting camps, co-operative farming squads or settlements, mechanical aid units for village self-help projects and low cost housing teams are examples. The variation covers a wide range but to be effective and workable the scheme would have to be flexible with teams coming into and going out of existence according to the needs of the country and the capacities of the offenders likely to be available for the work. It would certainly involve more personnel per offender than are now employed. There would have to be a special organization for working up the schemes, listing future needs and devising services from the prisoners available. There would have to be special liaison men with the ministries or agencies, official or unofficial, in the country likely to be needing the assistance that the prison service (or should it be called the 'rehabilitation' or 're-integration' service?) can give. Technical instruction would have to be provided by craftsmen employed by the prison services to work alongside the offender. And qualified group leaders might have to be provided to develop the community aspects of each camp. It might cost more in recurrent expenditures but capital costs should be less than with larger prisons and there should be fewer problems about expanding or reducing the service as necessary.

The effect of all this might be to provide a country with an adaptable, dynamic, mobile type of prison service in place of the static and relatively staid system of immovable real estate. It would be far less secure than the older pattern and therefore some risks would have to be accepted by the authorities as well as the community. There would always be one central maximum security prison in any case for those individuals with whom no risks can afford to be taken. Escapes from the more numerous, smaller camps would be easier, however, and the emphasis would be on the challenge and variety of the work providing the necessary assurance that offenders would become integral parts of the teams with which they would be working—and so would be ultimately prepared for their release into the community after sentence.

This major structural change in the prison system in Africa does not exclude the additional development of the modern services for gradually returning prisoners to the community such as those which have been developed recently in the United States, Sweden, England and Belgium—to mention only a few of the countries experimenting. Half-way houses from which prisoners can be allowed to accept regular jobs in the community before their release; week-end imprisonment to cut down the number of short sentences otherwise likely; attendance centres to interfere with leisure time by requiring regular reporting to police stations or other public centres for periods of work or training; detention centres designed to apply short, sharp training bouts; permission for wives to spend time with husbands in prison and vice-versa, and home leaves—some of these are already being applied in African states and could be extended.

One thing which experience has already made very clear in Africa is that effective prison work depends upon effective after-care and parole. Generally speaking, this has been lacking in African countries for the reasons already given—the vastness of the territory to be covered and the limited resources to spare for nation-wide probation and parole services. Nevertheless, parole and after-care services have been applied on a considerable scale in some countries with excellent results. The distances and disproportionate costs make it unlikely that uniformly applicable systems staffed by full-time professional workers throughout will be feasible in many places. Thus, the full scale exploitation of parole and after-care work in Africa awaits the invention of a system which mobilizes some of the existing facilities, services and means of communication for new ends. This might mean teachers acting as voluntary supervisors, local government officers as after-care officers on a part-time or voluntary basis; perhaps even the use of headmen or traditional chiefs as agents of regional professional officers. It seems certain, however, that for such a scheme drawing in so many diverse interests for a common cause, there will have to be a variety of forms of specialized training for those who are going to become involved. There is a great deal to be said for the use of voluntary or lay services to extend penal and correctional work and to provide the background of community-based services which are necessary: but this does not suggest that responsibilities of this kind can readily and without preparation be laid on the shoulders of people untrained and unprovided for the kind of thing that they will be expected to do. On the other hand training of this kind can be given if there is sufficient interest and sufficient finance available. It can be given in evening courses or in intensive sessions in the more remote areas by mobile teams. Whole populations can be educated in the need by means of suitable radio or television programmes.

The effort is well worth while. The cost of present prisons in any country greatly exceeds the cost of community alternatives of this kind. It is apposite that as this is written the prison systems in the Western world appear to be moving into a state of crisis. Apart from the quelling of the prison riot at Attica in New York State where hostages were held and so many persons killed in the action to restore order that the country was thrown into a turmoil of reform consciousness, there was the subsequent killing of hostages at Clairvaux prison in France and reports of disturbances from a number of other countries. Even in Sweden, so long famed for its progressive approach to corrections and for its realistic approach to the needs of prisoners, there is a call for more attention to be given to this question.

There are a great many factors at work. Certainly there have been years of talk about rehabilitation in some places without realization in practice except perhaps for a minority of the inmates. Certainly the overcrowding has accentuated the problem as crime has been rising and the police and courts have sent more to prison either on conviction or to await trial. But also in several countries the ex-offenders themselves have organized for political and social action to induce reform encouraged by the new evidence of the effectiveness of confrontation politics for minorities. And political activists of various persuasions have sometimes deliberately resorted to crime either to 'beat the system' or show their contempt for it—or both. When imprisoned they have frequently assumed leadership of the prisoners to campaign for their rights. Not infrequently political opportunists from outside have seized the opportunity to use prisoners or ex-offenders for their own ends, exploiting the genuine public interest in the need for reform. It would be shortsighted not to observe that prisons are always a kind of exaggerated version of the life outside, and the clash of values outside some of the Western prisons is highlighted inside. Clearly there are abuses and it is not difficult to make the case for reform. Since 1955 the United Nations' Standard Minimum Rules for the Treatment of Prisoners have been available to member countries but frequently they have been ignored. In 1967 when the Secretary-General called for reports on their implementation only forty-four countries replied and of these there were many with acknowledged difficulties in applying the rules.

Naturally therefore, the tendency is to go for more community-based schemes. Everywhere the evidence seems to be accumulating that the prison has failed to improve inmates and the recidivist rate in many countries is rising: the aim becomes simply to avoid a prison making a person worse if it cannot make him better. So, half-way houses from which a prisoner can take ordinary jobs, leaves or furloughs so that he can go home from time to time, conjugal visits from his wife, early parole and more probation are fostered. Naturally, as more men or women qualify for this general release to community care the remainder in prison are the hard core who cannot be released and who are extremely difficult to handle. Now they are without the leavening of the better types of offenders, and more than ever the prison houses the violent, the psychopathic, the seriously disturbed and the dangerous. More than ever it needs to have the maximum security conditions that are so much in disrepute. More and more the guards or wardens need to be persons of high quality—but at the same time the work becomes less and less attractive except for the very dedicated.

In this kind of situation the need for good quality community care for the majority of offenders is self evident. Prison must be a last resort and a wider variety of community programmes are necessary with a diversity of sanctions which do not involve imprisonment. This means shifting resources in a developing country to the community based schemes before the troubles in the prisons begin—and in the developed countries it means not losing any more time. For the prisons which will have to remain there must be high quality personnel with the best training it is possible to provide. For both sides of the situation the flow of better trained personnel for institutional and non-institutional treatment has to be assured. In this way the recourse to imprisonment can be reduced to a minimum and the prisons can become more effective and efficient in the work which they have to do.

Finally, it should be mentioned that basic humanitarian conditions for offenders have no necessary relevance to the reformative or rehabilitative efficiency of a prison or community programme. As a matter of basic civic or human rights it is necessary for certain standards to be maintained in institutions and in the administration of justice generally. This is true whether or not these conditions help or hinder reformation or rehabilitation. Perhaps harsh and inhuman treatment is an effective deterrent; but whether it is or not it cannot be used if human dignity is to be preserved. Perhaps good conditions for prisoners make rehabilitative training programmes more difficult to administer; even so they are necessary to keep a sufficient standard of civilization in our treatment of offenders. Most of those who share correctional ideals believe that it is possible to combine good conditions with successful programmes of rehabilitation. In nearly every case, however, this means incarcerating a person for as short a time as possible. And this is a lesson which Africa can learn while there is still an opportunity to choose directions.

(c) Other Institutions

Borstals, approved or reform schools and centres of re-education are widely used in Africa and mean rather different things according to the laws and concepts of the different countries. Most are intended, however, as devices for keeping the young offender out of prison and providing him with a constructive and educational régime to fit him more effectively for life outside. Some deal with older youths, others with the younger elements. Only a few countries have corresponding facilities for women and girls, preferring to use *ad hoc* alternative institutions (convents, schools, homes, etc.) for the few who become delinquent, and having separate sections of the prisons for the small number of serious or hardened offenders of the fair sex.

The history of the majority of these institutions goes back to the Second World War and the immediate post-war years, but there are notable exceptions. We learn that Kenya's Reformatory School was established in 1909, that fifty-nine boys were sent there in its first four years and that it really began its improved operations from the early thirties after a Crime Committee had reported on its 'unsatisfactory atmosphere'.[16] Ghana had a Boys' Home at Ada from 1929 run by the Salvation Army,[17] and Ethiopia's Training School and Remand Home was set up in 1942.[18]

Such evidence as is available would appear to indicate that these institutions have had very beneficial effects upon the incidence of crime and the degree of recidivism amongst younger offenders. Where trade training and education is a feature of these centres they frequently provide a preparation for work and personal advancement which is not nearly so readily available to the general public. Indeed, some people have complained that institutions of this type do too much for the delinquents and that they may actually be encouraging crime amongst young people unable to obtain such fine training facilities outside. It is very doubtful whether this is true. It is an argument which has been heard in most countries whenever the conditions for prisoners or convicted persons were improved. It is a reaction typical of the difficulty of making the transition from a punitive approach to incarceration to a reformative approach; and the claim that better conditions or prospects actually increase crime—or induce people outside to try to get inside—has never been substantiated.[19] Nevertheless, the question of justice arises whenever the conditions or opportunities being offered not only match but exceed those for the population as a whole. In Africa, this is particularly relevant in countries where there may be thousands of law-abiding young people with no chance at all of getting to school. It is extremely unlikely that they would deliberately commit crime to get the training, if only because they cannot be certain that they would be given this kind of sentence. It seems unjust, nevertheless, if their law-abiding conduct actually places them in a less favourable position for employment and advancement than those who are convicted of offences.

As other countries have found, there is really no answer to this apart from avoiding the contrast between the inside and outside becoming too obviously unfair. For no matter how bad the conditions in the institutions there will always be some people outside living in worse; and keeping conditions to a minimum will do nothing to reform, however much it may satisfy the public feeling for revenge or retribution. From a slightly different angle there is always the possibility that with education at such a premium in Africa the lack of stigma attached to the receiving of vocational training in a penal institution or re-educational centre may contribute to a reduction in the rate of recidivism.[20]

Whilst Africa is rather a special case and the arguments and philosophies of Europe may not fit, it would appear that there is a strong case for pressing on with the development of these special establishments for young or special offenders and for making them as effective as circumstances allow in terms of equipment, training facilities and education. It should not be overlooked that in the case of younger 'delinquents' sent to these schools, many of them are only there because of domestic neglect and for very minor offences. A good number are at the schools simply because there was nowhere else that they could be sent. In these circumstances there is little in the unfairness argument. There is very little 'criminality' in the sense of any serious or largely irredeemable conditions and it would be an obvious improvement if schools of this kind could be available to such people in trouble *before* conviction or a finding of guilt and not afterwards. This comment of course does not apply to countries which have removed criminal liability from minors under eighteen, but it is still true that it would be better to have such schools available to young people in difficulties before they had to be considered as being in need of 're-education'. However, there are a number of countries which allow young people to be sent to such schools without having to go through the courts (see the example of Togo given above) and this is a degree of flexibility which should be retained.

Practically everywhere in Africa these 'alternatives to imprisonment' seem to have done rather well. But this may be a superficial judgement and a great deal more needs to be done in the way of evaluation and follow-up studies. In any general consideration of crime prevention it can only be recommended that institutions of this kind be continued, improved, extended, varied, and as far as possible integrated into the national drive for economic and social progress. These centres, properly conceived and managed, can succeed not merely in preventing crime and the worst effects of family disruption amongst the young but can also reduce the flow to prisons and provide the country with a pool of capable, well trained and efficient manpower for greater positive achievements.

(d) Probation and Parole

Probation, meaning in its essential sense the opportunity for a person to prove himself, probably has a larger and more venerable place in the chronicles of African customary law than can ever be proved.

There may be little direct evidence of its use down the years, but since in most of the world's legal systems the practice of sending an offender (especially a first or young offender) back to his kin or guardians or superiors—often with an injunction that he be supervised and kept out of trouble in future—may be traced to early times, it would be unusual to find something different in Africa. Moreover, long familiarity with such a practice is suggested by the fact that in modern customary courts in Africa this is a procedure still regularly followed, once an order for compensation (for any damage done) has also been made.

As a specifically enacted form of written law, probation, which received full statutory recognition in America and Europe towards the last quarter of the nineteenth century, reached South Africa first (in 1906) with a legal provision for the conditional release of first offenders. Then the Prisons and Reformatories Act (No. 13 of 1911) gave the Governor-General of South Africa the power to frame regulations *inter alia* for the conditional release of convicts and prisoners. As promulgated some time later, these regulations provided for the appointment of probation officers and set out the duties of such offenders in connection with persons whose sentences had been suspended, with prisoners who had been conditionally released and with children and juveniles.

In fact, the voluntary use of probation, according to the models established by religious societies in Europe and America, had been practised in South Africa before this time. There being no provision for a 'bind over' procedure in Roman/Dutch law, it was not until 1914 that the practice was formally linked with the device of the suspended sentence (Act. No. 40 of 1914). Of course, it will be appreciated that at this period in South Africa, before and during the First World War, the written law applied mainly to Europeans and there were vast areas of the country, as well as millions of people, relatively unpoliced and subject mainly to customary laws and sanctions.

Elsewhere in East, West and Central Africa, probation as a statutory instrument for the treatment of offenders was introduced from the metropolitan countries rather late in the colonial era. Even then, the legal provisions were sometimes ahead of the services to implement them. In Zambia, for example, a legal provision for probation for first offenders can be traced to 1933 (Criminal Procedure Code Cap.

7. 5. 287 (1)) but a separate probation ordinance permitting a more general use of the system did not appear on the statute book until 1953, and not until 1955, when probation officers had been appointed, did it come into operation. There were still many areas of the country which were excluded from the provisions of the probation ordinance up to independence because of the shortage of probation officers.

In Kenya, the Probation of Offenders Ordinance (Cap. 64) was enacted in 1943: in Tanganyika and Uganda in 1948. In Sierra Leone the Probation Act was No. 19 of 1950. In francophone countries the introduction of special measures for minors and an extension of *liberté surveillée* belongs to the same post-war years.

These were occasions for the upsurge of measures for juveniles—and especially for the invoking of probation in the years during and after the Second World War. And most of these flowed from the increasing urbanization in Africa. It was generally the young people who flocked into the towns, some to take up work, some to find schooling, others to escape the confines of traditional ways of living. Many were without families and homes. As they appeared on the streets and committed offences they came before the courts in such numbers and with such frequency that it was soon clear that the older sanctions of a fine, corporal punishment or imprisonment did not apply.

They could not pay fines—and often were out of touch with relatives who might have been liable to fines for their young peoples' misdemeanours. Imprisonment was obviously to be avoided since the provisions for the segregation of juveniles were frequently inadequate and contamination was certain. Corporal punishment was widely applied but often ineffectually. One doctor in Central Africa charged with the task of examining young persons before sentences of caning were carried out, found the marks of previous canings so often that he eventually left to take further studies in forensic psychiatry.

Moreover, the cases of juvenile offenders were increasingly examples of child neglect and the lack of care and education rather than real delinquency. There were no extended child care services to cope with these and the traditional methods of dealing with crime were more likely to perpetuate the wrong-doing than to prevent it in the future.

It was in these circumstances that, casting around for other solutions, the various governments in Africa hit upon the need for special schools for reform or re-education and upon probation to prevent the need for institutional treatment at all. It was in this period that Africa received its first professional social workers and probation officers from Europe who began to train their African counterparts.

The results have been promising. Nearly everywhere in Africa where probation has been tried the results have been similar to those obtained with probation in the states of America and the countries of Europe. Roughly 70 per cent of those placed on probation do not offend again during the period of the probation order. The meaning of such statistics has yet to be probed however. The very fact that they are so similar in dissimilar cultures suggests that they may be a function of the probation structure itself. If the pattern of treatment is foreign to a group of people it is at least possible that the results are foreign too. The test would be to follow up the cases for years after the completion of the supervision, but this is very difficult to do in Africa. Nor has it been possible yet to produce in-depth studies of probation work in action in cultures other than in the West.

The geographical problems still abound. Hardly any country can be said to have a probation system applied uniformly throughout the nation. Sometimes the laws are so designed that probation is suitable to the courts only where—and when—the trained staff have been appointed. In other countries the law applies everywhere in principle but in practice it is limited to urban areas where the staff are available to supervise offenders. In still a few countries there is no probation to speak of simply because the personnel to implement it does not yet exist.

There are some other problems. The systematic, individualized type of social case work characteristic of probation in Western nations does not apply naturally in Africa. Here confidentiality is sometimes suspect in a group and the best form of social work to ensure an offender's reabsorption by his peers might be that in which group skills and community services are much more in evidence. Again, the probation *relationship* is a different entity in countries where all paid officials are government officials and the officer's status (and influence) is reflected by his position in the government hierarchy. Thirdly, the probation officer in Africa does not have the range of social services behind him which have nearly always been his support in Western countries. The poor law, the houses for homeless, the special treatment for alcoholics or epileptics, the special institutions for children and the refuges for the aged, have from the nineteenth century provided a background for probation work in America or Europe. In Africa, probation is being tried where nearly all of the other services are either non-existent or still very rudimentary. Instead the older social supports and controls of the extended family apply, but where these may be ineffective, as in many urban situations, the probation officer needs to show imagination and resourcefulness of no small order to cope with the varied and acute social needs of his clients—needs which may be shared by thousands of others who have not committed offences.

It is for reasons such as these that the probation system as it applies to Africa needs careful and constant review in the years to come. There are some fundamental questions still to be answered such as the extent to which probation really applies to the indigenous scene in modern Africa; the relevance of the assumptions and values of Western social work; and the role of the probation officer himself—as a court official, independent government official with social service responsibilities broader than probation, or as a community guide or leader. There are some lesser issues to be resolved: how to extend probation throughout the country; whether to use volunteers or appoint other local officials on a part-time basis; whether to experiment with probation without supervision, and what periods of supervision are likely to be the most effective. There is a need for better communications and links between towns, and between towns and rural areas, to ensure the coverage necessary with highly mobile probationers—or simply to obtain the information which courts need as part of a pre-trial investigation—or maybe to link an offender with his family. This problem of communications which might have been a major difficulty a few years ago should now be amenable to solution by means of short-wave radios where telephone connections are inadequate. It could, of course, be used for social purposes far wider than probation.

The better use of probation, its extension and improvement, is a fundamental part of any plan in Africa to adopt and redirect the penal system to fit local and modern conditions. The trend everywhere is to keep offenders out of prisons, to deal with them in community and to release them as soon as possible if they should have to go to prison. The key to reforms of this kind is obviously a strong, flexible and efficient probation system which could also serve as a parole system and provide an after-care service for several institutions (even mental institutions). It is important therefore to explore the issues connected with the most effective functioning of probation as soon as possible so that it can be expanded to become the basis for a new approach to penal methods.

There is a real sense in which the new approaches to the treatment of offenders for which most of the industrialized countries seem to be striving are natural and already basic to the way of life of most people in Africa. Here it has always been traditional to rely upon the community—and in particular upon each kin group within the larger society—to preserve order, encourage conformity and to reform those of its members who misbehaved or seemed inclined to do so. As in every other part of the world this involvement of the community has tended to decline over the years with the concentration of urban populations and mass living in industrial or commercial centres. Nevertheless the basic family structure remains and kin or group solidarity is much more a fact of social and economic life in Africa than in the West. This is why some form of probation and/or parole system is the logical base from which to begin building a penal structure appropriate to African conditions—and why Africa begins with real advantages in the movement to involve the community in the treatment of the problem.

The question is, of course, what kind of probation and parole is most suitable to the African situation? Some indications of the direction in which it might be possible to proceed can be obtained from the experience of probation and parole systems in both industrialized and developing countries. For example, it seems reasonably well established that the vital period of any order for supervision is the first six months. Often if the first six months are completed successfully the rest of the supervision period will be covered satisfactorily. It is possible therefore to provide for a greater turnover of cases with a reasonable hope of nearly the same degree of success by making probation or parole orders for a period of six months only. There are aspects in which this is not really satisfactory, of course, but it would be a way of making the most economical use of scarce resources.

Secondly, with such large areas to cover, it is clear that developing countries cannot really afford the professional staffs which would be necessary to extend the system extensively. The point would quickly be reached at which a probation officer or parole officer would be spending the greater part of his time travelling and only a fraction of it on the actual work for which he is appointed. Moreover, in terms of national priorities it is unlikely that the probation system would be sufficiently important to warrant the expenditure it would incur. This being so, the alternatives are clear—either to limit the use of probation to selected areas in which trained and professional officers can operate effectively without too much travelling, or to extend the system in a form which would require only a minimum of the time and attention of professional staff. The first approach has usually been the one adopted up to now; but if probation/parole is really to be made the backbone of a future community-based penal structure then it seems impossible to avoid the need to experiment with a less professional but more extended form of probation. This need not mean that the training of those to be responsible for an extended service needs to be abandoned. Short training courses and mobile training teams are part of the total operation. It does mean part-time probation officers and probably incorporating local government services. It probably means paying by the time actually spent in supervision or giving some kind of honorarium for the additional work. Finally, where local officials are too busy with their own work to accept additional commissions or this kind it might mean using the older people who might otherwise have little or nothing to do. The fact that some of them might still be illiterate should not inhibit their use at this period of development: they could still be valuable aides to centrally placed professional officers.

It is not usual in a discussion of this kind to raise the question of using the police for probation work. Normally, their law enforcement duties are thought to exclude them from consideration. It is thought that they would not be able to win the confidence of offenders and there would be a conflict of interests where they have to prosecute infringements of the law and help people to reform. It is assumptions of this kind which developing countries should be prepared to challenge, however. Undoubtedly the reservations are well founded and the possibility of a conflict of roles is very real. On the other hand, the modern efforts to bring the police into close touch with the community plus the many recorded instances of police officers helping to keep offenders out of trouble, as well as the success of some juvenile liaison services by which police seek to avert court action, all imply that there may be something to be said for experimentation where the police are the only ones with time and facilities for the kind of supervision required. Once again special training would be necessary and greater discretion would need to be vested in the individual officer. Certainly his power would be extended and he would have to be trained for the new role. There would be little point in setting up new specialized probation departments within the police departments, however, since this would defeat the object of involving the ordinary policeman in probation or parole work.

It is a difficult concept to elaborate and only a trial and error approach would reveal its limitations and its potential. But the idea of using the police for reform as well as law enforcement should not be ruled out simply because it has seemed to be out of the question in the more developed or more industrialized countries.

Finally, the work of probation officers need not be as individually direct as it has been in the industrialized countries. Even those countries are moving more and more towards community organization and towards reaching the individual effectively via his community or group relationships. In Africa this is a requirement for any effective probation work as we have already seen. It arises here because it also affects the administrative or organizational structure of the probation service itself. It is not enough to indicate that group workers might be more relevant to the African situation than case workers. There is a need to consider just how indirectly the profession of group workers might function so as to extend their influence more widely. Here the status, prestige and role of the part-time, voluntary or other type of probation extension worker has to be taken into account. In looking for valuable persons to extend probation as a means of keeping people out of trouble it might be wise to look not only for official status in the community but also for the natural leadership which is to be found in any small group or community. It might be possible to conceive of probation as a movement more than a service—with its local volunteer or partly-paid leaders and with probationers grouped for various kinds of public service. After all, special holiday camps for probationers have proved effective in England and elsewhere and some of the most dramatic reforms have been the work of organizations relying heavily on volunteers such as Alcoholics Anonymous. Elements of these experiences could well be carried over to the developing countries of Africa where it would seem that the local climate is favourable.

(e) Fines and Compensation

It will already be clear that compensation is and will continue to be the penalty most relied upon by African countries. Not only is it the traditional form of disposal for civil and many criminal wrongs committed; it is a procedure too long neglected (in fact if not in principle) by the industrialized countries—and one to which they are now returning. Canada has recently (1969) expanded a 1967 Ontario law providing for aid to persons killed or injured whilst helping a police officer to include victims of crime who were not engaged in helping the police. Similar laws are already in force in Newfoundland, Saskatchewan and Alberta. New York State has had a Compensations Board for victims of violent crimes since 1967 and England had also enacted a measure of this type.

There is, however, a fundamental difference between these modern statutes and the traditional use of compensation. In the immemorial tradition it is the offender or his kin who are responsible for compensating the victim. Whilst this power for a court to order restitution to be paid by the offender to his victim remained in the older laws and could be enforced by civil suit, or sometimes more effectively by the criminal court making the order, in practice this measure was not always used and it was rendered worthless in many cases by the penury of the offender or his skill in placing his possessions in the names of others who could not be reached by any order for the seizure of property to discharge the debt. Modern statute laws for compensation therefore meet this problem by transferring the burden from the offender to the community. Compensation is paid out of public funds.

It is doubtful whether this transfer of responsibility would meet African conceptions of the way to deal with offenders. On the other hand, the effectiveness of the compensation system as it has survived in Africa depends upon the kinship pattern of social life. Here too it was often likely that the offender could not pay, but his relatives then had to shoulder the burden—and it was unlikely that the offender would be able to shrug off his obligations to them. As urban living spreads and populations converge on the large centres, as families become more scattered and informal social controls become less effective, it is altogether likely that compensation will become more difficult to implement without recourse to public funds or to some alternatives to the kinship system. Even so it may be questioned whether the offender being unable to pay it is proper to consider his punishment a reform unrelated to the damage he has done. It would seem good sense to seek a penal structure of a kind which would allow an offender to work off his debt to the person offended. Where this is tied to halfway houses for the semi-release of prisoners so that they can earn a living to pay such compensation, there would be a continuation of the traditional principle of compensation

Fines are also likely to continue in Africa but they are rather more difficult to rationalize. On the one hand, they are distinctly retributive—calculated amounts which one must pay for the different kinds of wrongdoing. They can be increased to determine proportions, however, when it becomes necessary to discourage certain offences; and, as a rule, the law allows fines to be combined with other penalties.

On the other hand, fines are really only appropriate as penalties for those able to pay them. This has both negative and positive implications. To impose a fine on a destitute offender is only to delay his imprisonment in default—or to introduce the acceptance of long delays in payment and a form of debt collecting which brings the law into disrepute. When properly applied to those able to pay, however, fines can make law enforcement quite profitable.[21]

Where the imposition of fines has been used as a means of raising revenue, the monies received being paid into state or local treasuries, there are obvious dangers of a vested interest in law enforcement and it might even be argued that crimes are needed to help finance the services necessary to prosecute them.

Fines have nearly always been associated with reparation to authority for disregarding orders. They emerged in Europe as a form of atonement for the breach of the peace or order which had been decreed by the king, the prince, the lord or other ruler of the area within which the offence had been committed. Even if the damage done had been made good and the victim fully satisfied by compensation, the outrage to authority which the offence implied had still to be vindicated.

The earliest traces of fines in Africa have a similar rationale. They were associated first with the early kingdoms in which one tribe had domination over other tribes and imposed penalties over and above the compensation which a local customary court might award in order to underline its authority and to discourage offences which might appear to question its power.

Fines appear to make little sense to the African victim of a crime or his relatives—particularly if they are not accompanied by a form of compensation. Many of the misunderstandings in colonial days arose from the practice of district commissioners (who acted as magistrates) imposing fines or imprisonment without adequate attention to the need for compensation in minor criminal cases. Treating the offender was not treating the situation as it appeared to those involved.

(f) Juvenile Courts and Administrative Tribunals

There are still one or two countries without adequate legal facilities for the separate treatment of young offenders. Most of Africa understands, however, that some such screening device or system has to be provided within the criminal justice system so as to separate out the younger offenders for study and special treatment. This is the most logical way of rationalizing the criminal justice system in any country. It is the best way to reduce prison populations.

In most countries, however, the juvenile court system has been hampered by not having sufficient probation officers or social workers available to collect the background information required for more judicious disposal of the cases. Most countries have not yet been able to provide the juvenile court judges or magistrates with the range of treatments and methods needed to ensure individual and specialized treatment of the cases. Usually there are inadequate facilities for medical or psychiatric examinations when the whole country is taken into account. In some places there is still a great need to train the judges and magistrates for their specialized work with young offenders. More consideration of some of these problems with the present juvenile court system provides indicators for future developments. Moreover it should not be forgotten that in the highly industrialized countries, where welfare has so often taken priority over the ordinary machinery of the law, it has sometimes been found necessary to introduce a better system of legal representation for the young offender to protect his rights. His welfare alone has frequently justified unjust treatment. 'Juvenile justice' rather than 'juvenile delinquency' is a modern preoccupation in some developed countries.

There is nothing wrong with the juvenile court system in Africa which the allocation of more resources could not overcome. However, there is a need for a series of studies to show exactly how these courts are working and to compare the advantages of the different approaches. In some countries the juvenile court is no more than the regular judge or magistrate for the area hearing the cases of children and youths at a different time or place. In other areas the juvenile court judge becomes not only a specialist in handling the juvenile cases but he takes a regular interest in the reformative methods in use and becomes a leader and an instigator of improvements in the system. There are places where the juvenile judge or magistrate sits alone and other areas where, by law, he is required to sit with lay assessors. Sometimes lay judges have been appointed who have a special interest in children and young people. An area of criminological interest as yet practically untouched by the investigators is the reaction of the young people dealt with by these tribunals to the system under which they are being dealt with. There have been few studies of attitudes to the courts, the police or the judges, and it is possible that much of the work being done for young people is based on assumptions about what they need or require which may be far from the facts. In his study of such attitudes in Zambia in 1964, the writer found no differences between delinquents and non-delinquents in their attitudes to crime generally, to the police or to the courts, but this needs wider validation. A better knowledge in this area might enable the courts to adjust more effectively to the situation they are trying to handle.

Again, the juvenile courts of Africa are based nearly everywhere on Western patterns. It could well be that there is scope for experimentation in Africa with courts more immediately attuned to the local customs and ways of thinking. It may be that better use could be made of the elders and symbols of traditional authority (or of the newer educational or political symbols of authority) to invest the juvenile courts with greater relevance for the local scene. These, however, are refinements: usually the juvenile courts are working reasonably well and simply need to be better supported as soon as the resources become available.

If one is thinking of keeping people out of prisons and avoiding the stigma of the criminal justice label, there is virtue in examining the extent to which administrative tribunals can take over some of the work of the courts. Traffic offences immediately come to mind, and Germany has very recently decriminalized traffic offences (except the most serious). This means a separate courts' arrangement but it relieves the criminal courts of a burdensome duty and the unnecessary labelling of many otherwise law-abiding citizens.[22]

In Africa, the customary courts, urban and rural, have often acted in a sense as administrative tribunals, and there may be areas where this kind of approach could be developed. For, although they frequently have a criminal jurisdiction to deal with minor offences, these courts do not carry a criminal stigma and could still be accorded rather more flexibility. Japan and certain other countries have established special family courts to ensure that domestic cases can receive more considerate attention and are less rigidly invested by the law. In Africa the customary courts have again frequently performed this function and it might be possible to develop the theme. Finally, tax offences have helped to fill some of the African penal institutions with persons who might be defaulters but were not criminal in the usual sense. Here again special tribunals with appropriate powers could help to relieve the congestion.

It will be seen that this consideration of the courts and the ways in which they might be augmented or varied to reduce the flow of persons into penal establishments is another move towards a greater measure of decriminalization which has been discussed above. The snag is, that however varied these methods, the ultimate sanction for all such administrative or 'extra-legal' measures has still to be imprisonment, unless a suitable alternative can be found. With corporal punishment and other harsh methods reduced or prohibited the dependence upon the prison tends to increase. Africa, like so many other areas of the world, is seeking variations on the imprisonment theme which will enable it to deal more effectively with the problems which are increasing with urbanization.

PREVENTION AND TREATMENT BY IMPROVED ECONOMIC AND SOCIAL CONDITIONS

Ever since crime began to attract scientific attention, it has been thought that improved levels of living would serve to reduce crime rates. Even those most inclined to play down the environmental factors in crime have rarely denied them a limited influence. For administrators, social reformers and criminologists alike it has seemed logical to conclude that the amount of crime which might be attributed directly or indirectly to such things as unhealthy shanty towns, slums, poverty, overcrowding, the monotony and stress of living on the edge of subsistence or to the debilitation of general neglect would be necessarily reduced by improvements in conditions such as these.

As we have seen, however, the causal relationship between such circumstances and crime remains largely elusive and it is now arguable that countries which have made the most progress in eliminating the worst of negative environments are often those with the highest crime rates. Certainly, the connection between environment and behaviour has been either over-simplified or else misunderstood. It might then mean that higher incomes and better material conditions do not necessarily affect the frustration or resentment which 'less eligibility' arouses. If so, then inequalities at any level will be criminogenic. On the other hand, the persistence of crime in socialistic countries makes even this premise doubtful, and Japan's experience raises other possibilities.

There is the question then of whether African countries with their relatively small and still manageable problem of crime should:

(a) deliberately invest in improving levels of living in order to prevent crime; or,

(b) hope to benefit indirectly by a reduction in the crime rate from their more general efforts to improve economic and social conditions.

Merely to state the question in this form is to demonstrate its incidental nature. For, crime or not, there is unlikely to be any easing of the world-wide efforts to increase wealth. Whether or not improved economic and social conditions decrease or increase crime they will continue to be sought for their own sake. Their effect upon crime is incidental to the commitment of most countries (and especially the developing countries) to work for increased productivity, a higher national income, more equitable distribution of benefits and general progress in both economic and social conditions.

On the other hand, there is a difference between general hopes of improvement in social conditions decreasing crime and a deliberate effort to make them do so. It is probable that if the work to raise levels of living were to be undertaken with the problems of crime specifically in mind, the developing countries might achieve something higher, better and more wholesome from the development process than has been possible in the older industrialized nations.

This subject has been discussed earlier in this book, but to summarize, it would seem that with closer study of the results of developmental changes on the crime rate it should be possible for developing countries in Africa to make more direct and fruitful use of their national development measures as crime prophylactics. It is less a question of devoting greater funds to this than a need for careful evaluation and adaptation at each stage. It involves a recognition, however, that the prevention of crime is not just an aside to general economic and social growth but a factor of efficiency in the total process. Corruption, extortion, and other types of crime, so frequently impoverish a majority to enrich a minority in the total process of development —and reduce its benefits. But there might be a better, problem-centred approach to better living conditions.

[1] See p. 45 above.

[2] Since this was written the writer has been able to confirm that the World Health Organization is aware of the work being done in Belgium to discover the precise combination of herbs.

[3] See *Report of Pan-African Catholic Education Conference*, O.I.E.C., Brazzaville, 1965, especially pp. 227 ff. where the origin of the school as a European institution is discussed.

[4] The effects on child rearing are probably significant. No longer can the child be kept in such close proximity to its mother in the first two years. Weaning has to come much earlier. The socialization process becomes more problematical

with so many changes and such differences of values. Studies of juvenile delinquents carried out so far attest to the great significance of home security and good family relationships.

[5] See Clifford, *Juvenile Delinquency in Zambia*, op. cit.; also Le Brun's *Délinquance Africaine en Milieu Urbaine*, CEPSI, no. 58, September 1962. But note that the Zambian study showed that the group of delinquents studied had a rather better than average opportunity of schooling. Many young people never have the chance of going to school because primary education is still far from being universal in Africa south of the Sahara.

[6] These figures for Ghana and Togo were collected by the writer. For Zambia see figures given in *Annual Conference Report*, Zambia Council of Social Service, 1965 and Police *Reports*.

[7] ibid.

[8] Richard Quinney, *British Journal of Criminology*, 1965, 5, p. 132.

[9] W. Clifford, *Criminal Cases in Urban Native Courts*, Lusaka: Government Printer, 1960.

[10] Hayden, *Law and Justice in Buganda*, 296 (1960) quoted by James S. Read, 'Kenya, Tanzania and Uganda' in *African Penal Systems*, op. cit.

[11] Television News Report. In 1970 this centre was the scene of a prison riot!

[12] Uganda has claimed to be an exception: see address of the Commissioner of Prisons, Mr F. L. Okwaare, to Fourth United Nations Congress on the Prevention of Crime and Treatment of Offenders, Kyoto, Japan, August 1970.

[13] A recent study of numbers of persons imprisoned per 100,000 population suggests that while the USA imprisons 200 per 100,000, Japan 50 and the Netherlands only 20 per 10,000, Africa tends to imprison about 400 per 100,000 of population. The study is incomplete because data is scarce but this confirms the writer's own experience of the regular recourse to imprisonment in Africa.

[14] Act No. 29 of 1963.

[15] Mr F. L. Okwaare claims that Uganda is already doing this and that its prison system is fully integrated to the country's economic and social development. See his lecture to the Fourth UN Congress, Kyoto, Japan, op. cit.

[16] J. S. Read in *African Penal Systems*, op. cit.

[17] R. B. Seidman and J. D. Abaka Eyison in *African Penal Systems*, op. cit.

[18] S. Lowenstein in *African Penal Systems*, op. cit.

[19] This is the problem of 'less-eligibility' which is fully discussed by Herman Mannheim in his *Criminal Justice and Social Reconstruction*, London: Routledge and Kegan Paul, 1946.

[20] See Lambo and Clairmonte, op. cit.

[21] For example New York City alone, on a single Saturday morning, earns about US $12,000 from the illegally parked cars which the police tow away and this is but a fraction of the total traffic fines on a Saturday morning (*New York Times*, Sunday, 12 October 1968).

[22] Japan in the late 1960s relieved its criminal justice system of 4½ million traffic cases by allowing police officers to fix fines.

APPENDIX

PLANNING FOR FUTURE CRIME IN AFRICA

How much future crime will there be in Africa? Past experience and the inexorable spread of urbanization suggest that there will be a great deal of crime. This introduction to criminology will have failed if it has left any impression that crime can be completely eradicated.

The faint hope that it might be is still entertained, however, by people who fall into two main categories:

(a) *The stubborn idealists* who are still loath to abandon the possibility of a perfect earthly society. More specifically, this includes those who interpret human behaviour as a function of the environment and still believe that the right adjustment of material conditions will develop a crimeless society, eradicating selfishness, greed, lust, aggressiveness, personal inadequacies and all the motives for criminal conduct.

(b) *The indulgent realists* who see the criminal label as largely artificial and who would fain remove it from all kinds of behaviour in society which are prevalent but no longer morally or socially reprehensible. This would still leave murder, violence, theft, rape and several other types of crime to be dealt with: but criminal behaviour going beyond permissible bounds would be regarded as eccentric, strange, or sick rather than as wrong. Society would either get used to such conduct or treat it by other than legal procedures. According to this 'realism', crime is not difficult to get rid of because it is either a mislabelling of behaviour which ought to be tolerated or it is a form of disease to be dealt with medically, psychiatrically, socially or in other ways than by holding people responsible and punishing them for actions which others do not like.

Whether, in either case, crime would be truly eliminated becomes a question of semantics.

Neither of these extreme arguments (and, of course, they are not necessarily opposite or opposed arguments) seeks to exclude the need for law. It might be a different law with different definitions of the illegal—and new forms of disposition or treatment—but usually it is admitted that even in such 'perfect' conditions, there would be some forms of behaviour which could not be tolerated.

Perhaps in a wholly permissive society it would be the intolerant persons who would be outlawed. It may be that in a society where the doctor is the judge, the outcasts would be those who did not respond to 'treatment'. We know that in an authoritarian system where conventional labels change, offenders are prone to be those construed as 'enemies of the state' or 'counter-revolutionaries'. The fundamental point is that there would still be some people in the community to be 'dealt with'. Presumably, there would still be law to define behaviour which is proscribed, and this means a form of 'crime', whatever other name may be given to the phenomenon of anti-social, abnormal or reprehensible conduct. This is why the question of whether crime really survives or not becomes a terminological issue.

It may be noted that the proposition that there will always be some level of crime has been underlined by Durkheim, Tarde, Maine, Merton and other scholars who regard crime as a functional or normal feature of any society—even societies of saints and criminals. Other psychiatrically inspired writers have discussed crime as the necessary acting out of society's own guilt feelings and oppression, so that criminals are society's scapegoats, quite apart from the circumstances of their individual offences.

Thus, by definition, function and need, we may expect to find crime in any view of the future of man and men. In the course of the United Nations Consultative Group Meeting on the Prevention of Crime and the Treatment of Offenders held in Geneva in August 1968, it was remarked that probably every society needs an inoculation of crime to avoid more serious disorders and disruptions.

This is the factual situation: crime is inevitable in one form or another. This does not mean that a defeatist attitude is being recommended. Probably we will always have disease in one form or another, but we try to eradicate it, and we live in the hope of a great diminution of morbidity. That there *will* always be crime is not the same as saying that there *should* always be crime, and it is on this normative foundation that most criminology is built.

No African state is yet in a position to dispose neatly of its conventional crime by political redefinition, or to afford the luxury of tolerating extremes of deviation. Practical policy in Africa calls for a more immediately pragmatic approach beginning from the fact that crime can neither be planned nor legislated out of existence in the foreseeable future. This being so, it becomes possible to consider what might be done about the crime it is reasonable to anticipate.

It will be for each country in Africa to decide for itself, probably through experience spread over a period of time, the approximate level of its *real* crime (i.e. as compared with reported crime or with behaviour which society otherwise tolerates but which is still out-modedly forbidden by law). It would then be for the country to decide for itself, at any given time, roughly what proportion of real crime it can afford to regard as normal and acceptable.

To put it another way, it is for each society to determine for itself the amount and types of crime it might regard as tolerable, i.e. as a normal cost of its degree of personal freedom and its level of social and economic advancement. If this seems altogether too abstract an idea or too intangible a concept for practical application, it should be remembered that a society usually does this anyway, but unconsciously. Its levels of toleration and its decisions on crime are implied rather than expressed and they are reflected in such things as its legislation, its prosecution policy, the line its courts take in interpreting the law and the directions under which its police operate.

The suggestion here is that such decisions should be made more consciously, more deliberately: the decisions should be openly made for planning purposes. Having arrived, no matter how roughly, at some notion of what is normal, tolerable, acceptable or to be expected, it begins to be possible for a government to plan to contain crime within such predetermined limits and to reduce it even further if circumstances allow.

To arrive at the limits for which it would be desirable to plan, a country will naturally have recourse to its past and current experiences, to its criminal statistics, such as they are, and to any social indicators (levels of education, population growth, housing, mobility, etc.) which might provide clues as to the trends. Those criminologists aware of the limitations of their own science will admit that in making such an attempt the planners will be moving in uncharted regions.

It can be said in advance, for instance, that statistics now available will be but a poor guide to real crime in any country; they are particularly unreliable in most of the African countries. Experience is made up of far more than statistics, however, and there are a few useful indicators for planning purposes which are amenable to use in this part of the world with or without statistics. In any event, if the planner is to plan, he will have to find a way of achieving a base line.

(a) The Industrial and Urban Over-Culture

We have seen that an important aspect of crime in Africa is that it seems to be developing in response to the processes of industrialization and urbanization. As man concentrates in towns and orders his life around machinery with all the consequent social implications, so crime becomes a greater problem. This is an unfolding of illegal behaviour related to economic and social problems in a pattern which has already become very familiar in the so-called developed countries. Indeed it underlines a fact which is worth noting—namely, that in the criminological sense, there are really no 'developed' or 'developing' nations. All are faced with the same problem of crime, and none have found really effective solutions.

What is significant for our purposes is that crime, although differing in many aspects culturally, appears to grow in line with the common forms of industrial and urban development. It seems that these modern ways of living, earning and producing constitute a 'new', pervading and, at least potentially, criminogenic culture which overlays and dominates any local traditions and mores. Town boys, hoodlums, prostitutes, pimps, housebreakers, pickpockets, robbers, confidence tricksters, gamblers, protection racketeers and the rest may go under different names but whatever their language, style of clothes, or cultural background, they are clearly recognizable as modernization proceeds anywhere in the world. In fact, there is accumulating evidence that such offenders are motivated and produced psychologically and sociologically by much the same process everywhere—as families break up, the older social controls decline, new urban sub-cultures and sub-divisions develop, and, of course, as the opportunities of crime increase alongside, a perceptible decrease in the prospects of detention.

From this concept of an industry/urban over-culture, certain conclusions can be drawn, if only tentatively. First, it must be acknowledged that there is a possibility that this uniformity of crime growth with the development of towns and industry may yet prove to be less consistent or inevitable than it now seems. The familiarity of the growth pattern might turn out eventually to be no more than a reflection of the regular and similar fashion in which societies evolve and distribute their legal administration and enforcement services. The concentration of crime in towns and industrial settings could well be a direct outcome of there being more courts, police and correction services in such areas. We may yet find that it is our methods of legislating, categorizing or compiling statistics which give the impression of a common criminal growth pattern, and that in fact this common growth denominator may not exist. Juvenile delinquency may be as much a legal as a social creation.

Nevertheless, the association of crime and urban or industrial growth remains the persuasive fact and at least two African studies have questioned the supposed increase in crime as a simple function of an increase in police available. Whatever alternative or contributory explanations there may be, therefore, it remains true that wherever it has been studied, crime grows (apart from a few local exceptions) in a more or less predictable fashion with the development of industry, commerce and town living. It is on this basis that planners must work until the association has been challenged much more effectively than it has been to date.[1]

(b) Prospects of Planning

It was such considerations which induced the writer to suggest to the United Nations Congress on the Prevention of Crime and the Treatment of Offenders (held in Stockholm in August 1965) that:

(a) It should be possible to project future crime trends in developing countries from experience in developed areas of the world;

(b) It should be possible for developing countries to take control measures and to achieve a higher proportionate level of crime prevention than developed countries because:

(i) They could avoid some of the obvious mistakes which developed countries now know they had made in the past;

(ii) They could examine more closely the criminogenic aspects of future development efforts and guard against them;

(iii) They could experiment and evaluate crime prevention and control techniques to a degree impossible in complex systems with rigid and sometimes fossilized professional and administration divisions;

(iv) It might well be possible for developing nations, in the course of their action, to prevent crime (on the experience of countries which have travelled a similar road before) and to derive information on crime control which could be of great interest and inestimable value for the rest of the world.

The concept is quite simple. If, as seems possible from experience, crime does grow predictably with urbanization and industrialization, then countries already advanced in these directions could provide African nations with ample information on what to expect: what levels of crime seem to go with what levels of urban and industrial growth; what types of crime to anticipate; what the aetiological possibilities are; what difficulties may be expected in applying crime prevention and control policies; what actions to avoid that might aggravate the problem.

Then, in return, by trying out new preventative schemes and bolder, more imaginative control techniques—by tempering development efforts with a deeper sensitivity to their social cost and criminal implications—the developing countries might lead their advanced neighbours to a better understanding of their own problems and to the evolution of better control and prophylactic systems. To put it another way, by striving for maximum growth consistent with tolerable levels of crime—or perhaps the least crime consistent with maximum growth—the developing third of the world could be in the vanguard of the effort to achieve a more wholesome, satisfying and ultimately genuine form of development.

At the present time, the issues have become much clearer, and the prospects of an approach to crime in Africa on these lines have been very greatly enhanced. Crime and violence are now, more than ever before, recognized to be problems which the more economically advanced societies have failed dismally to solve. Not only has organized crime increased, but in the larger cities the streets have become dangerous after dark and the parks are not always usable in complete safety during the day. Assassination and kidnapping as political weapons have staged a comeback and police efficiency has been shown to be no direct function of larger numbers of officers, increased equipment, a higher technology or more sophisticated training.

It may well be that in these developed and complex countries the extensive social and corrective services which exist have helped to avoid crime becoming even worse than it is, but despite all efforts to prevent and control it, the levels of total crime have risen progressively. Viciousness and depravity have conspicuously increased, psychopathic offences and crime 'for the sheer hell of it' have struck new notes in the relationships between affluence, family disintegration, child neglect, mental health and the rising tide of non-conformity, alienation and crime. Most disturbing and significant of all, the involvement of young people in crime has not only become more general and pronounced, but is often defended as a part of life's experience (for example drug-taking, vandalism, and that form of student protest which uses illegalities to sharpen confrontation).

The developing nations of the world have fewer such problems and they usually enjoy stronger traditional safeguards and social controls. Most of their present difficulties with crime stem directly from their lack of resources to provide even minimal services. This means that they must husband their resources carefully, use some of their more general investments (e.g. in education) in more crime preventative ways and rely upon professions of multi-purpose workers rather than narrow but deeper specialists to do their preventive and corrective work. Here, however, necessity, as the mother of invention, can become (often has become) a virtue.

The possibility of the developing countries having a more significant part to play in the general world search for answers, remedies, preventatives, expedients and controls has been notably increased in recent years by the more extensive use which these countries are making of the process of planning for conscious national development. One gets very close to the link between crime control and planning for national growth when one takes into account the mounting disenchantment of the newly developing countries with the older forms of external capital aid and technical assistance as local growth stimulators—and their more recent interest in the enormous long-term potential of investments in human resources. It needs no restating here that human resources through better education, health and social services can mean not only more economic and social development but, if properly handled and appropriately refined, a good deal less crime.

(c) Past Planning in Developed Areas

A planning approach to the reduction of crime is not really new as an idea; it is new only in the shape which it could take in such developing areas as exist in Africa. The socialist countries of the world have long planned their social defence, like everything else, centrally and comprehensively. Central planning has been, for a generation or more, the only form of organized growth, and social defence has been included either directly or by implication. Ideologically, in these countries, crime was held to be a problem growing out of the economic evils of capitalism. It could not be expected to disappear at once with the revolution, but in so far as it remained, it was essentially a health or educational problem

—delinquents were either sick or badly trained; independent social problems by definition could not exist.

The results of all this planning on the levels of crime in these countries have not been entirely clear. Obviously the revolutionary action on all human behaviour in the nation had its impact on the forms of, and the opportunities for, committing crime; but social problems do not seem to have been very amenable to any casual dismissal by redefinition. For instance, Poland's experience of urban juvenile crime appears to be similar to that of many non-socialist countries. Russia, on the other hand, claims a falling delinquency rate. It all depends on what one means by crime. There is ample evidence to suggest that mass society living produces similar problems everywhere. The technocratic society is emerging in the socialist as well as the capitalist world. There is more planning in the countries devoted to free enterprise than there has ever been before; and the profit incentive has been partially re-established in the state industries of socialist areas. There is reason to believe, therefore, that crime problems in the two regions are not dissimilar. Still, results from socialist countries have suffered from the general lack of data and from certain ideologically determined concepts which have made comparison with earlier periods practically impossible.[2]

Planning in other developed countries has, for a long time, been viewed with suspicion and is often regarded as socialistic and inefficient and as unwarrantable interference with the freedom of industrial or commercial choice. The profit motive and incentives of material gain are felt to be more efficient than the socialist attempt to act like the Almighty in deciding what people should be having and how they should get it. Pure *laissez-faire* of this kind has never been easy to find in practice, however, and the trade cycles, occasional depressions as well as state intervention to fix social minima, have all served over the years to manoeuvre planning into a more respectable position even in the non-socialist areas of the economically developed world. It may not be such a direct operation as in the socialist areas, and there is still considerable latitude for individual freedom of choice. Nevertheless, the use of budgetary surpluses and deficits, regulation of credit and money supply, the direction of government spending and a variety of export, import and exchange controls, not to mention direct and indirect taxation, are extremely powerful in implementing national policy. Moreover, the giant conglomerates in industry have adopted planning wholeheartedly even when governments have been tardy.

Two things make this approach to national planning in the non-socialist developed countries relatively ineffective for crime control purposes, however. First, the situation is usually far too involved and complex. An overview which brings social defence into line with economic planning is never easy to obtain and sometimes impossible to implement satisfactorily. Social effects are secondary and remote as a rule, and there may be constitutional, legal or administrative barriers to keep a planning exercise at least one remove from reality or to slow it down so that it never catches up with events. Social change seems to have out-paced planning (in so far as there was such planning) in Western Europe and America: even in Eastern Europe and Russia, there are signs that the pace of change is a little too much for the planners. The integration of social defence planning and programming into the national plan has not yet been achieved anywhere and only piecemeal approaches have so far been considered.

Secondly, the planning has rarely been consciously social defence planning of a purposeful kind at a national level. The government at any given time may have had an identifiable social defence policy *in action*, but it has rarely been explicit, unequivocal or meant to permeate all the layers of society which it would have to permeate to be truly preventative or corrective. Indeed, social defence policy in the non-socialist developed areas has often been evolved by voluntary social reform groups and pushed step by step through the legislative process with the government simply and openly allowing itself to be pushed in this way.

In Africa and the developing areas generally, the planning procedure is generally more comprehensive, more public and specific, and it has defined social and economic objectives which could well be a help in embracing social defence. An overview is therefore more easily obtained, and the prospect of integrating social defence and national development is brighter.

Thirdly, there are reasons why developing countries *must* integrate planning in this way, if only to reduce wastage from the economy and the draining of essential resources. Fourthly, the whole process is simpler, more direct, yet less ideologically predetermined than in the socialist countries which are more developed. The implementation of planning is untrammelled as a rule by sub-divisions and less clogged with administrative and professional spheres of influence and interest. The enthusiasm of newly-won independence can be used to unite people in national efforts which quickly overcome such barriers.

From an economic planning angle, the possibility of controlling crime effectively means a reduction in the social costs of economic growth and a rare chance to avoid not only the drain of resources but also the diversion of benefits which so blatantly contradict all the precepts of social justice lying behind the development programmes of most newly independent nations.

[1] It is important, however, for Africa to take special note of the one major exception to this general rule of association between free enterprise, industrialization, urbanization and crime. This exception is Japan which has managed to urbanize rapidly and to concentrate industry at an unprecedented pace since 1950—but with a progressive fall in its crime rates both quantitatively and qualitatively. Now, with over 70 per cent of its population urbanized and more concentrated than anywhere else in the world, Japan has some of the world's safest cities. This is due to the special features of the Japanese social structure which may have relevance for future African development.

[2] But cf. p. 43 above.

INDEX

Printed by Kenya Litho Limited, Changamwe Road, P.O. Box 40775, Nairobi, Kenya and prepared for press, designed and published by Oxford University Press, Electricity House, Harambee Avenue, P.O. Box 72532, Nairobi, Kenya.

Schenectady County Community College
HV7138.C55
Clifford, W., An introduction to African
3 0313 00037615 3